BASIC ATONAL THEORY

Consulting Editor: Gerald Warfield

BASIC ATONAL THEORY

JOHN RAHN

SCHIRMER BOOKS
An Imprint of Simon & Schuster Macmillan
NEW YORK

Prentice Hall International
LONDON • MEXICO CITY • NEW DELHI • SINGAPORE • SYDNEY • TORONTO

Copyright © 1980 by Schirmer Books
An Imprint of Simon & Schuster Macmillan

All rights reserved. No part of this book may be reproduced or transmitted in any form or by any means, electronic or mechanical, including photocopying, recording, or by any information storage and retrieval system, without permission in writing from the Publisher.

Schirmer Books
An Imprint of Simon & Schuster Macmillan
1633 Broadway, New York, NY 10019-6785

Library of Congress Catalog Card Number: 87-1665

printing number

       7 8 9 10

Library of Congress Cataloging-in-Publication Data
Rahn, John.
  Basic atonal theory.

  Reprint. Originally published: New York : Longman,
c1980.
  Bibliography: p.
  Includes index.
  1. Atonality.   2. Music—Theory—20th century.
I. Title.
MT46.R33   1987   781'.22   87-1665
ISBN 0-02-873160-3

PREFACE

Basic Atonal Theory aims to induce an enjoyable understanding of atonal music, for listening, composing, or performing. It presents some basic underlying structural features of the system of twelve pitch-classes, a system common to all atonal and serial music. The use of the integers modulo 12 (numbers 0 through 11) as a model for this music theory is carefully taught. Consistent definitions are offered in place of informally opaque concepts, and proven theorems are offered in place of previously obscure assumptions.

The concepts and skills taught here are often cursorily and variously presented, referred to, or simply assumed in the professional literature. Indeed, much of this theory has been transmitted by "oral tradition," a very frustrating situation for those in the wrong place and time. Through its systematic approach to the concepts of atonal music, *Basic Atonal Theory* should prepare its reader for the professional literature in the field.

The Analysis sections (1 and 2) provide an antidote to mechanical application of the "important-looking" formulae of atonal theory. These chapters in particular emphasize both the particularity of atonal pieces and the contrasting high level of generality of systematic basic theory. They also emphasize the necessary *audibility* of any music-structural features worthy of notice.

The book is designed for flexible use as either a primary or adjunct text in courses dealing with the analysis or composition of atonal music, or for use as a reference work. It can also be used for self-programmed study independent of class work, especially by more advanced students. Sections marked with an asterisk and, in general, all footnotes, are intended only for the graduate student, specialist, or other interested person. These sections should be omitted from most undergraduate courses.

As a primary text, the book contains more than enough material for one term's class use, with minimal supplementation by the instructor in the form of explanations, analyses, instruction in how to compose, and correction of student analyses and compositions. This volume stops where it does—before any theory of serialism per se—mainly because, when it is used as a primary text, experience indicates that any more material would glut the one-term-long digestion of most undergraduate music majors. The theory of particularly serial relations is an *extension* of the basic atonal theory here presented, not an alternative to it.

In an analysis-oriented course, the first serious, independent analytic assignment can be given as soon as the class has finished chapter 4. The generation by the students of each such analysis and class discussion of the completed assignments can consume three to six class periods. It is suggested that, in an analysis course, several such substantial "mid-term" or "term paper" type analyses be assigned, to allow the students to profit from experience.

As a primary text for a course oriented around the composing of atonal music, the book provides preparation for the assignment of compositions several times during and after chapter 4, and again several times during and after chapter 5. The generation, class performance, and discussion of completed composition assignments may be expected to consume three to six class periods.

As an adjunct text, the book allows the instructor to pick and choose sections to be assigned, providing more formal instruction than usual in various concepts and skills so freely assumed in the professional literature. Students may be supplied with answer sheets, so that they may independently monitor their own progress in acquiring the skills as assigned. Self-correction of this sort is recommended for chapter 2 in all cases.

Dearest to my own heart is the use of this book for self-programmed individual study (with answers supplied for exercises in chapters 2–5). Often I have been approached by an undergraduate composer or theory major wishing to acquire the elementary concepts and skills of his or her discipline, or by a graduate in any discipline who wishes to be able to read the professional literature on twentieth-century music. And at last I may say to them all: "Read this book. Do the exercises as necessary to assure yourself that you understand what you have read and to practice the skills that the book teaches. Then, having graduated from the nursery, come play with me in the kindergarten of contemporary atonal theory."

ACKNOWLEDGMENTS

Acknowledgments for a book of this sort must be extended to the entire music-theoretical community. In particular, the general formative role of Milton Babbitt in the development of serial theory since 1948 cannot be overestimated. Lists of his published articles and compositions up to 1977 may be found in *Sounds and Words: Milton Babbitt at 60,* a special double issue of *Perspectives of New Music* (14/2 and 15/1, 1976). As that issue may indicate, Milton Babbitt's influence as a teacher, through direct and indirect "oral tradition," far exceeds even the influence of his publications. Benjamin Boretz—as theorist, teacher, composer, and editor of *PNM* since its inception—has been a foreman among the gardeners of music theory. I am pleased to acknowledge the personally transmitted musical influence of both these gentlemen.

I am grateful also to those students at the University of Washington who suffered through early versions of this text with courageous and generous spirit. The book would be a better one had it been able to incorporate simultaneously all of their very helpful suggestions. I am grateful to the Graduate School Research Fund of the University of Washington for a gift of valuable time. Finally, my love to my wife, Suzanne, who stole time from her own career to type large sections of illegible manuscript, and whose support also took less tangible but more important forms.

The musical examples are reprinted by the kind permission of Belmont Music Publishers, G. Schirmer, Inc., Boosey and Hawkes, Inc., European American Music Distributors Corporation, and C.F. Peters Corporation.

SELECT BIBLIOGRAPHY

A very short, minimally annotated bibliography suggests a few avenues for future travels.

Journals:
Journal of Music Theory (JMT). Yale School of Music, New Haven, Conn. 06520.
  Music theory of music of all periods.
Perspectives of New Music (PNM). Annandale-on-Hudson, New York 12504.
  Articles of all kinds around contemporary and twentieth-century music and composition.
Both journals can be rather formidably technical reading; *Basic Atonal Theory* will give you a leg up. Browse through at least their tables of contents for all their issues.

Books:
Boretz, Benjamin, and Edward T. Cone, eds. *Perspectives on Contemporary Music Theory.* New York: W.W. Norton, 1972.
  An anthology of articles from *Perspectives of New Music,* including several crucial ones.
———. *Perspectives on Schoenberg and Stravinsky.* Rev. ed. New York: W.W. Norton, 1972.
  An anthology of articles from *Perspectives of New Music.*
Forte, Allen. *The Structure of Atonal Music.* New Haven: Yale University Press, 1973.
  A research book. Much basic theory appeared for the first time in book form in Part 1. Forte's theory of set-complexes is developed in Part 2. Forte's terminology and the set-type labels of his Appendix 1 are widely used.
Lang, Paul Henry, ed. *Problems of Modern Music: The Princeton Seminar in Advanced Musical Studies.* New York: W.W. Norton, 1962.
  Articles of varied levels of difficulty and interest.
Perle, George. *Serial Composition and Atonality: An Introduction to the Music of Schoenberg, Berg, and Webern.* Berkeley: University of California Press, 1962.
  An easily-read research book, including many musical examples and short analyses.
Wuorinen, Charles. *Simple Composition.* New York: Longman, 1979.
  A textbook in serial composition by a distinguished composer.

CONTENTS

Preface	v
Acknowledgments	vii
Chapter One: Introduction	1
Analysis One: Webern's *Symphonie* op. 21: Thema	4
Chapter Two: The Integer Model of Pitch	19
Chapter Three: Basic Operations	40
Analysis Two: Schoenberg's Five Pieces for Orchestra: *Farben*, op. 16 no. 3	59
Chapter Four: Set Types	74
Chapter Five: Common-Tone Theorems	97
Bibliography	124
Appendices	133
Answers to Selected Exercises	144
Index	155

CHAPTER ONE
INTRODUCTION

1.1 THE GREAT ADVENTURE

To analyze music is to find a good way to hear it and to communicate that way of hearing it to other people. Probably there is no single best way of hearing any given piece, but some ways are generally recognizable as being better than others. Each person makes his own decision as to the degree and quality of insight communicated to him by a particular analysis of a particular piece. If these individual judgments did not tend to converge into clumps, music theory would be even more anarchical than it is.

An essential ingredient for this clumping process is willingness to pursue actively someone else's truly alien insight. Without such willingness no music-analytical conversation (however heated it may become) can occur, no mutual accommodation, no synthesis of two formerly separate and alien viewpoints; no learning.

Since infancy you and I have been surrounded by "tonal" music, in home, supermarket, elevator, and dentist's chair. After twenty years or so of this most of us have evolved ways of "making sense" out of this music, and in analytical conversations about such music all viewpoints involved are likely to be relatively sophisticated (in content, if not in means of expression of that content). Let us call up a metaphor: your way of "making sense" out of this ambient tonal music is your set of "tonal filters." The sounds pass through and are organized by your "tonal filters" into music that "makes sense."

After a lifetime of such constructive brainwashing you are exposed, for the first time, to "nontonal" music. You try to "make sense" out of it with your existing listening skills; you hear it through your "tonal filters" and *it sounds terrible*. Truly, a "nontonal" piece makes a terrible tonal piece; and vice versa. In an environment of "tonal" music, hearing Western "classical" "serious" "atonal" music—like Schoenberg's or Boulez's—subjects you to the same kind of "culture shock" experienced in listening for the first time to, say, Javanese Gamelan music. In fact, the shock is more acute, because there is no expectation of dealing with a radically different culture, because the similarity of basic materials (such as pitch scale) and continuity of musical tradition can tempt you into believing (implicitly) that your "tonal filters" *should* make sense of the music, and because the relational structures of pitch, duration, etc., involved in "nontonal" Western music may well be *more* alien than the structures in some (not all) non-Western music.

Moreover, "atonal" music is very diverse. (The process of creating categories of pieces of music is discussed in Analysis 1.) As a categorical label, "atonal" generally means only that the piece is in the Western tradition and is not "tonal." Subcategories do exist, built on various sets of criteria. Is the music one is attempting to categorize notated in Schoenberg's kind of traditional music notation? Or is it notated in a relatively "indeterminate" notation designed to guide improvisation, as in Stockhausen's *Zyklus?* Is the music marked by a notation designed (paradoxically) to eliminate any influence of the composer on the sounds produced? Are individual sounds only "stochastically" organized (à la Xenakis)? Is the music "content-determinate" or "order-determinate" as to pitch? Does the music borrow some structures or materials from tonal music? Does it quote fragments of tonal music? Pride itself on being only a very subtle distortion or adaptation of tonal music? Is timbre a primary dimension of organization? Pitch? Time? Such subcategories are not necessarily mutually exclusive, and certainly no list of categories known to me is inclusive in the sense of providing a determinate and accurate characterization for every piece of "atonal" music.

Nevertheless, there does exist a relatively coherent tradition from Wagner, Brahms, and Mahler; through Schoenberg and his pupils Webern and Berg; through European (Boulez, Stockhausen, Nono, Dallapiccola, Ligeti, etc.) and American (Stravinsky, Babbitt, Carter, Wuorinen, Davidovsky, Martino, etc.) serial or serially-influenced music of the 1950s and 1960s; to much present-day composition concerned with determinate radically nontonal pitch organization. The keystone to this kind of music is the classical free atonal and serial music of Schoenberg, Webern, and Berg.

This book attempts to provide the basics of a theory for this "keystone" kind of music, just as texts on tonal theory may concentrate on the tradition of Bach, Beethoven, and Brahms.

The relations taught here are basic to *all* atonal music, whether that music is serial or nonserial. Indeed, serialism arose partly as a means of organizing more coherently the relations used in the preserial "free atonal" music. There are relations—those deriving from syntactical order—that are peculiar to serial atonal music. The theory of these particularly serial relations is an *extension* of the "basic atonal theory" given here; serial theory builds on basic atonal theory as its foundation. Thus many useful and crucial insights about even strictly serial music depend only on such basic atonal theory. The treatment of serial theory in itself is a more advanced topic.

Please remember that this is, in a sense, a first-year theory book. It *must* first return to "boring" basics (such as interval) because these are *different* basics from those used in tonal theory. Atonal music is radically different from tonal music, demanding radically different theory. An understanding of these basics is needed for the sake of the really exciting musical structures that will be built upon them.

A knowledge of grade school mathematics is required (e.g., ability to add and subtract). Before reading chapter 2, you should skim over Informal Explanations of Assumed Notations and Concepts (Appendix 1) and refer to this material whenever an unfamiliar notation or concept crops up in the text. Beyond this, the completion of a high school algebra course should leave no terrors even for the minimally mathematical person in any of the explained notations and concepts.

A newly acquired conscious understanding of the principles behind atonal music, along with intensive listening to the music, will reward you with a new world of musical understanding. If you enjoy Bach, Beethoven, or Brahms, you should be able to learn to enjoy Schoenberg, Webern, or Berg, and the music of their tradition. Remember that your "tonal filters" are worse than useless. The theory of atonal music should build you a set of "atonal filters." There are, however, some additional difficulties.

First, some of this atonal music—such as the Webern *Symphonie* op. 21 discussed first in Analysis 1—demands a great deal of intense listening concentration. The change in concentration level can be a hurdle comparable to that stumbled over by a hypothetical exclusive devotee of the songs of Stephen Foster attending his first "classical music" recital—a performance of Book I of Bach's *Well-Tempered Clavier*. Other atonal music may ask you to dilute your concentration over vast periods of time, or to concentrate on unaccustomed aspects of the sounds presented (particularly in electronically produced music).

Secondly, even within the keystone atonal tradition of Schoenberg—in fact even among Schoenberg's works considered by themselves—each piece is more radically different from every other piece than is the case within the tonal tradition. One's "atonal filters" are at best a scaffolding or basic framework to be filled out differently for every piece. This puts on the listener a large burden of flexibility of musical understanding, of skill in creating structures that fructify his or her sonorous experience.

Thirdly, not all atonal music is *good* music. In fact, most contemporary music is not very good. The average concert of newly written music will probably include several pieces that are mediocre, if not just plain awful; if you are lucky, it may contain one or two wonderful pieces. This has been the case for newly written music of all historical periods, and the present is no exception. Nor is any label—like "tonal," "atonal," "serial," "improvisatory"—a guarantee that the piece so labelled will be either good or bad. A consensus may gradually appear; but the majority is not always right. Tastes differ.

But these very "difficulties" and "burdens" are better perceived as challenges and opportunities. No other kind of music is more intensely exciting, or better suited to a vigorously active, creative listener, performer, or composer.

> Day!
> Faster and more fast,
> O'er night's brim, day boils at last:
> Boils, pure gold, o'er the cloud-cup's brim
> Where spurting and suppressed it lay,...
> But forth one wavelet, then another, curled,
> Till the whole sunrise, not to be suppressed,
> Rose, reddened, and its seething breast
> Flickered in bounds, grew gold, then overflowed the world.
> Robert Browning, *Pippa Passes*

EXERCISES

1. In preparation for Analysis 1, listen at least twice to the *Symphonie* op. 21 of Anton Webern. Do not follow a score; just listen.

2. Listen to a good performance of the complete opera *Wozzeck* by Alban Berg. Follow a score and libretto if possible.

ANALYSIS ONE

Webern's **Symphonie** op. 21: Thema

1. EAR-TRAINING: WITHOUT SCORE

Having listened to the Webern *Symphonie* op. 21 at least twice, you should be convinced that this music does not make sense as tonal music; but you may at least harbor a lurking suspicion in your listening brain that it does make sense some way (or ways). This chapter concentrates on the Thema (mm. 1–11) of the Variationen that are the second movement, in an attempt to lead your ears on a path of some comprehension through one small section. Understanding the nontonal audible relations that make sense of this section can be a seed around which comprehension of other sections of the *Symphonie* may crystallize.

Listen to the Thema three times, without following a score; ignore the violin entrance at the end (m. 11).

> *Play Thema, three times.*

In many performances the French horns are out of balance with each other and with the other instruments, but it still should be apparent that this Thema has a fairly strong character of being a "tune plus accompaniment." The clarinet, which plays more or less continuously, has the tune.

> *Play clarinet tune alone. If played on a piano, note that dynamics and expression are inaccurate—e.g., a piano note cannot crescendo; neither can a piano play the articulation of m. 1 (in which the attack of the first F is accented but the tail end of the first F is no louder than the end of the second F).*
>
> *Play clarinet tune again.*

Now listen for that clarinet tune in the orchestral recording.

> *Play Thema.*

Can you hear the clarinet tune as a tune? (If not, replay recording until clear.) Exactly what instruments are playing?

Play Thema.

Clarinet, harp, and two French horns; you should be able to follow each instrumental part. (Replay if necessary. Poor recording quality may make it more difficult to identify instruments.)

My way into this piece (the Thema) is through its middle (mm. 5-7), which stands forth as (paradoxically) the "first" thing to be noticed:

Play mm. 5-7.

Play Thema.

The eighth-note movement in m. 6 is faster than its surroundings, but a more important signal is the voice-crossed interchanged *tritones* in m. 6.

Play Thema.

Play clarinet mm. 5-7.

Play harp mm. 5-7.

Play clarinet m. 6.

Play harp m. 6.

Play clarinet and harp m. 6.

Play Thema.

Can you hear that the clarinet in m. 6 and the harp in the middle of m. 6 are playing linear tritones—in fact, the *same* tritone (E♭/A as it turns out) in reverse order? The clarinet plays A-E♭ while the harp plays E♭—A.

Play clarinet m. 6.

Play harp, middle two eighth-notes of m. 6.

This results in a voice-crossed *repetition* of a *simultaneous* E♭/A in the middle of m. 6:

EXAMPLE 1

Play Ex. 1. (Note that piano cannot articulate voice-crossing.)

6   Basic Atonal Theory

Thus two instances of a *linear* interval combine to form the same interval as a repeated simultaneity; such minimally varied repetition compels our attention.

Play Thema.

Our attention having been drawn to tritone intervals, we now recognize more easily the tritone-ness of the rest of mm. 5-7 surrounding those middle E♭/A's.

Play mm. 5-7.

The clarinet plays B♭—E in dotted quarter-notes in mm. 5 and 7, while the harp plays E—B♭ (again, the same tritone, reversed) on the first and last eighth-notes of m. 6, "nesting" inside the clarinet tritone.

EXAMPLE 2

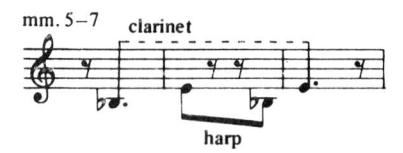

Play Ex. 2.

Notice that each instrumental part alone in mm. 5-7 shows the same kind of nesting of one tritone inside another:

EXAMPLE 3

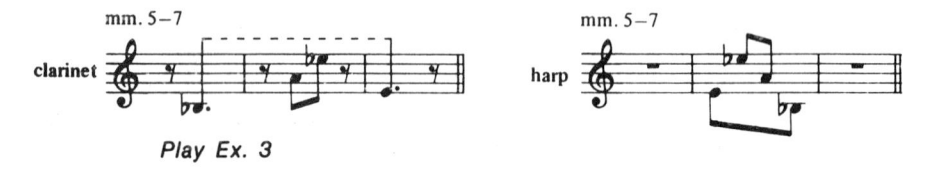

Play Ex. 3

Moreover, in mm. 5-7 played on the piano, or listened to while ignoring the instrumental lines, a linear tritone B♭—E can be heard followed by two identical tritone simultaneities E♭/A which are followed by a repetition of the initial linear tritone B♭—E; the E♭/A's nest inside the B♭—E's. See Ex. 4.

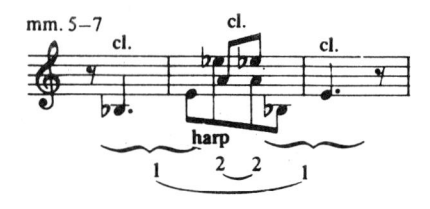

EXAMPLE 4

Play Ex. 4

As Ex. 4 shows, this pitch-sensitive but instrumentation-deaf version can be regarded as a 1 2 2 1 pattern. This kind of pattern—which is the same going backwards as it is going forwards—is called a *retrograde-symmetrical* pattern. Similar retrograde-symmetrical patterns are exemplified in mm. 5-7 by the instrumentation alone (ignoring pitch, duration, etc.):

```
                2   1
    1   2   1   2   2   1
   cl. hp. hp. cl. hp. cl.
           cl. hp.

or: 1   2   3   3   2   1
```

and by the durational patterns alone, both within single instrumental parts:

and of the ensemble:

By paying attention to tritones, multiple cooperating retrograde-symmetrical patterns have been made more clear in mm. 5-7. On the other hand, the presence of these patterns undoubtedly helped draw our attention to the tritones in the first place—a "by your own bootstraps" process typical of analysis. Certainly it would be well to keep retrograde symmetry in mind as a possible principle of organization for larger chunks of this piece.

Do you hear how all these structures fit together to make mm. 5-7 a memorable spot?

Play Thema.

The general effect of mm. 5-7 (a very hearable thing here) is shimmer—a *structured* shimmer—around those two tritones, B♭—E and E♭/A.

Play Thema three times.

Since tritones have been such a reliable guide so far, in this *particular* piece, it would be reasonable to listen for tritones in the rest of the Thema, to find out whether they can guide us out of the "first," middle section (mm. 5-7).

Listen to just the first few notes (m.1).

Play m.1.

What's that interval? Sing it.

Play m. 1.

8 Basic Atonal Theory

(Sing it. Identify it by ear.) The actual pitches are given in Ex. 5. The first *linear* interval heard is the B—F between the clarinet and harp; the first *simultaneity* heard is also B/F (on the second beat). Does this remind you of mm. 5-7? In mm. 5-7 there are two linear tritones (B♭—E), inside of which are nested two simultaneous tritones (E♭/A), which are, inside of themselves, produced by two linear tritones (A—E♭, E♭—A).

EXAMPLE 5

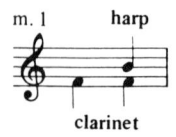

This suggests another possible organizational principle, to be either corroborated or denied for this piece by further exploration: that structures which are presented linearly can also be presented simultaneously; that the *same kinds* of structures can be simultaneities and successions, lines and chords. (This is in contrast to tonal music, where certain "scale-step" relations are, generally, reserved for linear structures alone.) Schoenberg called this principle "the unity of musical space."

To recapitulate, there are three possible organizational principles of different kinds that have been suggested by our examination of the piece so far (listed in an order that will later be shown to be significant): 1) "unity of musical space"—that is, linear and simultaneous structures may grow out of one another and be identical in content; 2) retrograde symmetry; and 3) the structural preeminence of the tritone. Without jumping to conclusions (and thereby failing to enjoy the intervening scenery, even if the jumped-to conclusions are not disconfirmed), let us further follow audible tritones through the Thema.

Notice that the clarinet part may be divided into repeated notes and single notes. The first and last three are repeated; the middle six are single.

Play Thema.

The outer two of those six single clarinet notes are a tritone apart—F♯ and C—extending the nested-tritone, retrograde-symmetrical structure of mm. 5-7 outwards (see Ex. 6).

EXAMPLE 6

Becoming aware of the F♯—C tritone yields a further dividend. Almost immediately previous to the clarinet F♯, the harp has a C (m. 3); soon after the clarinet C (m. 8), the harp has an F♯. The rather far-apart F♯—C in the clarinet is nested inside an even farther-apart C—F♯ in the harp, but in such a way that a much more immediate F♯/C relation is heard *between* the clarinet and harp, reinforcing the audibility of the longer-range, within-instrument relations (see Ex. 7).

EXAMPLE 7

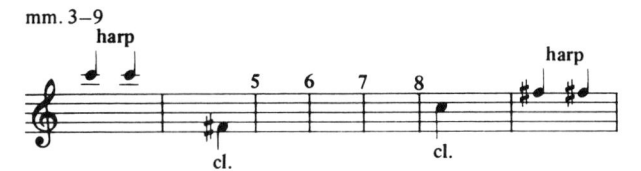

[music notation: mm. 3–9, harp and cl. parts, measures 5, 6, 7, 8, with harp notes]

Play Thema

The harp's C is further connected to its F♯, across the intervening (E (E♭—A) B♭) in m. 6, by the fact that the harp's C and F♯ are the two highest notes heard in any instrument in the Thema.

Play Thema.

This nesting C/F♯ harp/clarinet relation encourages us to hear the first note of the harp, a B heard in conjunction with the clarinet's initial F, connected by a tritone to the last note of the harp, an F heard in conjunction with the clarinet's final B. The Thema begins and ends with a B/F, with switched instrumentation (see Ex. 8). This naturally also connects the first and last clarinet notes.

EXAMPLE 8

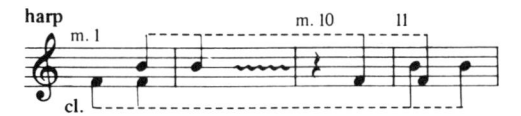

[music notation: harp m. 1, m. 10, 11, cl.]

Play Thema.

The entire harp part can now be heard as a complex of successively nested tritones (see Ex. 9).

EXAMPLE 9

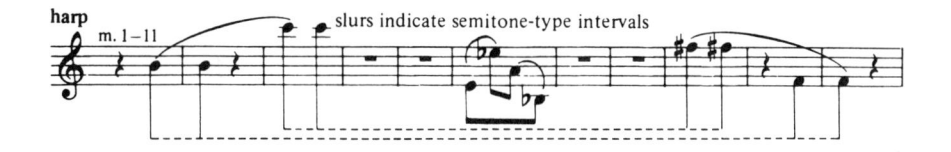

[music notation: harp m. 1–11, slurs indicate semitone-type intervals]

Play Ex. 9.

But while the large-scale structure is of nested tritones, the more immediate, "local" successions are by means of one semitone, up or down, plus or minus an octave (that is, "unordered pitch-class interval 1"—see chapter 2): B—C; E—E♭; A—B♭; F♯—F (see slurs in Ex. 9). Could this be another principle of organization for this piece—that, at least within each instrumental sound, large-scale relations are articulated by tritones, and local relations by semitones?

Listen to the harp and, this time, the horns:

10 Basic Atonal Theory

Play Thema.

It should be obvious that the large-scale linear intervals in the horns are tritones. What is the local relation between the horns, that is, the interval of simultaneity?

Play Thema.

Corroboration for the principle above is found in the horns: the local relations are semitone-type intervals; the large-scale relations are linear tritones (see Ex. 10).

EXAMPLE 10

There remains only the clarinet part.

Play clarinet part, mm. 1-11.

We have already heard the middle six notes, and the first and last notes, as being structured in nested tritones. It should come as no surprise that the entire clarinet part is so structured. In Ex. 11, brackets connect nested tritones and slurs show semitone-type intervals.

EXAMPLE 11

Notice that all immediate adjacencies (without intervening rests) are semitone-related, except the crucial A-E♭ in the very middle which, as a local detail in conjunction with the harp part, led us outwards to listen for the tritones in the larger structure. In fact, it is only at that point (mm. 5-7) that rests do separate semitone adjacencies (B♭—A, E♭—E). If they did not, the crucial middle A—E♭ tritone would lose its uniqueness and therefore would be less compelling to our attention, making the rest of the structure more difficult to hear.

Play Thema.

Analysis One 11

To recapitulate: four possible organizational principles have so far emerged for the Thema: 1) "unity of musical space"—that is, lines and simultaneities may grow out of one another and be identical in content; 2) retrograde symmetry; 3) general structural preeminence of the tritone; and 4) within one kind of instrumental sound, articulation of large-scale relations by (usually nested) tritones, and local relations by semitones.

Play Thema.

Analytical generalizations (such as those used in arriving at the four organizational principles just named) can be produced and applied from either of two viewpoints: primary or secondary.[1]

Primarily, the composer, performer, or listener must generalize (consciously or unconsciously) within a specific piece of music over the population of the sounds of that piece, in order to understand that piece enjoyably. The four principles of organization above—arrived at through primary generalization—justify their existence only by the increased audible coherence they bring to the Thema's collection of particular sounds.

Secondarily, a principle of organization may be found manifesting itself legitimately in more than one piece of music. A music historian or theorist may then generalize over populations of pieces of music, saying that "such-and-such an organizational principle is found in all these pieces" (handing you a list of titles). When many different pieces have many of their primarily generated organizational principles in common, an historian or theorist is liable to use the common principles as a criterion by which to *categorize* these pieces. When told that an unfamiliar piece is "tonal," one initially takes more or less on faith the correctness of the implied assertion that that piece will, upon analysis, be found to share certain organizational principles with other "tonal" pieces already known. Because you are told what kinds of structures to listen for, you are saved the labor of generating the organizational principles afresh from the sounds of that piece.

Secondary generalization and categorization of this sort are undoubtedly useful, but beware of two pitfalls. First, the categorization may encourage shallow understanding. Every piece of music is unique, with idiosyncratic organizational principles and structures shared with no other piece of music. Such idiosyncratic principles and structures are just as important for understanding and enjoying the music as are the principles it happens to share with other members of its category. Secondly, it may be that a piece does not legitimately manifest *all* the principles of its category. An attempt to hear a piece in terms of inapplicable (or fruitlessly applicable) principles may obscure the beauties of a more idiosyncratic organization.

A particularly noisome example of the first pitfall lies in the still widespread fallacy that a "serial" piece is nearly completely understood by "12-counting" it (identifying the row-order function or functions of each pitch). This analysis of the Thema of Webern's *Symphonie*—a "serial" piece in category—is meant to be a counterexample to that fallacy. "Serialism" need be invoked only in larger contexts with respect to this piece of music, providing relations at a relatively high level of abstraction that tie together the Thema with the other variations and the *Symphonie* as a whole. As to the second pitfall, a dogged, beat-by-

12   Basic Atonal Theory

beat "roman numeral analysis," abounding in eleventh and thirteenth chords, of a piece by Debussy, would be a flagrant case in point.

Take with the above grains of salt the following ex cathedra secondary generalizations with respect to our four discovered principles of organization for the Thema.

The above principles have been listed always in order of increasing secondary particularity: 1) applies to many if not most atonal compositions; 2) applies to many sections of Webern's *Symphonie* and to various other pieces and sections of pieces; 3) applies to the Thema and could apply to other sections and pieces; and 4) is less likely than 3) to apply to pieces or sections other than the Thema.

2. ANALYSIS WITH SCORE

We have been led from small-scale to large-scale structure, and have heard a remarkable coherence. The instrumental parts have been examined separately, and, in the middle part of the Thema, together. Most of the structures have emerged from relatively easily heard features of the music. We have yet to examine the whole Thema. Its structure is, of course, supported by the structure of its parts, but there are unifying features of the whole, that are less easy to hear, and to which we should progress.

Now follow the score as the Thema is played.[2]

Anton Webern *Symphonie* op. 21. Copyright 1929 by Universal Edition. Copyright renewed. All rights for the U.S.A. and Canada owned exclusively by European American Music Distributors Corporation. Used by permission.

Play Thema, twice.

Ex. 12 shows the pitches of the Thema in the order in which they occur. Brackets connect the closest tritone-related pitches between the clarinet and the other instruments, and the resulting tritones are numbered in the order in which they occur.

EXAMPLE 12

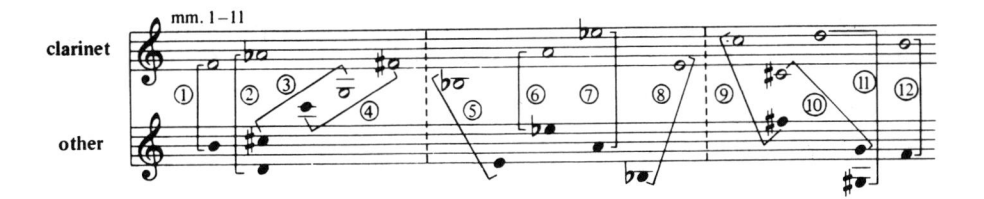

Notice that the six *large-scale* tritones *within* the clarinet part (see Ex. 11) each occur as *local* tritones *between* the clarinet and the other instruments in each half of the Thema (see Ex. 12). The local tritones occur in the same order as the members of the large-scale nested tritones in the clarinet—naturally, since each pitch-class can participate in only one tritone-pair. Each clarinet pitch functions doubly, as a member of a large-scale nested tritone within the clarinet part, and as a member of a local tritone between the clarinet and the other instruments. The two similar functions reinforce each other's audibility.

We have heard before (in part I of this analysis) how the harp and horn parts are structured *individually* by large-scale tritones. It now appears that all of these "other" instruments taken together are structured in large-scale nested tritones, just like the clarinet part; and, as in the clarinet part, each pitch of an "other" instrument also functions doubly, as a member of a local tritone with the clarinet, and as a member of a large-scale, nested-tritone structure of the pitches of the "other" instruments. Ex. 13 shows the local tritones (numbered in order of occurrence) and the nested structure of tritones within the clarinet and within the "other" instruments. Now compare with Ex. 12. The double function of each pitch is easy to see.

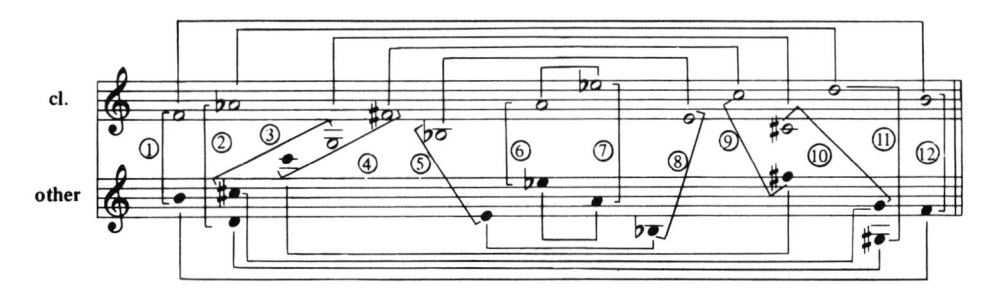

EXAMPLE 13

14   Basic Atonal Theory

Listen to the Thema for these relations. Again, the large-scale and local tritone structures reinforce each other's perceptibility. Such mutual perceptual reinforcement among large-scale and local, successive and simultaneous structures, is one reason why the principle of "unity of musical space" has proven so popular.

Play Thema, three times.

As a result of the local and nested structures shown in Ex. 13, the pitch-class structure of the entire Thema can be heard as one of nested tritones forming a retrograde-symmetrical pattern. Ex. 14 shows only local tritones, in order, with their nested, retrograde-symmetrical structure.

EXAMPLE 14

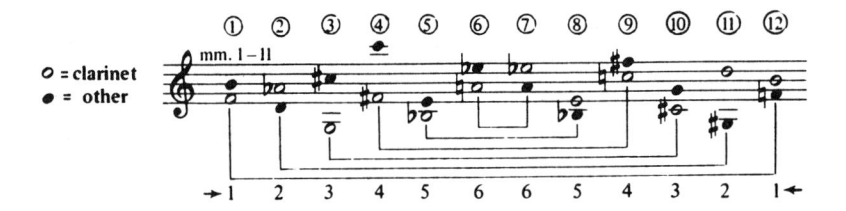

Can you hear this retrograde-symmetrical structure?

Play Thema.

The middle section from which this whole analysis started, incorporating the tritones numbered ⑤ through ⑧, is by far the easiest to hear. One reason for the relative obscurity of the rest of the structure is the more dense, *overlapped* presentation of the tritones numbered ②-④ and ⑨-⑪ (see Ex. 12). But this very obscurity provides an even more obviously audible clue to the retrograde symmetry of the Thema: the texture is hearable as retrograde-symmetrical (Exx. 15 and 16).

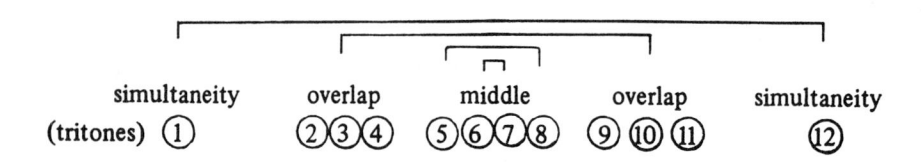

EXAMPLE 15

EXAMPLE 16 Number of Pitches per Attack Time, per Measure

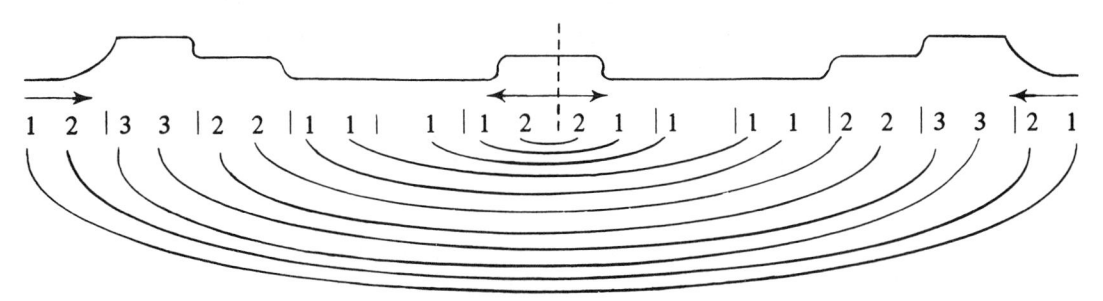

Play Thema.

There is yet another reason for the relative obscurity of the overlapped tritones (②-④, ⑨-⑪). Corresponding tritones ① and ⑫, ⑤ and ⑧, and ⑥ and ⑦ consist of identical pitches (in the same octaves), helping to produce that easily identifiable "structured shimmer" in the middle section (see Ex. 14). But corresponding overlapped tritones ② and ⑪, ③ and ⑩, and ④ and ⑨ correspond only in pitch-class content. For example, for tritones ④ and ⑨, not only are the F♯ and C of ④ in different octaves from the F♯ and C of ⑨, but their registral order is also reversed: in ④, F♯ is lowest; in ⑨, C is lowest. Moreover, the actual *pitch* interval of ④ is 18 pitch semitones (an octave plus a tritone), while the pitch interval of the corresponding ⑨ is 6 pitch semitones. See Exx. 14 and 17.

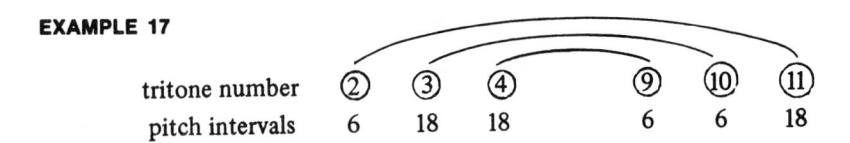

EXAMPLE 17

tritone number	②	③	④	⑨	⑩	⑪
pitch intervals	6	18	18	6	6	18

Such reversals are true of ② and ⑪, ③ and ⑩, as well as ④ and ⑨ (again, see Exx. 14 and 17). Every possible *pitch* difference is made an actual difference, retaining only pitch-class content identity of the corresponding tritones in these overlapping, obscured sections. The contrast with the middle and ends could not be sharper.

Play Thema.

Exx. 18 and 19 show respectively the pitches of the clarinet part and of the other instruments, with the interval in *pitch* semitones between adjacent pitches.

EXAMPLE 18

cl.
→ 3   13   11   8   11   6   11   8   11   13   3 ← unordered pitch interval
← -3 +13 -11 +8 -11 -6 +11 -8 +11 -13 +3 ←
→ +3 -13 +11 -8 +11 +6 -11 +8 -11 +13 -3 → } ordered pitch interval

16   Basic Atonal Theory

EXAMPLE 19

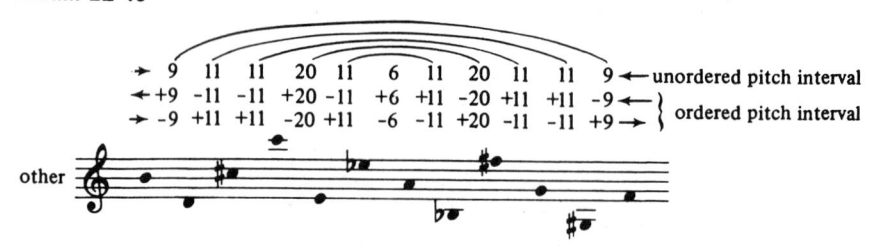

```
→  9   11   11   20   11    6   11   20   11    9  ← unordered pitch interval
←  +9  -11  -11  +20  -11  +6  +11  -20  +11  -9 ←  ⎫
→  -9  +11  +11  -20  +11  -6  -11  +20  -11  -11 +9 → ⎬ ordered pitch interval
                                                      ⎭
```

other [musical staff notation]

Notice that, while the interval series of Ex. 18 are quite different from those of Ex. 19, each example separately exhibits a retrograde-symmetrical structure. In each case, the series of *unordered* pitch intervals (see chapter 2) is retrograde symmetrical (the same backwards as forwards); and the series of ordered pitch intervals from left to right differs only in the sign of the middle "6" from the series of ordered pitch intervals taken from right to left on the same pitch series. Further comments are found in chapter 2.

Moreover, the clarinet part, and the nonclarinet parts both separately and together, are retrograde-symmetrical as series of *durations* of sounds and rests, and as series of *dynamic and articulation markings,* and even as series of *orchestrational patterns* (which instrument is chosen to play which note)! See Exx. 20 and 21.[3]

EXAMPLE 20

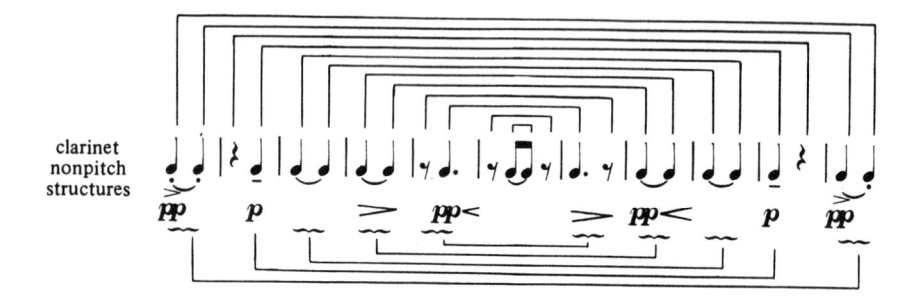

clarinet nonpitch structures [musical notation with pp, p, >, pp<, >, pp<, p, pp dynamics]

EXAMPLE 21

harp = x
horns = ♩
nonpitch structures [musical notation with pp<, p, pp<>, p, pp> and pp<, p> dynamics]

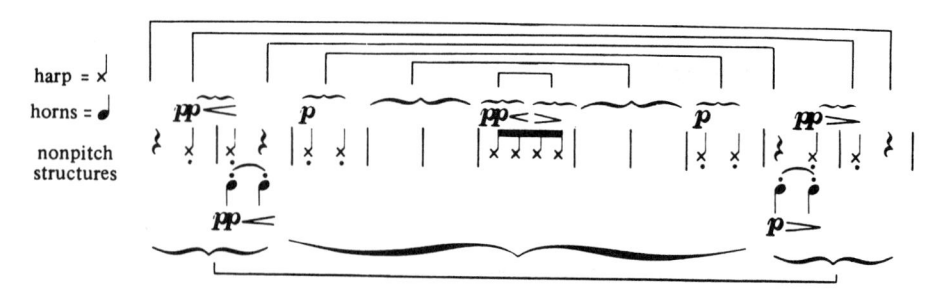

If Exx. 20 and 21 were superimposed, the result would again be a retrograde-symmetrical structure, of all nonpitch aspects of the Thema. Under such overwhelming circumstances, the *lack* of a straightforward retrograde-symmetrical structure of *pitches* (see Exx. 12 and 14) is curiously refreshing.

But it should come as no surprise that the clarinet part is a *pitch-class* retrograde of the "accompaniment" and vice versa, making the pitch-class structure of the whole retrograde-symmetrical (see Exx. 22 and 14).

EXAMPLE 22

clarinet	F	A♭	G	F♯	B♭	A	E♭	E	C	C♯	D	B
accompaniment	B	D	C♯	C	E	E♭	A	B♭	F♯	G	A♭	F

Remember that the ordering of the accompaniment pitches (see Ex. 22) is not the time-order of their attacks in the music, but was induced by the structure of local tritones between the clarinet and the accompaniment (see Exx. 12, 13, 14).

Thus all aspects of the Thema except pitch—durations, orchestration, dynamics, and articulation markings—combine their individual retrograde-symmetrical structures to form a very audible compound retrograde-symmetrical structure of the whole, reflected around the middle of m. 6. The pitches of the Thema form many nested structures, some of them retrograde-symmetrical, around this middle point of reflection, but are, taken altogether, only indirectly retrograde-symmetrical, as pitch-classes in an order induced by a structural criterion (local tritones).

Play Thema, three times.

EXERCISES

1. In preparation for later chapters and analyses, listen intensively to the following works:
    Schoenberg: *Five Pieces for Orchestra (Fünf Orchesterstücke)* op. 16
    Drei Klavierstücke op. 11
    Klavierstück op. 33a
   Be prepared to identify each of the five pieces of op. 16, as well as each of the three pieces of op. 11, and op. 33a, from hearing a short excerpt from each of them. You may be given such a "listening test."

2. Other sections of the Webern *Symphonie* are audibly retrograde-symmetrical in some way or ways. Listen to the entire *Symphonie*. Then listen again, following a score and paying particular attention to the sections given below. Continue listening until you can easily identify these sections without the score, experiencing the retrograde symmetry of each section:

    a) I mm. 25b—(34-35)—44 (Contrast mm. 45-60.)
    b) II mm. 34—(39)—44 (III. var.)
    c) II mm. 67—(72)—77 Kl., Bkl. only (VI. var.) (Contrast horn.)
    d) II mm. 78—(83)—88 (VII.var.) (Notice differences brought about by treatment of grace notes.)
    e) II mm. 89—(94)—99 (coda)

Notice various treatments of the "middle" (measure number in parentheses) from which each of the above sections starts its self-retrograde, as the middle of m. 6 functions in the Thema.

3. Listen repeatedly to Webern's *Variationen* for piano op. 27. Can you hear the ways in which retrograde symmetry is used, especially in the first movement?

4. Explore some of the many audible relations in the Thema that were not mentioned in our analysis.

5. Listen several times to Schoenberg's *Pierrot Lunaire* op. 21. Read the text (in translation if necessary) and follow the score. Then listen to it again, preferably late at night with all the lights off. (If you enjoy listening this way, try also Schoenberg's *Serenade* op. 24 and his third *String Quartet* op. 30.)

NOTES

[1] If primary generalization generalizes over a population of the sounds of a particular piece, and secondary generalization generalizes over a population of pieces of music, is it a kind of "tertiary" generalization that generalizes over a population of primary and secondary generalizations (as we do here)? Such tertiary generalization is heady and sinister stuff. A more innocent kind of tertiary generalization is used to generalize over populations of *categories* of pieces, either synchronically (over categories of pieces written in a common historic era) or diachronically (over categories of pieces written in differentiated historic eras)—e.g., generalizations arising from comparison of the serial works of Schoenberg with those of Berg and Webern, or from a comparison of the English Renaissance madrigal with the fourteenth-century Italian madrigal.

[2] N.B.: the harp notes with circles over them (mm. 1-3, 9-11) are harmonics sounding one octave higher than notated; otherwise this score sounds as notated.

[3] With regard to Exx. 20 and 21, the only fly in the ointment is the *pp* in the harp in m. 10. To retrograde the harp in mm. 1-2, mm. 10-11 "should be" marked:

I have always regretted not being able to hear more clearly the harp/clarinet F/B in m. 11. As marked in the score, the harp's F there is *less* than *pp* in dynamic.

It is assumed that the horns crescendo to a *p* in m. 2, and diminuendo to a *pp* in m. 10. Notice the score's strange placement of the *p* in the clarinet's m. 10. This placement (under the legato note) corresponds spatially and temporally to the clarinet's m. 2. But are we not to assume that m. 9 after the crescendo is played *p*, corresponding to m. 3?

CHAPTER TWO
THE INTEGER MODEL OF PITCH

2.1 TERMS AND ASSUMPTIONS

Tonal theory has been around so long and so pervasively that many of its concepts are built into our basic musical terminology. To call a particular pitch a C♯ is to accept at least two theoretical assumptions about structures of pitches. The first is the assumption of *pitch-class equivalence:* that all pitches that are called C♯, in whatever octave, have enough in common (for purposes of musical structure) that it is useful to give all of them the same name—"C♯". The second is the assumption of *diatonic functionality:* a C♯ cannot function (for example) as the fourth degree of an A♭ major scale, even though a C♯ and a D♭ (which can so function) may both be produced by hitting the same key on a piano. Of these two assumptions, that of diatonic functionality is more elaborate, more sophisticated, further along the tree of theoretical development, and more peculiarly "tonal."

The theory of atonal music can retain the assumption of pitch-class equivalence, but must reject diatonic functionality as being too particularly "tonal." Hence there is a need for a way to notate pitches which does not incorporate diatonic functionality. For decades, theorists have been solving this problem by using *integers* (nonfractional numbers) to notate pitches. This less specialized notation has allowed us also, as a bonus, to *construct* (rather than assume) the structures of diatonic functionality in tonal music. Tonal theory can in this sense be regarded as a special case of atonal theory, just as atonal theory is a special case (incorporating pitch-class equivalence) of a more general theory of music.[1]

But the use of integers also carries with it assumptions which must be carefully examined. Integers have a structure of their own (unlike the letter-names of tonal theory). Integers are ordered: of any two different integers, one is greater. Integers are equally spaced: a chain can be constructed of all integers such that the next integer along is always greater than the last by exactly "one": ..., −4, −3, −2, −1, 0, 1, 2, 3, 4, 5, ... In fact, all sorts of things can be proven true of integers—see any book on number theory. It does *not* follow that, because we are using integers to name pitches (or grapes, or housemaids), all those things that are true of integers are going to be true of pitches (or grapes, or housemaids). We must carefully determine the limits of similarity between integers (with their structure) and pitches (with their possible structures). To do otherwise would be to fall into the *numerological fallacy.*

20 *Basic Atonal Theory*

It turns out that pitches can share with integers at least the properties of being ordered and equally spaced. The next section will describe a way of correlating pitches and integers that preserves this useful similarity. When two structures are so correlated, they are called *models* of one another. In this case, we are using the integers as a model of a pitch structure. A manipulation of the model will correspond to a manipulation of what is modelled, so long as the manipulation involves only those structural features of the model (such as order and equal spacing) that can also be features of what is modelled. This gives a much stronger reason (than the mere denial of diatonic functionality) for using numbers to model pitch: many things can easily be proven about integers, within our limitations, which are then also proven about pitch. We are given then, if not carte blanche, at least carte beige to apply the riches of algebra and number theory to pitch.

2.2 PITCH AND ITS INTERVALS

2.21 Pitch

A trained listener can tell which of any two different pitches is higher than the other (if he can't, they're not different). This ordering by "higher than" can be correlated to the "greater than" ordering of integers by assigning smaller integers to lower pitches. In any "equal-tempered" system (such as our 12-pitch-per-octave system) pitches are equally spaced—that is, the perceived interval between any two adjacent pitches is a constant. This allows us to correlate the minimum difference between integers (one) with the minimum difference between pitches (a "semitone"). The result is a correlation between chains of integers and chains of pitches (chromatic scales).

We might now number the notes of the piano 0 to 88 from lowest to highest; or from −88 to 0, etc. No particular pitch seems uniquely to deserve being called "0", and yet 0 must be assigned to *some* particular pitch. Let us adopt the convention that C4, middle C on the piano, will be called "0", unless otherwise specified. Ex. 1 shows some pitches (not all pitches) named in this way; all accidentals are sharps and are not meant to imply any diatonic functionality.

EXAMPLE 1

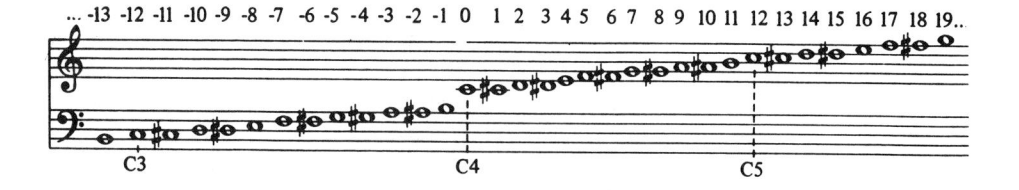

2.22 Ordered Pitch Interval

The number of semitones between two pitches may be obtained by subtracting the name of one from the name of the other, which leads to a definition of ordered interval for pitch.

DEF For any two pitches x and y, the ordered interval between x and y equals y minus x.

Symbols can be introduced to abbreviate this definition. (Review Appendix 1 for fuller explanations of mathematical notations and concepts as they appear in the text to follow.) Let "ip $<x,y>$" denote the ordered interval between pitches x and y. The "ip" means "pitch interval;" the angles "$<$,, '' $>$" indicate that what they enclose is *ordered* from left to right. Then the abbreviated definition reads:

DEF ip $<x,y> = y-x$

Notice that this definition distinguishes between an interval upward and an interval downward. For example, the interval from C4 to E4 (in that order) is ip $<0,4> = 4-0 = 4$, but the interval from E4 to C4 (in that order) is ip $<4,0> = 0-4 = -4$. A positive value indicates an upward interval, a negative value a downward interval. Other examples follow (see Ex. 2). In this example the interval from D4 to B4 = ip $<2,11> = 11-2 = 9$; the interval from F4 to G#3 = ip$<5,-4> = -4-5 = -9$; the interval from D#3 to A3 = ip$<-9,-3>=-3-(-9)=-3+9=6$; the interval from D3 to B2=ip$<-10,-13>$ $=-13-(-10)=-13+10=-3$; the interval from C4 to G5=ip$<0,19>=19-0=19$; the interval from A4 to E3=ip$<9,-8>=-8-(9)=-17$. In each case, the name of the first pitch is subtracted from the name of the second pitch.

EXAMPLE 2

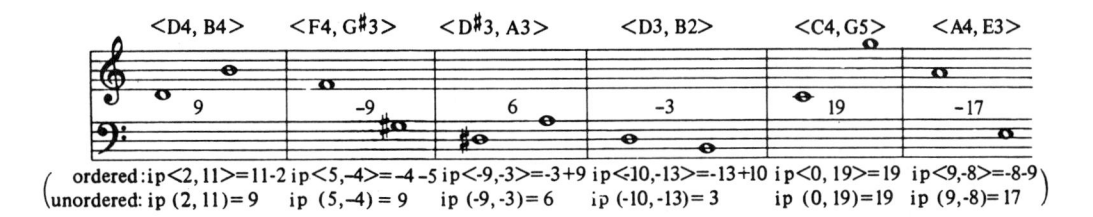

$\begin{pmatrix} \text{ordered: ip}<2,11>=11-2 & \text{ip}<5,-4>=-4-5 & \text{ip}<-9,-3>=-3+9 & \text{ip}<-10,-13>=-13+10 & \text{ip}<0,19>=19 & \text{ip}<9,-8>=-8-9 \\ \text{unordered: ip }(2,11)=9 & \text{ip }(5,-4)=9 & \text{ip }(-9,-3)=6 & \text{ip }(-10,-13)=3 & \text{ip }(0,19)=19 & \text{ip }(9,-8)=17 \end{pmatrix}$

Tonal theory also defines ordered interval for pitches, but many different tonal intervals (in principle, an infinite number of them) correspond to the same number of semitones; for example, "1" corresponds to a minor second, an augmented unison, a doubly diminished third, etc. But until you get used to using numbers, you may be "translating" tonal intervals into number of semitones, for which the following list may prove helpful.

perfect unison	0		perfect fifth	7
minor second	1		minor sixth	8
major second	2		major sixth	9
minor third	3		minor seventh	10
major third	4		major seventh	11
perfect fourth	5		perfect octave	12
tritone	6		minor ninth	13

22   Basic Atonal Theory

2.23   Unordered Pitch Interval

It is also useful to define a measure of distance, irrespective of direction, between two pitches whose relative order is not taken into account. There are 4 semitones between C4 and E4 or between E4 and C4, up or down. This measure is useful when dealing with sets (unordered collections) of pitches.

DEF   For any two pitches x and y, the unordered interval between x and y equals the absolute value of (y minus x).

The operator "absolute value of" converts any negative numbers to positive ones of the same magnitude. In symbols, the abbreviated definition reads:

DEF $ip(x,y) = |y-x|$

Notice that the unorderedness of x and y is given by the fact that they are enclosed in parentheses (x,y) rather than (ordering) angles $\langle x,y \rangle$. The result of the calculation is the same as for that involving ordered pitch interval, except that negative numbers become positive.

For example:

$$ip(17,8) = |8-17| = |-9| = 9$$
$$ip(-10,-13) = |-13-(-10)| = |-13+10| = |-3| = 3$$
$$ip(-9,-3,) = |-3-(-9)| = |-3+9| = |6| = 6$$

See Ex. 2.

2.3   PITCH-CLASS AND ITS INTERVALS

2.31   Pitch-class

Much of music theory talks not about pitches, but about pitch-classes. A "pitch-class" in this sense is an equivalence class of all pitches that are exactly octaves apart. More precisely, using our integer model of pitch:

DEF   Two pitches b and c are in the same pitch-equivalence class if and only if for some integer n, $b = 12 \cdot n + c$, or equivalently (for some non-negative integer n) $ip(b,c) = 12 \cdot n$.

For example:

$$ip(1,13) = 12$$
$$ip(-5,19) = |19-(-5)| = 19+5 = 24 = 2 \cdot 12$$
$$ip(46,-2) = |(-2)-46| = |-48| = 48 = 4 \cdot 12$$

Then, according to the above definition, pitches 1 and 13 are in the same pitch-equivalence class; pitches −5 and 19 are both in a (different) class; and pitches 46 and −2 are both together in yet a third pitch-equivalence class.

Pitches in the same pitch-class are some "integral multiple" of 12 semitones apart; that is, the unordered pitch interval between them is 0, 12, 24, 36, etc. We can then simply define a "pitch-class" ("pitch-class" and "pitch-classes" are abbreviated "pc") to be a set of all such pitches.

DEF   **A "pitch-class" or "pc" is a set of all pitches such that for any two members of the set b and c, ip (b,c) = 12·n for some non-negative integer n.**

For example:

$$ip(-14,-2) = |(-2)-(-14)| = |-2+14| = |12| = 1\cdot 12$$
$$ip(-2,10) = |10-(-2)| = |10+2| = 1\cdot 12$$
$$ip(-14,10) = |10-(-14)| = 10+14 = 2\cdot 12$$

so the pitches −14, −2 and 10 are three members of the same "pitch-class."

It is easily seen that there are just 12 distinct such pitch-classes (see the list that follows); *each pitch-class is named by its least non-negative member*. The names of the 12 pitch-classes are then "0", "1", "2", "3", "4", "5", "6", "7", "8", "9", "10", "11". Pitch 12 is in the same set as 0, pitch 13 as 1, pitch 14 as 2, etc.

$$0 = (...-36, -24, -12, \ 0, 12, 24, 36, 48...)$$
$$1 = (...-35, -23, -11, \ 1, 13, 25, 37, 49...)$$
$$2 = (...-34, -22, -10, \ 2, 14, 26, 38, 50...)$$
$$3 = (...-33, -21, -\ 9, \ 3, 15, 27, 39, 51...)$$
$$4 = (...-32, -20, -\ 8, \ 4, 16, 28, 40, 52...)$$
$$5 = (...-31, -19, -\ 7, \ 5, 17, 29, 41, 53...)$$
$$6 = (...-30, -18, -\ 6, \ 6, 18, 30, 42, 54...)$$
$$7 = (...-29, -17, -\ 5, \ 7, 19, 31, 43, 55...)$$
$$8 = (...-28, -16, -\ 4, \ 8, 20, 32, 44, 56...)$$
$$9 = (...-27, -15, -\ 3, \ 9, 21, 33, 45, 57...)$$
$$10 = (...-26, -14, -\ 2, 10, 22, 34, 46, 58...)$$
$$11 = (...-25, -13, -\ 1, 11, 23, 35, 47, 59...)$$

Since we want to treat the members of these sets as "equivalent," it is fortunate that the sets meet the criteria for being "equivalence classes": they are non-overlapping, and exhaustive of the set of all pitches.

Mathematics has already developed a system of *arithmetic modulo 12* which meets this case. The word "modulo" is abbreviated "mod." "Mod 12" means "in the measure of 12" in English, but the mathematical meaning of "mod 12" lies mainly in the definition that follows: two integers b and c are "equivalent mod 12" if and only if b = 12·n+c for some integer n. Of course, this is the same formula that appeared in the previous two definitions about pitch-class. For example, the expression 25 = 12·2+1 shows that pitches 1 and 25 are members

24   Basic Atonal Theory

of the same pitch-class. The "pitch-classes" shown in the chart of 12 pitch-classes are in mathematics the "residue classes mod 12" of the integers.

From now on, all talk about pitch-classes will be in terms of a quirky *mod 12 arithmetic,* in which for any integer smaller than 0 or larger than 11, *add or subtract 12 until you get an integer between 0 and 11 inclusive.* For example, $5+9=(14=14-12=)2$, and $5-6=(-1=-1+12=)11$. (Clock time is a familiar example of a mod 12 system: 9 hours past 5 o'clock is 2 o'clock; 6 hours earlier than 5 o'clock is 11 o'clock.) This may seem confusing initially, but as you progress through the text it will quickly become second nature.

Under the convention that middle C is pitch 0 unless otherwise specified, pitch-class 0 contains all C's (in whatever octave); pitch-class 1 contains all C♯'s (or D♭'s or B𝄪's, etc.); pitch-class 2 contains all D's (or E♭♭'s or C𝄪's, etc.); and so on. Comparing Ex. 3 with Ex. 1, you can see that pitch 12 "equals" (is contained in and labeled by) pitch-class 0, pitch 13 equals pitch-class 1, pitch 14 equals pitch-class 2, and so on, just as in arithmetic mod 12.

EXAMPLE 3

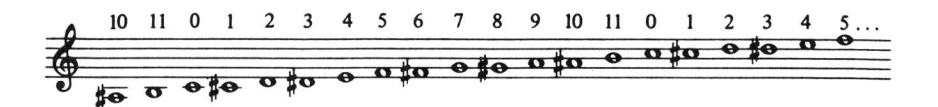

Sometimes, when looking at a particular piece of music, it is useful to have "0" denote some other pitch-class than C (although *within* any piece of music or analysis, the zero, once established, cannot be moved without destroying useful relationships). Ex: 4 gives the opening tune of the Schoenberg Piano Concerto op. 42. Since this starts with an E♭, it is not unreasonable to take E♭ as pitch-class 0; then B♭ is pitch-class 7, D is 11, F is 2, and so on, in whatever octave. Informally, the name of a pitch-class other than 0 is the least number of semitones *above* a pitch in pitch-class 0 that any of its pitch members can be. (Some pitch B♭ is 7 semitones *above* an E♭, some pitch D is 11 semitones *above* E♭, etc.) Alternatively, just shift the pitch numbers above Ex. 1 until 0 is over some D♯ (see Ex. 5). Then 7 is over A♯, 11 over D, etc., and these least non-negative members will name their corresponding pitch-classes (consisting of all D♯'s, all A♯'s, all D's, etc.).

EXAMPLE 4

Arnold Schoenberg Concerto op. 42. Copyright © MCMXLIV, by G. Schirmer, Inc. International copyright secured. Used by permission.

EXAMPLE 5

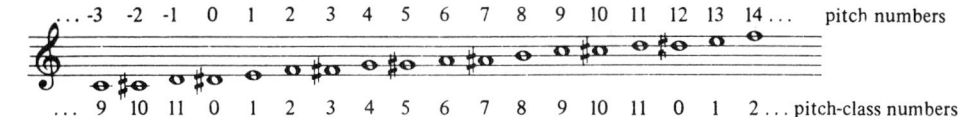

...-3 -2 -1 0 1 2 3 4 5 6 7 8 9 10 11 12 13 14... pitch numbers

... 9 10 11 0 1 2 3 4 5 6 7 8 9 10 11 0 1 2 ... pitch-class numbers

2.32 Ordered Pitch-class Interval

We have defined interval for pitches, but not for pitch-classes. The "ordered interval" between two pc (Milton Babbitt calls this "directed interval") might be thought of as the interval "up" from the first to the second pc. But "up" is no longer as unambiguous as it was for pitches. Given two pitch-classes, either one will have a member pitch that is higher than any given pitch member of the other. Pick any C; then some C♯ is higher. Pick any C♯; then some C is higher (by at least 11 semitones). Purely for convenience, we could decide to correlate "higher" with "having a greater integer for a name," so that pitch-class 1 is higher than 0, pc 5 is higher than 1, and so on. (Then C♯ is the higher pc if C=0, but C is the higher if C♯=0.) But regardless of this problem, the definition of ordered interval for pc "i<a,b>" can be similar to that of ordered interval for pitch:

DEF   i<a,b> = b−a **(for any two pitch-classes a and b, the ordered pitch-class interval between a and b in that order equals the number b−a mod 12.)**

This definition and all following definitions about pitch-classes assume that *all numbers are converted to their least non-negative equivalent, mod 12*. For example, i<5,1> = 1−5 = (−4) = 8, but i<1,5> = 5−1 = 4. In dealing with negative numbers, it is important to remember that 0 = 12 = 24 = 36...so that −4 = 0−4 = 12−4 = 8; −13 = 0−13 = 24−13 = 11.

For calculating intervals, the following table is handy:

−1	−2	−3	−4	−5	−6	−7	−8	−9	−10	−11
11	10	9	8	7	6	5	4	3	2	1

Assuming that C=0, here are a few more examples, in which the interval from

C to B = i<C,B> = i<0,11> = 11−0 = 11

B to C = i<B,C> = i<11,0> = 0−11 = −11 = 1

B♭ to D = i<B♭,D> = i<10,2> = 2−10 = −8 = 4

E to G♯ = i<E,G♯> = i<4,8> = 8−4 = 4

A to F = i<A,F> = i<9,5> = 5−9 = −4 = 8

G to C♯ = i<G,C♯> = i<7,1> = 1−7 = −6 = 6

F♯ to D♯ = i<F♯,D♯> = i<6,3> = 3−6 = −3 = 9

A♭ to E♭ = i<A♭,E♭> = i<8,3> = 3−8 = −5 = 7

26   *Basic Atonal Theory*

Employing this definition the intervals between successive notes of a tune can be obtained. The following intervals are the intervals between successive pc of the Schoenberg tune of Ex. 4 (see Ex. 4). Notice that, in a sense, each interval does give the number of semitones "up" from the first to the second pc: place a pitch member of the second pc as closely as possible above a pitch member of the first pc and then employ ordered pitch interval. (There are 7 pitch semitones from E♭ up to B♭; 4 from B♭ up to D; 3 from D up to F; 11 from F up to E; etc.)

$$i\langle 0,7\rangle = 7-0 = 7$$
$$i\langle 7,11\rangle = 11-7 = 4$$
$$i\langle 11,2\rangle = 2-11 = -9 = 3$$
$$i\langle 2,1\rangle = 1-2 = -1 = 11$$
$$i\langle 1,9\rangle = 9-1 = 8$$
$$i\langle 9,3\rangle = 3-9 = -6 = 6$$
$$i\langle 3,5\rangle = 5-3 = 2$$
$$i\langle 5,5\rangle = 5-5 = 0$$
$$i\langle 5,5\rangle = 5-5 = 0$$
$$i\langle 5,10\rangle = 10-5 = 5$$
$$i\langle 10,6\rangle = 6-10 = -4 = 8$$
$$i\langle 6,8\rangle = 8-6 = 2$$
$$i\langle 8,10\rangle = 10-8 = 2$$
$$i\langle 10,6\rangle = 6-10 = -4 = 8$$
$$i\langle 6,8\rangle = 8-6 = 2$$
$$i\langle 8,8\rangle = 8-8 = 0$$
$$i\langle 8,4\rangle = 4-8 = -4 = 8$$

EXERCISES 2-1

Consider the following musical excerpt. A line of pc is produced for this excerpt by taking the pc of the pitches in the order in which they are attacked:
C G E D E♭ B F A A♭ B♭ C♯ F♯

The Integer Model of Pitch 27

1. Write out this line of pc as a succession of pc numbers, with C = 0.

2-12. Give the ordered pc intervals between successive pc in the line:

  2. i<C,G>   = i< , > =
  3. i<G,E>   = i< , > =
  4. i<E,D>   = i< , > =
  5. i<D,E♭> = i< , > =
  6. i<E♭,B> = i< , > =
  7. i<B,F>   = i< , > =
  8. i<F,A>   = i< , > =
  9. i<A,A♭> = i< , > =
  10. i<A♭,B♭> = i< , > =
  11. i<B♭,C♯> = i< , > =
  12. i<C♯,F♯> = i< , > =

A different line of pc is produced by taking the pc of pitches in the order of lowest pitch to highest pitch:

C F A♭ B♭ A C♯ G E♭ E D B F♯

13. Write out this line of pc as a succession of pc numbers, with C = 0.

14-24. Give the ordered pc intervals between successive pc in this line. Compare with 2-12.

2.33 Unordered Pitch-class Interval; Sets

Just as it is useful to simplify music to pitches (disregarding timbre, dynamics, etc.) and to simplify pitches to pitch-classes (disregarding octave distinctions), so is it useful to simplify ordered successions of pc to *sets*, or unordered collections of pc (disregarding distinctions of "which came first"). For a very simple-minded example, take the following succession of pc (from Bach's *Well-Tempered Clavier*, I:1 Prelude):

CEGCEGCE   CDADFADF   BDGDFGDF   CEGCEGCE

Taking every eight of these pc instances produces the following succession of sets of pc:

{C,E,G}   {C,D,A,F}   {B,D,G,F}   {C,E,G}

which could be labeled I, II^7, V^7, I respectively, while the set of all these pc {C,D,E,F,G,A,B} is the C major diatonic collection. The temporary obliteration of all distinctions except those of pc content makes it easier to see certain relations having to do *only* with pc content; this is perhaps even more true for atonal than for tonal music.

28 Basic Atonal Theory

The pc in a set have no ordering. The set of pc {0,7} does not determine whether 0 or 7 should be the first pc in obtaining an interval between them. (The curly braces "{ }" and the list they enclose notate a set.) The two possible ordered intervals are i<0,7> = 7 and i<7,0> = 5. A definition of *unordered pc interval* or *i(a,b)* is needed to make the interval between pc in a set unambivalent.

DEF   **i(a,b) = the smaller of i<a,b> and i<b,a>.**

Simply by convention, we take the *smaller* of the two possible ordered pc intervals to be the unordered pc interval. It turns out that, although the possible values for ordered pc interval are the integers 0 through 11, the possible values for *unordered* pc interval are 0,1,2,3,4,5, and 6, for reasons given below.

Any two numbers that add up to 12, or to 0 mod 12, are called "complementary mod 12" or "complements mod 12." *Reversing the order of two pc produces the complementary (mod 12) interval.* Notice that 0 and 6 are their own complements (0+0 = 0; 6+6 = 0).

i<0,1> = 1	i<0,4> = 4
i<1,0> = 11	i<4,0> = 8
i<0,2> = 2	i<0,5> = 5
i<2,0> = 10	i<5,0> = 7
i<0,3> = 3	i<0,6> = 6
i<3,0> = 9	i<6,0> = 6

integers mod 12:   0 1 2 3 4 5 6 7 8 9 10 11
mod 12 complements: 0 11 10 9 8 7 6 5 4 3 2   1

(See note [2].)

Therefore the smaller of i<a,b> and i<b,a> will always be the smaller of two complements mod 12: ⓪, ① and 11, ② and 10, ③ and 9, ④ and 8, ⑤ and 7, ⑥.

	(for a ≤ b)	
0 1 2 3 4 5 6	i(a,b) = i(b,a)	i<a,b>
0 11 10 9 8 7 6		i<b,a>

Notice that mod 12 complementary intervals are (in a sense that will be made precise later) inversionally related: 11 (a major seventh) is related under i(x,y) to the inversion of a major seventh, 1 (a minor second); 10 is related to 2; 9 to 3; and so on. Some examples of unordered pc interval are:

The Integer Model of Pitch

$i(11,0) = i(0,11) = 1$ $i<11,0> = 0-11 = -11 = 1$

$i(5,7) = i(7,5) = 2$ $i<5,7> = 7-5 = 2$

$i(6,3) = i(3,6) = 3$ $i<3,6> = 6-3 = 3$

$i(2,10) = i(10,2) = 4$ $i<10,2> = 2-10 = -8 = 4$

$i(1,8) = i(8,1) = 5$ $i<8,1> = 1-8 = -7 = 5$

$i(4,10) = i(10,4) = 6$ $i<4,10> = 10-4 = 6$

Unordered pitch-class interval is also known as "interval class" ("ic"), "interval distance," "undirected interval," and even (completely incorrectly) as "interval mod 6."

EXERCISES 2-II

25-35. Give the unordered pc intervals for the pairs of pc used for items 2-12 (Exercises 2-I).

36-46. Give the unordered pc intervals for the pairs of pc used for items 14-24 (Exercises 2-I). Compare with 25-35.

47. a) What are the "mod 6" equivalents of the integers 0,1,2,3,4,5,6,7,8, 9,10,11? (Remember that an equivalent integer "mod 12" is found by subtracting or adding 12 until the integer is between 0 and (12-1) inclusive.)

    b) Why then is "interval mod 6" an unsatisfactory definition of unordered pc interval?

48. Unordered interval for pitch was defined as the absolute value of the difference: $ip(x,y) = |y-x|$.

    a) Why can't you define unordered interval for pitch-class in the same way: $i(a,b) = |b-a|$?

    b) (optional) Can you make changes in the other definitions and conventions that would make this last definition work?

2.4 INTERVALS: A RECAPITULATION

The preceding definitions of ordered pitch interval ($ip<x,y>$), unordered pitch interval ($ip(x,y)$), ordered pc interval ($i<x,y>$), and unordered pc interval ($i(x,y)$) do make musically relevant distinctions. Although these distinctions become most useful in higher-order concepts that are constructed using the definitions of interval—for example, in the unordered-pc-interval-content/common-tone theorem found in chapter 5—the bare distinctions themselves can be usefully heard in music.

EXAMPLE 6

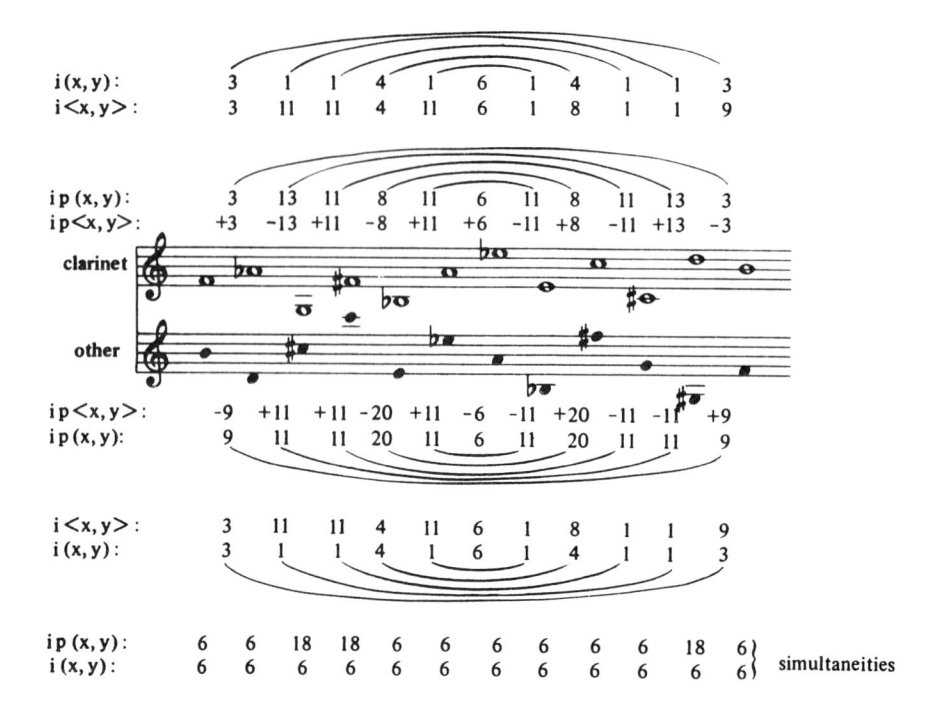

i(x,y):		3	1	1	4	1	6	1	4	1	1	3
i<x,y>:		3	11	11	4	11	6	1	8	1	1	9

ip(x,y):		3	13	11	8	11	6	11	8	11	13	3
ip<x,y>:		+3	−13	+11	−8	+11	+6	−11	+8	−11	+13	−3

clarinet

other

ip<x,y>:		−9	+11	+11	−20	+11	−6	−11	+20	−11	−11	+9
ip(x,y):		9	11	11	20	11	6	11	20	11	11	9

i<x,y>:		3	11	11	4	11	6	1	8	1	1	9
i(x,y):		3	1	1	4	1	6	1	4	1	1	3

ip(x,y):	6	6	18	18	6	6	6	6	6	6	18	6	
i(x,y):	6	6	6	6	6	6	6	6	6	6	6	6	simultaneities

Ex. 6 should recall our analysis of the Thema of Webern's *Symphonie* op. 21 in Analysis 1. Let us examine the intervals between adjacent pitches in each line of pitches. Ordered pitch interval—ip<x,y>—gives the most precise information. But the series of unordered pitch intervals—ip(x,y)—forms a retrograde-symmetrical structure. Thus, by *giving up* information about detail in moving from ip<x,y> to ip(x,y), we have *gained* information about structure. Unordered pitch interval is more "general" than ordered pitch interval because unordered pitch interval uses the same description for the two different orderings of a pitch pair, while ordered pitch interval distinguishes the two orderings. In losing particularity, one gains generality. The results of generality (here, the retrograde-symmetrical structure) can then reflect back on our more particular perceptions. Here, we can notice that ip<x,y> which correspond in the retrograde structure of the ip(x,y) are always of opposite sign (opposite pitch direction).

Further, i<x,y> is more general than ip<x,y> since it ignores octave placement, concerning itself only with pitch-classes. In this sense, i<x,y> is also more general than ip(x,y). But in another sense, ip(x,y) is more general than i<x,y> since ip(x,y) ignores distinctions of order and i<x,y> does not. The diagram below shows two directions in which various basic concepts are ordered from the particular to the general.

GENERAL
↑
  unordered (sets)
  partially ordered (e.g., lines containing chords)
  ordered (lines)

PARTICULAR ─────────────────────────────→ GENERAL

SOUNDS (pitch + timespan + instrument + dynamic + ...)   NOTES (pitch + timespan)   PITCHES   PITCH-CLASSES

With regard to Ex. 6, the move from ip(x,y) to i<x,y> does lose information about pitch detail (although gaining information about order). Again, the loss rewards us with gained information about structure: the series of i<x,y> for the clarinet line and for the "other" line are identical! As we shall see in chapters 3 and 4, and as common sense indicates, this identity of i<x,y> series means that the lines are *pitch-class transpositions* of each other. One would hardly have guessed from the ip<x,y> series that the two lines enjoyed such an intimate relationship.

Finally, the move from i<x,y> to i(x,y)—unambiguously in the directions of generality—again reveals structure (retrograde symmetry).

We can also look at the simultaneities between the two lines of pitches shown, measuring both ip(x,y) and the more general i(x,y) (which gives a very redundant series of sixes). Analysis 1 hints at some of the interesting structures behind the differences in these two interval series.

2.5 NORMAL FORM

The members of a set of pc may be listed in any order without changing the identity of the set. In order to be able to compare sets easily, it has been found necessary to choose one particular standard order to list them in. This standard listing order is called the "normal form" or "normal order" of a set of pc. The ability to take a set and quickly, almost automatically, list it in normal form is absolutely crucial to all subsequent use of nontonal theory. It may take a little practice to acquire this skill, but the acquisition is really not all that difficult.

Perhaps two examples of how the notion of normal form can make life easier will hearten you for the ministruggle ahead.

Ex. 7 gives the four 3-note simultaneities found in the Thema of the Webern *Symphonie* (see Analysis 1). It should be obvious that the first and fourth are transpositions of one another: transposing each pitch of ① down 6 pitch semitones gets ④ (see chapter 3 for more rigorous treatment).

32 *Basic Atonal Theory*

EXAMPLE 7

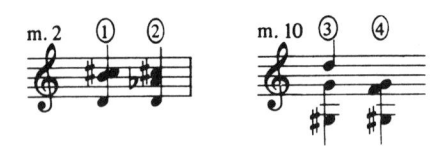

The relation between ② and ③ is neither that obvious nor too obscure, but becomes clear when ② and ③ are treated as sets of pc and put in normal form. The normal form of ② is A♭—C♯—D; the normal form of ③ is D—G—G♯. You can now see at a glance that the pc sets of ② and ③ are transpositions of each other by a pc interval of 6:

A♭—C♯—D

D —G —G♯

(This "see-at-a-glance" mechanism, among others, is made explicit in chapters 3 and 4.)

Ex. 8 gives two lines of pitches. Play them and listen. Are they in any way transpositions of one another?

EXAMPLE 8

Certainly not as *lines of pitches*. Perhaps more general concepts will reveal a relationship. (See diagram of particular/general directions in section 2.4.)

Are they related as *sets of pitches?* No. We can rule that out easily; for one thing, the pitch span of the first is from E♭ (pitch 3) to D (pitch 26) or 26−3 = 23 pitch semitones; but the pitch span of the second is only 13 pitch semitones from F (pitch 5) to F♯ (pitch 18).

Are they related as *lines of pc?* No. Take the ordered pc intervals between adjacent pc and compare:

1) { E♭   C♯   F♯   D   C   A   line
        10   5   8   10 9   i<x,y>

2) {   3   6   4   1   4   i<x,y>
     E   G   C♯   F   F♯ B♭   line

Only if the two series of i<x,y> were the same would the two lines of pc be transpositionally related. (Again, see chapters 3 and 4.)

The Integer Model of Pitch

Finally, are they related as *sets of pc?* By far the easiest way to find out is to list the sets in normal form and then see if the two normal forms are related as lines of pc.

```
1) { C    C#    D    Eb    F#    A           normal form
       1     1    1     3     3               i<x,y>

2) {       1    1     1     3     3           i<x,y>
     E    F    F#    G    Bb    C#           normal form
```

By placing the two pitch lines in normal form, we can see that these audibly very different pitch lines are, at a very high level of abstraction only (that of pc sets), transpositionally equivalent.

Procedure for Finding Normal Form

Intuitively, normal form is an ordering that increases (rises) from left to right "within an octave" and that occupies the least possible interval. We look first for a smallest outside interval (the ordered pc interval from first to last pc). If this produces a tie (two or more such intervals), look for the smallest next-most-outside interval until the tie is broken or you've gone all the way to the interval between the first and second pc. If the tie still is not broken, choose the remaining ordering having the smallest initial pc number.

This procedure will always produce one unique ordering for any pc set. A more rigorous definition of normal form and a shortcut procedure to finding normal form appear at the end of this section.

EXAMPLE 9

Ex. 9 gives pitches that are members of pitch-classes 0, 6, 2, 11 (with C = 0). This ordering—0 6 2 11—is not "within an octave" since i<0,6> and i<6,2> already add up to 6 + 8 = 14, more than 12 pc semitones. But another ordering may be tried to correct the situation. *Numerical order* (e.g., 0 2 6 11) *of pc numbers always results in one "increasing ordering within an octave"; the other increasing orderings can be produced by rotation:*

```
    0    2    6   11
    2    6   11    0
    6   11    0    2
   11    0    2    6
```

EXAMPLE 10

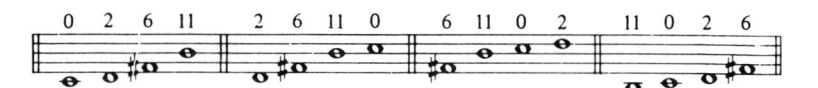

34 Basic Atonal Theory

Each of these increasing orderings is represented in Ex. 10 by pitches arranged in rising order within an octave. Each case is "within an octave" because the sum of the ordered intervals between adjacent pc is less than 12:

$$i<0,2> + i<2,6> + i<6,11> = 2 + 4 + 5 = 11$$
$$i<2,6> + i<6,11> + i<11,0> = 4 + 5 + 1 = 10$$
$$i<6,11> + i<11,0> + i<0,2> = 5 + 1 + 2 = 8$$
$$i<11,0> + i<0,2> + <2,6> = 1 + 2 + 4 = 7$$

The ordering with the smallest outside interval (which equals the sum of the adjacency intervals) is 11 0 2 6, with its outside interval of $i<11,6> = 7$ between its first and last pc. Therefore the normal form of {0, 6, 2, 11} is {11, 0, 2, 6}.

Rather than figuring the ordered pc intervals using numbers, you may find it easier to use pitch representatives of the pc involved, as in Ex. 10, but the results are the same either way. In Ex. 10, the interval from B to F♯ (7 semitones) is obviously the smallest outside interval.

EXAMPLE 11

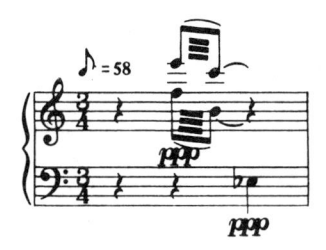

Anton Webern *Funf Satze*. Copyright 1922 by Universal Edition. Copyright renewed. All rights for the U.S.A. and Canada owned exclusively by European American Music Distributors Corporation. Used by permission.

Ex. 11 gives a piano reduction of the first measure of Webern's op. 5 no. 4 (for string quartet). With C = 0, this measure defines the set of pc {0, 3, 4, 5, 11}.

EXAMPLE 12

Ex. 12 gives the five increasing orderings within an octave for Ex. 11:

    0 3 4 5 11,
    3 4 5 11 0,
    4 5 11 0 3
    5 11 0 3 4, and
   11 0 3 4 5.

The smallest outside interval is $i<B,F> = i<11,5> = 6$, so the normal form is {11, 0, 3, 4, 5}.

Shortcut for Smallest Outside Interval

There is a shortcut to finding the smallest outside interval. Take any increasing ordering within an octave, such as the first ordering of Ex. 12: 0 3 4 5 11. Look for the *largest inside interval* (in this case it is the 6 semitones from F to B, pc 5 to 11). Rotate the ordering so that the right-hand, upper element of the largest inside interval (in this case, B = 11) is the first and lowest pitch. This process assures a smallest outside interval (11—0—3—4—5) without your having to write out all the rotations.

So far not more than one of the increasing orderings has had the smallest outside interval, so the outside interval has been enough to determine the normal form. Ex. 13 gives a piano score of mm. 1-6 from Schoenberg's *Die Jakobsleiter*.

EXAMPLE 13

Arnold Schoenberg *Die Jakobsleiter*. Used by permission of Belmont Music Publishers, Los Angeles, California 90049.

Look at the culminating chord in the right hand at m. 6. The set of pc of these pitches is {0, 3, 6, 9, 10, 11} with C = 0. Its six increasing orderings are:

0 3 6 9 10 11,

3 6 9 10 11 0,

6 9 10 11 0 3,

9 10 11 0 3 6,

10 11 0 3 6 9, and

11 0 3 6 9 10.

The six orderings are given in pitches in Ex. 14.

EXAMPLE 14

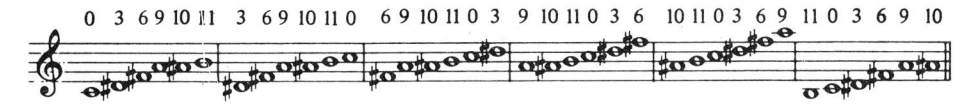

36   Basic Atonal Theory

Of these orderings, three have an outside interval of 9, and the other three an outside interval of 11. There are three orderings with a smallest outside interval of 9:

  3 6 9 10 11 0,

  6 9 10 11 0 3, and

  9 10 11 0 3 6.

So we look at the next-most-outside interval—the interval between the first and the next-to-last pc:

  i<3,11> = 8

  i<6,0> = 6

  i<9,3> = 6

This still doesn't settle it, so we look at the next-most-outside interval (between the first and third-to-last pc) of the remaining two orderings, 6 9 10 11 0 3 and 9 10 11 0 3 6.

  i<6,11> = 5

  i<9,0> = 3

Thus, we find that the normal form is {9, 10, 11, 0, 3, 6}. This process is equivalent to looking at the pitch orderings shown in Ex. 14 and choosing for the normal form that ordering which is *most closely packed to the left*—namely, 9 10 11 0 3 6.

EXAMPLE 15

EXAMPLE 16

Ex. 15 shows an "augmented triad," {1, 5, 9}, if C = 0. Ex. 16 shows the three increasing orderings within an octave for this triad:

  1 5 9,

  5 9 1, and

  9 1 5.

Each has the same outside interval:

  i<1,9> = i<5,1> = i<9,5> = 8

Each has the same next-most-outside intervals:

  i<1,5> = i<5,9> = i<9,1> = 4

So the criterion of "most packed to the left" does not determine a unique normal form here, and the remaining ordering with *smallest initial pc number* is chosen: {1,5,9} is the normal form. The criterion of "smallest initial pc number" does not come into play until the "most packed to the left" criterion has failed for all intervals.

EXAMPLE 17

Arnold Schoenberg Suite op. 29. Used by permission of Belmont Music Publishers, Los Angeles, California 90049.

Ex. 17 shows the first measure of the last movement of Schoenberg's Suite op. 29 (accidentals apply only to the note they immediately precede). This clarinet part may be heard as two subphrases of six notes, each of which is articulated the same way: ; and each of which has the same pitch contour: by twos, down, up, up. The pitches of the first subphrase define a set of pitch-classes, with E♭ = 0: {0, 4, 3, 7, 11, 8}. The six increasing orderings within an octave of this set (shown in pitches in Ex. 18) are:

    0   3   4   7   8 11,
    3   4   7   8 11   0,
    4   7   8 11   0   3,
    7   8 11   0   3   4,
    8 11   0   3   4   7, and
   11   0   3   4   7   8.

EXAMPLE 18

Three of the six orderings have the smallest outside interval 9:

    3   4   7   8 11   0,
    7   8 11   0   3   4, and
   11   0   3   4   7   8.

The next-most-outside intervals of the three orderings are all 8:

$$i<3,11> = i<7,3> = i<11,7> = 8$$

Their third-most-outside intervals are all 5:

$$i\langle 3,8\rangle = i\langle 7,0\rangle = i\langle 11,4\rangle = 5$$

Their fourth-most-outside intervals are all 4:

$$i\langle 3,7\rangle = i\langle 7,11\rangle = i\langle 11,3\rangle = 4$$

Their fifth-most-outside intervals are all 1:

$$i\langle 3,4\rangle = i\langle 7,8\rangle = i\langle 11,0\rangle = 1$$

So the one of the three orderings with the smallest initial pc number is the normal form: {3, 4, 7, 8, 11, 0}.

To recapitulate, it is now possible to define a unique "normal form" of a set in terms of the informally defined attributes "increasing within an octave" and "most packed to the left":

DEF **The "normal form" of a set is that ordering of its members which is increasing within an octave and most packed to the left; if there is more than one such ordering, it is the remaining ordering with the smallest initial pc number.**

Any set of pc is usually listed in normal form. The sets given in the answers to exercises 49 and 51 are in normal form. The normal form of {0, 2, 4, 5, 7, 9, 11}—the diatonic collection—is {11, 0, 2, 4, 5, 7, 9}.

Shortcut Procedure for Finding Normal Form

1. Arrange the set in numerical order.
2. Notice each adjacency interval.
3. Rotate so that the right-hand member of the largest inside adjacency interval is first, and the smallest intervals are to the left ("most packed to the left"); in case of tie at this stage, elect the remaining ordering having smallest initial pc number.

Example: {8, 3, 7, 0, 6, 9}

1. 0 3 6 7 8 9

2.   3 3 1 1 3   intervals
   0 3 6 7 8 9 (0)   pc

3. 0, 3, and 6 are each right-hand members of the largest inside interval 3; but only the ordering starting on 6 is most packed to the left:

      6 7 8 9 0 3   pc
       1 1 1 3 3   intervals

EXERCISES 2-III

In each case, form sets of pc from the notes indicated and write their normal form. Let C = 0.

49. Use all the notes in the left hand (bass clef) in m. 1-5 of Ex. 13 (compare with the notes in the right hand).
50. Use the first four notes of Ex. 17.
51. Use the last four notes of Ex. 17. Compare with 50.
52. Use the middle four notes (fifth, sixth, seventh, and eighth) of Ex. 17.
53. Use mm. 5, 6, and 7 (the last three measures) of Ex. 4.
54. Use the first six notes (from E♭ through C) of Ex. 4.
55. Use Ex. 4 from the F♯ in m. 3 to the end (the last six pc). Compare with 54.
56. Use mm. 1 through 4 (the first half-phrase, from E♭ through A♭) of Ex. 4.

NOTES

[1] Benjamin Boretz has developed in detail the growth of more specialized from less specialized musical concepts, in his *Meta-Variations* (see Bibliography).

[2] This can not only be illustrated, but (thanks to the modelling relation set up between integers and pc) *proven* using variables ranging over the integers mod 12:

$$i<a,b> + i<b,a> = 0 \quad \text{IFF}$$
$$(b-a) + (a-b) = 0 \quad \text{IFF}$$
$$b-a+a-b = (b-b) + (a-a) = 0+0 = 0$$

(for any two pc a and b)

CHAPTER THREE
BASIC OPERATIONS

3.1 TRANSPOSITION

Transposition and inversion each will be defined in the form of an *operation* of a particular sort, in this case, a "mapping." In other words, transposition or inversion will "operate" on one thing to produce another thing; it will "map" the first thing into the second. But any operation or mapping may be thought of also as a *relation* between the input and the output of the operation. We will informally use the words "operation," "mapping," and "relation" interchangeably.[1] (See Appendix 1.)

3.11 Pitch Transposition (T_n^p)

The transposition of a set or line of pitches adds the same number of pitch semitones to each pitch. Transposition can be defined in terms of the transposition of a single pitch, with the usual understanding that *the transposition of a set or line of pitches is the set or line of the transpositions of the individual pitches.*[2]

DEF   For any pitch x and any pitch interval n, $T_n^p(x) = x+n$

The definition may be read, "the pitch transposition of x by n semitones equals x plus n," or, "T sub n maps pitch x into pitch (x plus n)." (The equals sign "=" may be replaced in any of these operation definitions by an arrow "→", which indicates a "mapping" of x into x + n.) See Ex. 1.

EXAMPLE 1

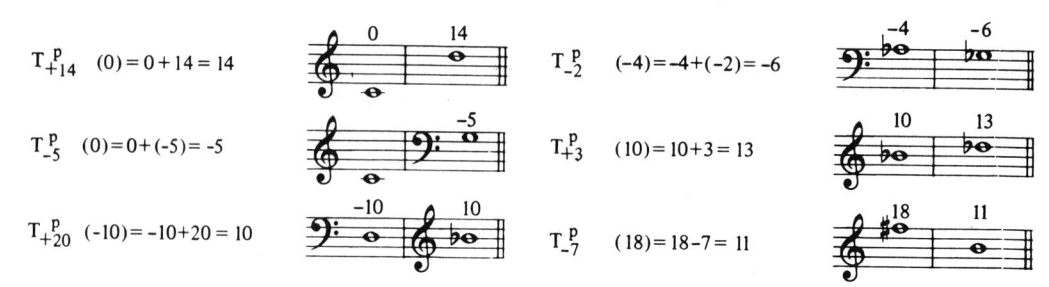

T_{+14}^p (0) = 0 + 14 = 14

T_{-5}^p (0) = 0 + (-5) = -5

T_{+20}^p (-10) = -10 + 20 = 10

T_{-2}^p (-4) = -4 + (-2) = -6

T_{+3}^p (10) = 10 + 3 = 13

T_{-7}^p (18) = 18 - 7 = 11

Basic Operations 41

The following notations are equivalent, that is, mean the same thing:

$$T_n^p(x) = x + n,$$

$$T_n^p(x) \rightarrow x + n, \quad \text{and}$$

$$x \xrightarrow{T_n^p} x + n.$$

All three can be read, "T sub n maps pitch x into pitch (x + n)." The superscript "p" in "T_n^p" distinguishes this transposition of *pitch* from the later-to-be defined transposition of *pitch-classes*, T_n.

In pitch transposition all intervals are preserved, and preserved in contour.[3] Therefore any two lines related by T_n^p will have the same intervals in the same order.

Here is a shortcut to transposing a line of pitches by some T_n^p: transpose the first pitch of the line by T_n^p, then take this transposed pitch and add the successive pitches to it to produce the same intervals as in the first line. This will produce the "same tune" at transposition T_n^p (see Exx. 2 and 3). This "shortcut" may plug in to your present musical skills more directly than the procedure of transposing each member of the line individually by T_n^p.

EXAMPLE 2   To transpose a line of pitches, transpose each pitch, in order.

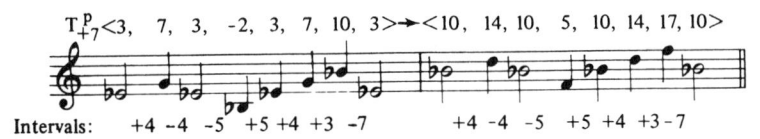

$$T_{+7}^p \langle 3, 7, 3, -2, 3, 7, 10, 3 \rangle \rightarrow \langle 10, 14, 10, 5, 10, 14, 17, 10 \rangle$$

Intervals: +4 −4 −5 +5 +4 +3 −7   +4 −4 −5 +5 +4 +3 −7

EXAMPLE 3

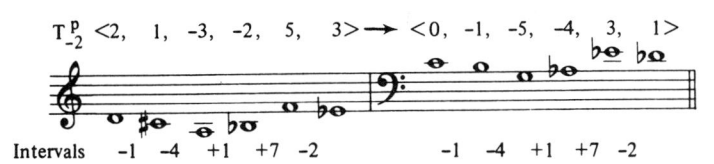

$$T_{-2}^p \langle 2, 1, -3, -2, 5, 3 \rangle \rightarrow \langle 0, -1, -5, -4, 3, 1 \rangle$$

Intervals: −1 −4 +1 +7 −2   −1 −4 +1 +7 −2

EXERCISES 3-1

1. $T_{+7}^p(7) =$ [staff] $T_{+7}^p(7)$ with middle $C(C^4) = 0$

2. $T_{-3}^p(-10) =$ [staff]

3. $T_{12}^p(-16) =$ [staff]

4. $T_{-13}^p(4) =$ [staff]

5. $T_{-5}^p \langle 6, 2, -1, 7, 6, 11, 10, 4, 3, 12, 11, 6, 5, 14, 13, 12, 13, 9, 6, 8, 6 \rangle$
   $\langle \qquad\qquad\qquad\qquad\qquad\qquad\qquad\qquad \rangle$

a) [staff]

42 Basic Atonal Theory

b) T_{-5}^p

6. $T_6^p <-2, -5, 2, 8, 1, 4>$

7. $T_{-6}^p <-2, -5, 2, 8, 1, 4>$

3.12 Pitch-Class Transposition (Tn)

Pitch-class transposition is similar to pitch transposition:

DEF   For any pc x and any pc interval n, $T_n(x) = x + n$ (mod 12)

This definition may be read, "the pitch-class transposition of x by n semitones equals x plus n." As usual for pc, all additions dealing with pc are *mod 12* and *all results are converted to a number between 0 and 11 inclusive*.

Pitch-class transposition (T_n) does *not* preserve "contour" of a line of pc, since a line of pc has no particular contour. But T_n does preserve both ordered pc interval and unordered pc interval: for any two pc x and y and any pc interval, the ordered (or unordered) interval between x and y equals the interval between the transpositions of x and of y. (See Ex. 4.)[4]

EXAMPLE 4

C equals zero. In the musical examples, pc are represented by pitches.

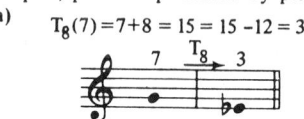

a) $T_8(7) = 7+8 = 15 = 15 - 12 = 3$

b) $T_{10}<0, 1, 4> = <0+10, 1+10, 4+10> = <10, 11, 14> = <10, 11, 2>$

   $i<x,y>: 1,3$ $<0, 1, 4>$ $\xrightarrow{T_{10}}$ $<10, 11, 2>$ $i<x,y>: 1,3$

c) $T_4<7, 8, 10, 0> = <7+4, 8+4, 10+4, 0+4> = <11, 12, 14, 4> = <11, 0, 2, 4>$ and for $<11, 0, 2, 4>$

   $i<x,y>: 1,2,2$ $<7, 8, 10, 0>$ $\xrightarrow{T_4}$ $<11, 0, 2, 4>$ $i<x,y>: 1,2,2$

d) $T_8 \{11, 0, 2, 4\} = \{11+8, 0+8, 2+8, 4+8\} = \{19, 8, 10, 12\} = \{7, 8, 10, 0\}$

   $\{11, 0, 2, 4\}$ $\{7, 8, 10, 0\}$

It is obvious from Ex. 4 that one way to transpose a line of pc by T_n is to:

1. represent each pc by a pitch;
2. transpose those pitches by T_n^p, using the T_n^p shortcut;
3. convert the resulting pitches to the pc of which they are members.

Since a musician can *hear* pitches (in his imagination) and usually can easily "finger" a transposition of a line of pitches, as part of his performing technique, this shortcut for T_n has advantages of musical immediacy. Remember, a pitch-class cannot easily be performed or heard, consisting as it does of all octave-related pitches; *rather, we hear pitches, qualified or colored by their membership in a pitch-class.*

Similarly, to transpose a set is to transpose each of its members. The members must be listed in *some* order—the "normal form" order is standard. So, in effect, what you are doing is transposing a line, the line of the set members in the order in which they happen to be listed. Thus the transposition of a set of pc can become the more musically immediate transposition of a line of pitches, experientially.

EXERCISES 3-II

Perform the following transpositions (C = 0) and write out the answers both in numbers and in pitch representation.

1. T_6 (6) =

2. T_2 <0, 6, 8> = < >

3. T_6 <0, 1, 4, 2, 9, 5, 11, 3, 8, 10, 7, 6> =
   < >

4. T_{11} <0, 8, 11, 4, 9> = < >

5. T_7 <0, 2, 4, 5, 7, 9, 11> = < >

6. T_6 <4, 1, 8, 2, 7, 10> = < >

44 Basic Atonal Theory

List each of the following sets in normal form, perform the indicated transpositions, and write out the normal forms in pitch representation. Let C equal zero.

	Set	Normal form	Transpositions in normal form
7.	{2, 7, 10, 4, 1, 8}		T_6
8.	{9, 10, 1, 0}		T_7
9.	{6, 1, 0, 4}		T_5
10.	{8, 1, 4, 7, 0}		T_2
11.	{8, 1, 5, 0, 4}		T_{10}
12.	{7, 4, 1, 5, 3}		T_7
13.	{2, 4, 9, 10, 8, 3}		T_3
14.	{9, 10, 1, 0, 8, 7, 4, 5}		T_5
15.	{4, 3, 10, 8, 2, 9}		T_9
16.	{2, 6, 11, 10, 7, 3}		T_{10}

3.13 Identity and Inverse Operations

Transposition by zero semitones does not change anything. Such an operation, which maps every element into itself, is called an *identity* operation.

$$T_0^p(x) = x + 0 = x$$

$$T_0(x) = x + 0 = x$$

Naturally, since T_0^p and T_0 map every element into itself, they are also identity operations for sets or lines of those elements.

That a system of operations has or does not have an identity operation is of crucial formal importance. For one thing, a system lacking an identity operation is not a "group," but rather a "groupoid" or "semigroup" or other system. Musically, and very informally, the lack of an identity operation would rule out repetition.

It would be musically useful if, having performed an operation on a set or line A to produce a different set or line B, we could then perform some operation on B that would get us back to A. Such an operation, that undoes the work of a first operation, is called the *inverse* of the first operation. (Do not confuse any "inverse" operation with the operation of inversion, T_nI, to be explained later in this section.) Thus, transposition maps x into x + n. The inverse operation would map x + n back into x; it must subtract n from x + n.

THEOREM
The inverse of any T_n is $T_{(-n)}$. The inverse of any T_n^p is $T_{(-n)}^p$.

$T_n(x) \rightarrow x+n$ $\qquad\qquad T_n^p(x) \rightarrow x+n$

$T_{(-n)}(x+n) \rightarrow (x+n)-n = x \qquad T_{(-n)}^p(x+n) \rightarrow (x+n)-n = x$

$x \xrightarrow{T_n} (x+n) \qquad\qquad x \xrightarrow{T_n^p} (x+n)$

$(x+n) \xrightarrow{T_{(-n)}} x \qquad\qquad (x+n) \xrightarrow{T_{(-n)}^p} x$

Each pair of the preceding formulas is an informal proof of the theorem. The two pairs of formulas in the left-hand column notate in two different ways a proof for T_n; the pairs in the right-hand column notate a proof for T_n^p. The idea is to perform an operation on a variable, x, and then to perform the "inverse" operation on the result, bringing back the original "x" again. For example, if x = 7, and the interval of transposition, n, = 2, then we have the following:

$T_2(7) \rightarrow 7+2 = 9 \qquad\qquad T_2^p(7) \rightarrow 7+2 = 9$

$T_{10}(9) \rightarrow 9+10 = 7 \qquad\qquad T_{10}^p(9) \rightarrow 9 + 10 = 19$

$7 \xrightarrow{T_2} 7+2 = 9 \qquad\qquad 7 \xrightarrow{T_2^p} 7+2 = 9$

$9 \xrightarrow{T_{10}} 9+10 = 7 \qquad\qquad 9 \xrightarrow{T_{10}^p} 9+10^p = 19$

Remember, for T_n, "(-n)" is expressed as the non-negative mod 12 complement of n: $-n = 0-n = 12-n$, so the inverse of T_2, for example, is $T_{-2} = T_{10}$.

3.2 INVERSION

Inversion will be defined as the compound operation *transposed inversion* in order to avoid certain otherwise all too common confusions. (See note 7, at the end of the chapter). This definition fits one of the tonal-music senses of the word "inversion," in that each interval of an inverted tune is merely reversed in direction, as in the "inversion" of a Bach fugue subject. (See Ex. 5, a–c.)

3.21 Pitch Inversion (T_n^pI)

DEF For any pitch x and any ordered pitch interval n, $T_n^pI(x) = -x+n$

(You may prefer to think of (−x+n) as (n−x).)

46 Basic Atonal Theory

For example, $T_n^p I(7) = -7+8 = 1$; $T_n^p I(5) = -5+3 = -2$.

This definition may be read, "pitch inversion maps pitch x into pitch (negative x plus n)." Pitch inversion preserves contours with *pitch intervals in the opposite directions;* each pitch interval changes sign (from positive to negative or negative to positive) but retains its absolute value. That is, for any two pitches x and y: 1) the interval between x and y equals (y−x); but 2) the interval between the inversion of x and the inversion of y equals the negative of (y−x), the same number of semitones but in the opposite direction.[5] For example, if x = 4 and y = 9, i<4,9> = 9−4 = 5; and $T_n^p I(4) = -4+n$ and $T_n^p I(9) = -9+n$, so i<(−4+n), (−9+n)> = (−9+n) − (−4+n) = −9+n+4−n = −9+4+n−n = −5: the same interval with opposite sign. (See Ex. 5, a–c.)

Again, a "musical" shortcut exists that will give the same result as applying $T_n^p I$ in turn to each member of a line of pitches. Apply $T_n^p I$ to the first pitch of the line to get the first pitch of the inverted line, then add the following pitches to produce the same intervals *in the opposite directions*. This will give a mirror reflection of the first tune at $T_n^p I$ (see Ex. 5).

EXAMPLE 5

Middle C equals zero.

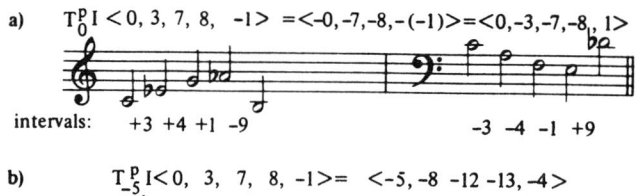

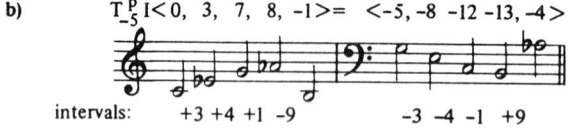

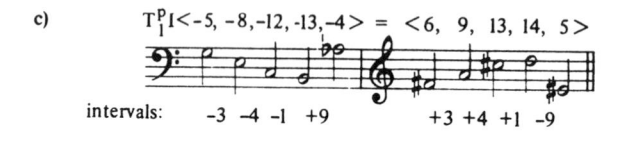

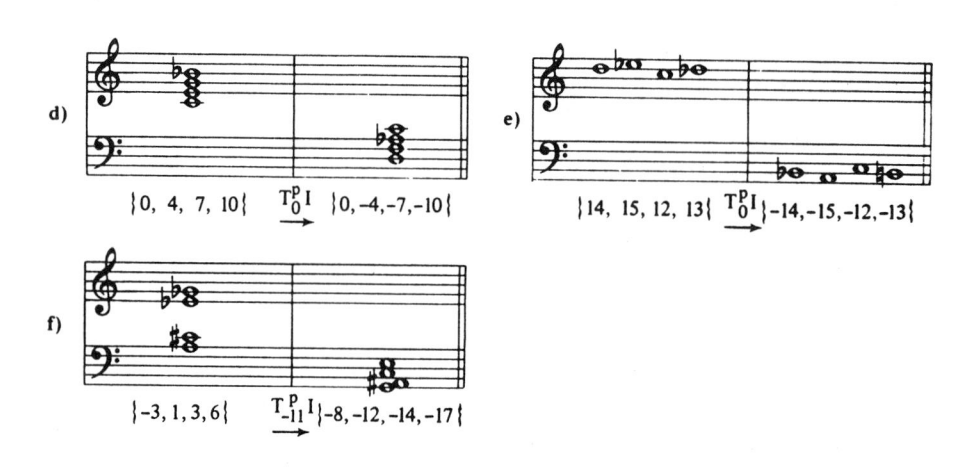

a) $T_0^p I <0, 3, 7, 8, -1> = <-0,-7,-8,-(-1)> = <0,-3,-7,-8, 1>$

intervals: +3 +4 +1 −9   −3 −4 −1 +9

b) $T_{-5}^p I <0, 3, 7, 8, -1> = <-5,-8 -12 -13, -4>$

intervals: +3 +4 +1 −9   −3 −4 −1 +9

c) $T_1^p I <-5, -8, -12, -13, -4> = <6, 9, 13, 14, 5>$

intervals: −3 −4 −1 +9   +3 +4 +1 −9

d) {0, 4, 7, 10} $T_0^p I$ {0,−4,−7,−10}

e) {14, 15, 12, 13} $T_0^p I$ {−14,−15,−12,−13}

f) {−3, 1, 3, 6} $T_{-11}^p I$ {−8,−12,−14,−17}

EXERCISES 3-III

Middle C equals zero.

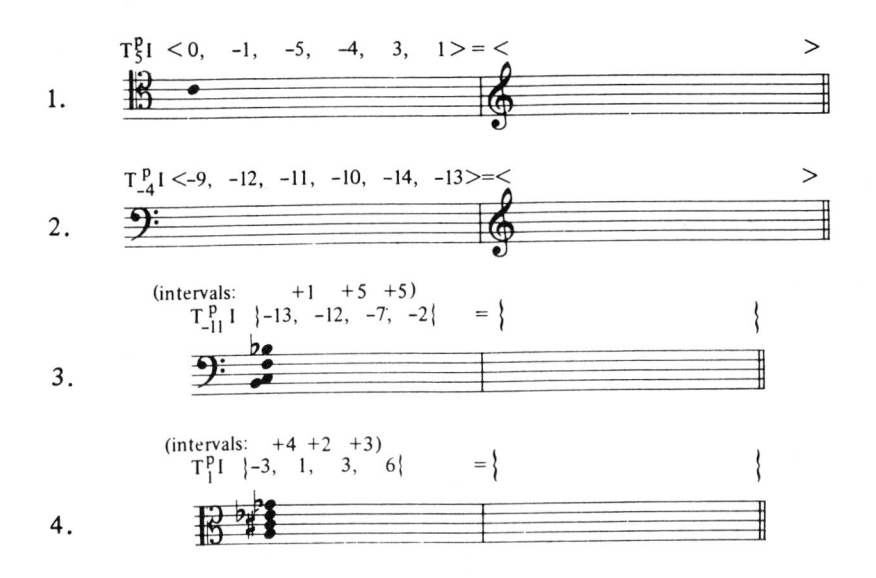

1. $T_5^P I \langle 0, -1, -5, -4, 3, 1 \rangle = \langle \quad \rangle$

2. $T_{-4}^P I \langle -9, -12, -11, -10, -14, -13 \rangle = \langle \quad \rangle$

3. (intervals: +1 +5 +5)
   $T_{-11}^P I \{-13, -12, -7, -2\} = \{ \quad \}$

4. (intervals: +4 +2 +3)
   $T_1^P I \{-3, 1, 3, 6\} = \{ \quad \}$

3.22 Pitch-class Inversion ($T_n I$)

DEF   For any pc x and pc interval n, $T_n I(x) = -x + n$ (mod 12)

This definition may be read, "$T_n I$ maps x into (negative x plus n)." For example, $T_{10}I(11) = -11+10 (= -1) = 11$; $T_2 I(6) = -6+2(= -4) = 8$. Again, while there is no contour to be mirrored (as there was for pitch lines), $T_n I$ does preserve the absolute value of intervals while "reversing their sign."[6] Using *unordered* pc intervals in $T_n I$, this amounts to no change (prove it yourself from the definitions). Therefore $T_n I$ is mainly interesting in using *ordered* pc interval in the operation. The proof follows that for $T_n^p I$, but with the reverse of sign—$(y-x)$ becomes $(x-y)$—producing the (non-negative) *complementary* (mod 12) interval; thus, 1 becomes $(-1) = 11$, 2 becomes $(-2) = 10$, 3 becomes $(-3) = 9$, and so on.

Note that if the interval of transposition is 0, $T_n I(x) = -x$, producing the complementary (mod 12) pc.[7] For example, $T_0 I(5) = -5+0 = -5 = 7$; 5 and 7 are complementary mod 12.

To invert a line by $T_n I$: (1) represent each pc by a pitch; (2) apply the $T_n^p I$ shortcut; (3) convert the resulting pitches to the pc of which they are members.[8]

To invert a set, invert it as a line in its "normal form." The result will be the inversion, usually ordered in the *retrograde* of the normal form of the inversion. (See Ex. 6.)

48   Basic Atonal Theory

EXAMPLE 6

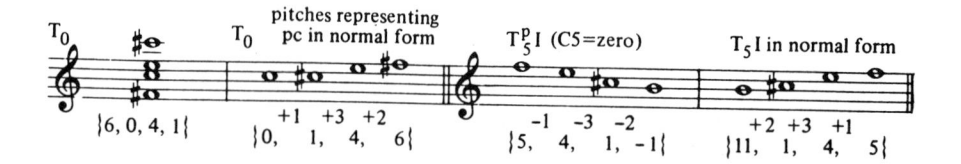

T_0 {6, 0, 4, 1}

T_0 pitches representing pc in normal form
+1 +3 +2
{0, 1, 4, 6}

T_5^pI (C5=zero)
−1 −3 −2
{5, 4, 1, −1}

T_5I in normal form
+2 +3 +1
{11, 1, 4, 5}

Summary: Invariance of Normal Form

The result of transposing a set in normal form will usually be the normal form of the transposition. The rare exceptions occur for sets that are transpositionally symmetrical (see 4.33), so that the criterion of "smallest initial pc number" comes into play, as in item 7 of Exercises 3-II. Thus, for most sets, once a set is put in normal form, all its transpositions come out in normal form. You usually don't have to "normalize" each of the transpositions separately.

For most sets, the result of inverting the normal form of the set is the retrograde of the normal form of the inversion. Many exceptions occur for inversionally symmetrical sets (section 4.32). When the normal form is not decided by the outermost interval, a nonsymmetrical set may be an exception: T_8I of $<0, 1, 4, 8>$ is $<8, 7, 4, 0>$, whose retrograde is $<0, 4, 7, 8>$. But the normal form of $\{0, 4, 7, 8\}$ is $\{4, 7, 8, 0\}$. Despite such exceptions, it is helpful, as a rule of thumb, to assume that the inversion of a set's normal form is the retrograde of the inversion's normal form, until it may prove otherwise.

EXERCISES 3-IV

For each set in the following exercises (C = 0): A) order in normal form; B) invert as indicated; and C) order inversion in normal form.

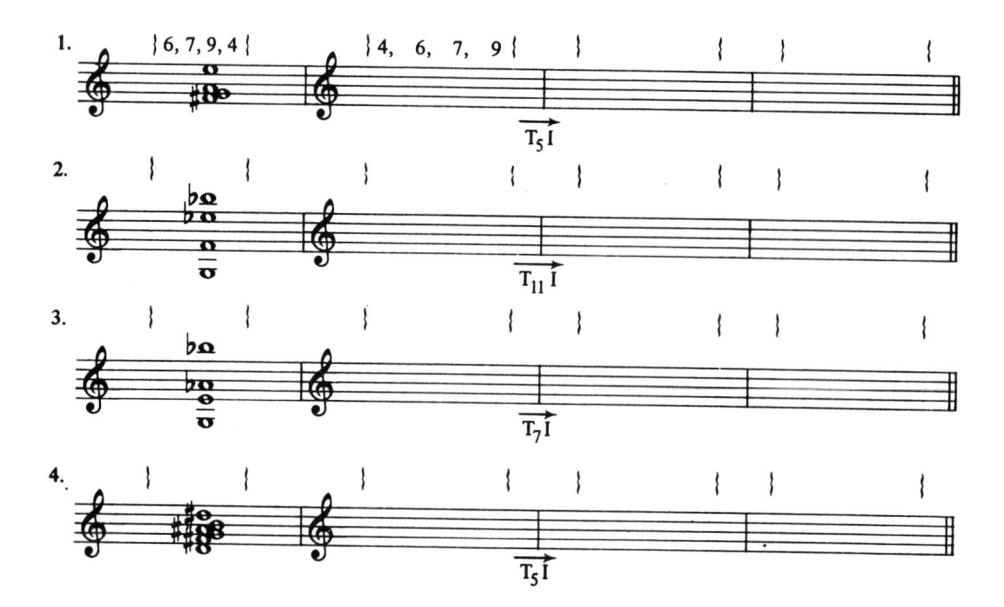

1. {6, 7, 9, 4}   {4, 6, 7, 9} $\overrightarrow{T_5I}$

2. $\overrightarrow{T_{11}I}$

3. $\overrightarrow{T_7I}$

4. $\overrightarrow{T_5I}$

5. (C=0) T_5I <5, 8, 7, 6, 10, 9> = < >

6. (E♭=0) T_8I <8, 0, 2, 3> = < >

7. (A=0) $T_{11}I$ <0, >

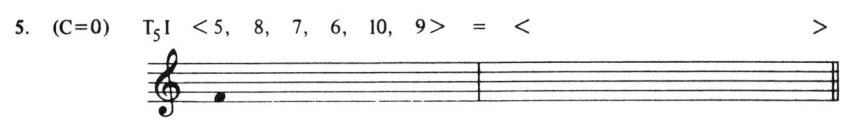

   < >

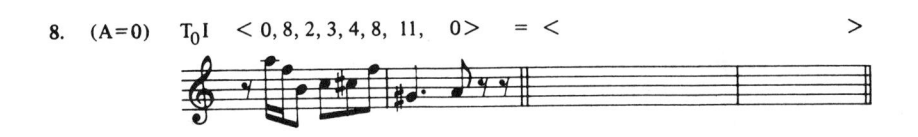

8. (A=0) T_0I <0, 8, 2, 3, 4, 8, 11, 0> = < >

3.23 Inverse Operations for Inversion. Sum, Index, Inversional Center

T_nI maps any element x into $(-x+n)$; the inverse of that operation maps $(-x+n)$ back into x. (Recall section 3.13.)

THEOREM
Every T_nI is its own inverse. Every T_n^pI is its own inverse.

The result of performing T_nI on any pc x is the pc whose number equals the expression $(-x+n)$. But the result of performing the same T_nI again on $(-x+n)$ is the original pc, x. Therefore every T_nI (inversion for every value of "n" separately) is its own "inverse" operation: $T_nI(T_nI(x)) = x$.

$$T_nI(x) = -x+n; \quad T_nI(-x+n) = x-n+n = x$$

The proof is identical for T_n^pI.

Sum. Notice that any two pc related by a T_nI must add up to the "n" of the T_nI: $x + (-x+n) = n$.

We can then make statements like the following: pc 10 and 8 are inversionally related by $T_{(10+8)}I$, or T_6I. The operation T_6I maps pc 10 into pc 8, and also maps pc 8 into pc 10; T_6I maps pc 8 and 10 into each other.

$T_6I(10) \to 8$ $T_6I(8) \to 10$

$10 \xleftarrow{\quad T_6I \quad} 8$

50   Basic Atonal Theory

Index. This sum is called (following, as usual, Milton Babbitt) the "inversional index" of any two pc related by T_nI, or of the operation T_nI itself; for example, the index of pc 8 and 10 is (8+10) = 6; pc 8 and 10 are (therefore) related by operation T_6I, whose index is its subscript, 6.

Inversional center. The "center of (inversional) symmetry" of two T_nI-related pc is one-half their index, or n/2. This holds equally for T_n^pI on pitches. For T_n^pI, this inversional center (n/2) is a place in pitch exactly *halfway between the two T_n^pI-related pitches.* (Since n equals the sum of the two pitches, the center is the numerical average of the two pitches.) All pairs of pitches related by T_n^pI for the same value of n have the same index (n) and the same center (n/2). See example at end of this section.

For T_nI also, the center of symmetry is always one-half the index, n, of each operation T_nI on pc. But for each T_nI on pc, there are always *two centers of symmetry 6 semitones apart*, since the system is now mod 12. (12 o'clock and 1 o'clock are equidistant from 12:30—by ½ hour—and from 6:30—by 5½ hours each.) This makes some sense in the mathematical model: every index n equals n+12 mod 12, so ½·n can be either ½·n or ½·(n+12) = ½·n+6.

The concepts of inversional index and center of symmetry may become clearer when you look at the effect of each T_nI mapping on all 12 pc. The mapping T_6I is shown below. (If necessary, review Appendix 1 on this notation for mappings.)

$$\begin{pmatrix} x \\ T_6I(x) \end{pmatrix} \begin{pmatrix} 0 & 1 & 2 & 3 & 4 & 5 & 6 & 7 & 8 & 9 & 10 & 11 \\ 6 & 5 & 4 & 3 & 2 & 1 & 0 & 11 & 10 & 9 & 8 & 7 \end{pmatrix}$$

sums   6 6 6 6 6 6 6 6 6 6 6 6

Notice that the sum of pc in each T_6I-related pair equals the index of the operation T_6I, namely 6. Ex. 7 shows this mapping for pitches representing each pc (C = 0).

EXAMPLE 7

Notice the characteristic "wedge" shape in Ex. 7. As one scale goes up, the other scale goes down. Observe that there are pc unisons at D♯ and at A; that is, D♯ maps into D♯ and A maps into A, under T_6I. The pc 3 and 9 are thus the two "centers of inversional symmetry" for T_6I, 3 being equal to one-half the index 6 and 9 being a tritone away from the other center, 3. (You can think of 9 also as one-half the index 18, since 18 = 6 mod 12.) In the pitch representation in Ex. 7, the center of symmetry 9 = A is halfway between each pair of T_6I-related pitches. The scales are mirror images of each other reflected through a line at pitch 9 = A. These two pc centers of symmetry can be regarded as centers of symmetry for the entire operation T_6I.

Similar wedge-shaped representations can be constructed for each of the other inversion operations, T_0I, T_1I, T_2I, T_3I, T_4I, T_5I, T_7I, T_8I, T_9I, $T_{10}I$, and $T_{11}I$. Each of the twelve operations is uniquely identified by its index, the "n" of its "T_nI", and each pair of pc related by such an operation adds up to its index. The two centers of symmetry for an inversion operation are always equal to one-half the index, and one-half the index plus six ($\frac{1}{2} \cdot n$ and $\frac{1}{2} \cdot n + 6$).

Keep the concepts of index and center of symmetry on ice. They are basic to many principles of serial and nonserial composition. The sections of this text on T_nI common-tone theorems (5.3, 5.4) and hexachordal combinatoriality (5.6) depend on the notion of index. Other developments of these concepts are foundational syntactical principles of serial dodecaphonic composition and are beyond the scope of this text. While Schoenberg pioneered the compositional use of combinatorial relations, Webern mainly eschewed combinatoriality in favor of such principles as "dyadic invariance under inversion"; and Berg's music is full of relations depending on the concepts of index and inversional center. (For those wishing to pursue this subject, I recommend the following articles and books—in this order, stop at any point—from the Bibliography (pp. 120–128): **Babbitt (4) and Westergaard (2), Lewin (8) and (13), Gamer and Lansky, Deyoung, Babbitt (7) and (9), Perle (8) and (9), and Lansky (1)**.)

$T_n^p I$ *inversional center example*. Ex. 8 shows a set of pitches centering around the A below middle C. If that A equals pitch zero, the series of pitches ordered from lowest to highest is

$$<-19, -14, -9, -6, -4, -1, 0, 1, 4, 6, 9, 14, 19>$$

The line maps into its retrograde at $T_0^p I$: -19 maps into 19, -14 maps into 14, ..., 0 into 0, 1 into -1, ..., 19 into -19. Each such pair of pitches adds up to the index 0. The center of symmetry is $\frac{1}{2} \cdot 0 = 0$. Such arrangements of pitches are not uncommon in serial and other atonal music.[9] This particular example consists of all the pitches in the first 22 measures of the Webern *Symphonie* op. 21.

EXAMPLE 8

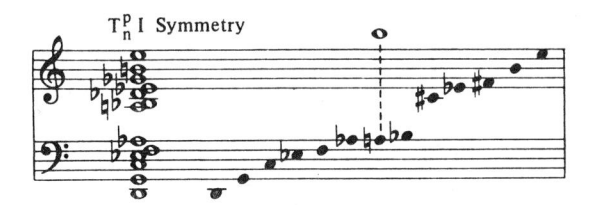

*3.3 COMPOUND OPERATIONS

A "compound operation" is an operation expressed as the "product" of two or more other operations. To "multiply" operation X by operation Y (in this sense), first perform operation X, then perform operation Y on the result. This "product" of X and Y is written "Y(X(z))" (where z is an element operated on by Y).

52   Basic Atonal Theory

The operations are performed from right to left in this notation; first X on z, then Y on the image of z under X. (Two operations are said to "commute" if and only if they may be performed in either order with the same result—that is, IFF $Y(X(z)) = X(Y(z))$ for all z. T_x and T_y commute for any x and y, T_n and T_nI do not commute.) For example, $T_5(T_2(x))$ is a compound operation defined by its final result: $T_5(T_2(x)) = T_5(x+2) = (x+2)+5 = x+7$. This particular compound operation is then equivalent to a simple operation, namely, $T_7(x) = x+7$.

The following table gives the simple operations equivalent to the four possibilities for compounding T_n and T_nI operations in pairs:

1. $T_b(T_a(x)) = T_b(a+x) = (a+x) + b = x + (a+b) = T_{(a+b)}(x)$
2. $T_b(T_aI(x)) = T_b(-x+a) = (-x+a) + b = -x + (a+b) = T_{(a+b)}I(x)$
3. $T_bI(T_a(x)) = T_bI(x+a) = -(x+a)+b = -x+(b-a) = T_{(b-a)}I(x)$
4. $T_bI(T_aI(x)) = T_bI(-x+a) = -(-x+a)+b = x+(b-a) = T_{(b-a)}(x)$

If the left-hand operation is a transposition, the subscripts add; if the left-hand operation is an inversion, the subscripts subtract. Two operations of the same kind (case 1—both T_n; and case 4—both T_nI) produce a transposition; two operations of different kinds (cases 2 and 3) produce an inversion.

Note that finding the inverse operations is very easy; set the simple result to be T_0 and, *for case 1:*

$$T_{(a+b)} = T_0 \quad \text{IFF } a+b = 0 \quad \text{IFF } a = -b$$

for case 4:

$$T_{(b-a)} = T_0 \quad \text{IFF } b-a = 0 \quad \text{IFF } b = a$$

The system of T_n and T_nI is "closed": a compound of any number of operations can always be reduced in pairs to a simple operation that is some T_n or T_nI.[10] For example:

$$T_{11}I(T_7(T_0I(T_2(T_5(x))))) =$$
$$T_{11}I(T_7(T_0I(T_7(x)))) =$$
$$T_{11}I(T_7(T_5I(x))) =$$
$$T_{11}I(T_0I(x)) =$$
$$T_{11}(x) = x+11$$

But this works both ways: any simple operation (such as $T_{11}(x)$) can be expressed as more than one compound operation of any given length—such as $T_{11}I(T_7(T_0I(T_2(T_5(x)))))$. Compositionally, this means that, if you have decided that you want to go *from* some set (or line or row or matrix, etc.) *to* some transformation of that set (or line or row, etc.)—for example, *from* $T_0(X)$ *to* $T_{11}(X)$—you can "prolong" this transition in many different ways by substituting an equivalent compound operation of any length you want. In the above example, the structure would "pass through" four forms between the initial T_0 and the final T_{11}: $T_0 — T_5 — T_7 — T_5I — T_0I — T_{11}$.

Of course, the musical relevance or irrelevance of this prolonged transition is determined by the particular structure (set, line, matrix, etc.) being transformed in relation to the particular transformations used, and especially by the way all this was composed into the audible music.

Shown below is a chord sequence from Schoenberg's op. 16 no. 3 *(Farben)* considered as two conjunct compound operations, from T_0^8 to T_4^9, and from T_4^9 back to T_0^8 (see Analysis 2).

operation $\quad T_{-1}^0 \quad T_3^9 \quad T_2^9 \quad T_{-1}^0 \quad T_{-1}^0 \quad T_{-1}^0 \quad T_{-1}^0$

chord name $\quad T_0^8 \to T_{-1}^9 \to T_2^9 \to T_4^9 \to T_3^9 \to T_2^9 \to T_1^9 \to T_0^8$

$T_2^9(T_3^9(T_{-1}^0(T_0^8))) = T_2^9(T_3^9(T_{-1}^9)) = T_2^9(T_2^9) = T_4^9$

$T_{-1}^0(T_{-1}^0(T_{-1}^0(T_{-1}^0(T_4^9)))) = T_{-1}^0(T_{-1}^0(T_{-1}^0(T_3^9))) = T_{-1}^0(T_{-1}^0(T_2^9)) = T_{-1}^0(T_1^9) = T_0^8$

The notion of compound operations is especially useful in the theory of invariance and combinatoriality.[11]

*3.4 MULTIPLICATIVE OPERATIONS

Mappings in which the argument is multiplied are called "multiplicative." (The "argument" in this sense is "that which is operated on"; for example, 4 is the argument of $T_6 I(4)$; x is the argument of $T_n(x)$; and z is the argument of $T_3 M7(z)$.) In mod 12 arithmetic, the mapping $x \to -x$ is identical to the mapping $x \to 11 \cdot x$. (For $x = 1$, $1 \to -1 = 11$ and $1 \to 11 \cdot 1 = 11$; for $x = 2$, $2 \to -2 = 10$ and $2 \to 11 \cdot 2 = 22 = 10$; etc.) Therefore pc inversion $T_n I(x) \to -x+n$ is identical to a multiplicative operation $T_n M11(x) \to 11 \cdot x + n$; in other words, first multiply x by 11 to get $11 \cdot x = -x$, then add n. The identity operation $T_0(x) \to x+0$ equals the multiplicative identity operation $M1(x) \to 1 \cdot x$; both leave x unchanged.

Since the middle 1950s many composers have found useful two additional basic operations, usually defined as $M5(x) \to 5 \cdot x$ and $M7(x) \to 7 \cdot x$. $M5(x)$ maps a chromatic scale into a circle of fourths, and is often called the "circle of fourths transform." $M7(x)$ maps a chromatic scale into a circle of fifths and is often called the "circle of fifths transform."

M5 (x)—"the circle of fourths transform"

$$x \quad \begin{pmatrix} 0 & 1 & 2 & 3 & 4 & 5 & 6 & 7 & 8 & 9 & 10 & 11 \\ 0 & 5 & 10 & 3 & 8 & 1 & 6 & 11 & 4 & 9 & 2 & 7 \end{pmatrix}$$
$5 \cdot x$

M7 (x)—"the circle of fifths transform"

$$x \quad \begin{pmatrix} 0 & 1 & 2 & 3 & 4 & 5 & 6 & 7 & 8 & 9 & 10 & 11 \\ 0 & 7 & 2 & 9 & 4 & 11 & 6 & 1 & 8 & 3 & 10 & 5 \end{pmatrix}$$
$7 \cdot x$

54   Basic Atonal Theory

Both M5 and M7 are their own inverse operations. (M5(M5(x)) = M5(5·x) = 5·(5·x) = 25·x = 1·x = x. M7(M7(x)) = M7(7·x) = 7·(7·x) = 49·x = 1·x = x.) The two operations commute: M5(M7(x)) = M7(M5(x)) = 35·x = 11·x. Note that the product of M5 and M7 is 11·x, or $T_0I(x)$. Neither M5 nor M7 commutes with T_n. The convention is, as it was for inversion, to "transpose last": $T_nM5(x) = 5·x + n$ and $T_nM7(x) = 7·x + n$ are standard. The inverse of T_nM5 is $T_{7n}M5$, and of T_nM7, $T_{5n}M7$; see Exercises 3–V, item 1.

The system of the operations T_n, $T_nM11 (= T_nI)$, T_nM5, and T_nM7 is closed under compounding of operations (see section 3.3). That is, for any values of "n" in "T_n", a compound operation of any length whose members are some T_n, T_nM11, T_nM5, or T_nM7 is always equivalent to some simple operation which is either a T_n, a T_nM11, a T_nM5, or a T_nM7.

In proof of this, matrix A shows all pairwise compounds. Every pair compound is some simple operation and every longer compound can be reduced recursively in pairs (see examples in section 3.3). The matrix is read as follows: the m-th entry in the n-th row is the compound of *first* the m-th operation listed above (m-th column) and *second* the n-th operation listed on the left (n-th row). For example, the third entry in the second row is the simple operation, of form T_nM7, equal to $T_xM11(T_cM5)$: for any pc "p", $T_xM11(T_cM5(p)) = T_xM11(5p+c) = 11(5p+c) + x = 55p + 11c + x) = T_{(11c+x)}M7(p)$.

matrix A	T_a	T_bM11	T_cM5	T_dM7
T_w	$T_{(a+w)}$	$T_{(b+w)}M11$	$T_{(c+w)}M5$	$T_{(d+w)}M7$
T_xM11	$T_{(11a+x)}M11$	$T_{(11b+x)}$	$T_{(11c+x)}M7$	$T_{(11d+x)}M5$
T_yM5	$T_{(5a+y)}M5$	$T_{(5b+y)}M7$	$T_{(5c+y)}$	$T_{(5d+y)}M11$
T_zM7	$T_{(7a+z)}M7$	$T_{(7b+z)}M5$	$T_{(7c+z)}M11$	$T_{(7d+z)}$

The situation can be simplified by letting all "n's" in the "T_n" operators equal zero. Then let $T_0 = M1$. Matrix B is read as follows: the m-th entry in the n-th row is the compound of *first* the m-th operation listed above (m-th column) and *second* the n-th operation listed on the left (n-th row). For example, the second entry in the third row is the simple operation equal to M5(M11): for any pc "p", M5(M11(p)) = M5(11p) = 5(11p) = 55p = 7p = M7(p).

matrix B	M1	M11	M5	M7
M1	M1	M11	M5	M7
M11	M11	M1	M7	M5
M5	M5	M7	M1	M11
M7	M7	M5	M11	M1

In this simplified case, each operator (M1, M11, M5, M7) is its own inverse and all operations commute (notice the diagonals of matrix B). Remember that M11 is inversion (T_0I) and M1 is identity (T_0). Then notice that the inversion of M5 is M7, and the inversion of M7 is M5. The M7 of M5 (or vice versa) is M11.

Basic Operations 55

The beauty of the way M5 and M7 fit into this structure of operations with inversion (matrix B) is one of the attractions of these operations.[12] Another attraction of great practical import may at first seem a bit abstruse. M1, M11, M5, and M7 are the only possible operators on the 12 pc that are "isomorphisms" in the group-theoretical sense.[13] Among other things, this means that (informally) *when you operate on two pc you operate identically on their interval*.[14] (See section 5.15.) For example, take pc 3 and 4. $i<3,4> = 4-3 = 1$; $i<M5(3),M5(4)> = i<5\cdot3,5\cdot4> = i<15,20> = i<3,8> = 8-3 = 5$; and $5 = M5(1) = M5(i<3,4>)$. This attribute can be used to build very nicely coherent pc structures.[15] It should be noted, however, that M5 and M7 do *not* "preserve interval," and that M11 preserves only *unordered* pc interval. Transposition, which does preserve both ordered and unordered interval, is not an isomorphism in this sense. (If it were, instead of preserving interval, T_n would map that interval y into interval (y+n).)

M5 and M7 are also useful in producing pc set *invariance*, about which we shall hear much more later. For example, T_0M7 leaves every *even* pc number the same, and maps every *odd* pc number a tritone away (adding 6), so that both "whole-tone scales"—or $(0, 2, 4, 6, 8, 10)_{Tn}$ type sets—map into themselves as *sets* of pc, in an interesting musical way.[16]

EXERCISES 3-V

1. Prove that the inverse operation of T_nM5 is $T_{7n}M5$, and that the inverse operation of T_nM7 is $T_{5n}M7$ (see 3.23 and 3.3).

2. Work out the following mappings on sets of pc as demonstrated (2a) and meditate on the results.

   a) $\{0, 2, 4, 6, 8, 10\}$ $\begin{pmatrix} 0 & 2 & 4 & 6 & 8 & 10 \\ 0 & 10 & 8 & 6 & 4 & 2 \end{pmatrix}$ $\begin{matrix} x \\ M5(x) \end{matrix}$

   b) $\begin{pmatrix} 1 & 3 & 5 & 7 & 9 & 11 \\ & & & & & \end{pmatrix}$ $\begin{matrix} x \\ M5(x) \end{matrix}$

   c) $\begin{pmatrix} 0 & 2 & 4 & 6 & 8 & 10 \\ & & & & & \end{pmatrix}$ $\begin{matrix} x \\ M7(x) \end{matrix}$

   d) $\begin{pmatrix} 1 & 3 & 5 & 7 & 9 & 11 \\ & & & & & \end{pmatrix}$ $\begin{matrix} x \\ M7(x) \end{matrix}$

3. Follow exercise 2.

   a) $\begin{pmatrix} 0 & 3 & 6 & 9 \\ & & & \end{pmatrix}$ $\begin{matrix} x \\ M5(x) \end{matrix}$ d) $\begin{pmatrix} 0 & 3 & 6 & 9 \\ & & & \end{pmatrix}$ $\begin{matrix} x \\ M7(x) \end{matrix}$

   b) $\begin{pmatrix} 1 & 4 & 7 & 10 \\ & & & \end{pmatrix}$ $\begin{matrix} x \\ M5(x) \end{matrix}$ e) $\begin{pmatrix} 1 & 4 & 7 & 10 \\ & & & \end{pmatrix}$ $\begin{matrix} x \\ M7(x) \end{matrix}$

   c) $\begin{pmatrix} 2 & 5 & 8 & 11 \\ & & & \end{pmatrix}$ $\begin{matrix} x \\ M5(x) \end{matrix}$ f) $\begin{pmatrix} 2 & 5 & 8 & 11 \\ & & & \end{pmatrix}$ $\begin{matrix} x \\ M7(x) \end{matrix}$

56 Basic Atonal Theory

4. Follow exercise 2.

   a) $\begin{pmatrix} 0 & 4 & 8 \end{pmatrix}$ x M5(x)

   b) $\begin{pmatrix} 1 & 5 & 9 \end{pmatrix}$ x M5(x)

   c) $\begin{pmatrix} 2 & 6 & 10 \end{pmatrix}$ x M5(x)

   d) $\begin{pmatrix} 3 & 7 & 11 \end{pmatrix}$ x M5(x)

   e) $\begin{pmatrix} 0 & 4 & 8 \end{pmatrix}$ x M7(x)

   f) $\begin{pmatrix} 1 & 5 & 9 \end{pmatrix}$ x M7(x)

   g) $\begin{pmatrix} 2 & 6 & 10 \end{pmatrix}$ x M7(x)

   h) $\begin{pmatrix} 3 & 7 & 11 \end{pmatrix}$ x M7(x)

5. Follow exercise 2.

   a) $\begin{pmatrix} 0 & 6 \end{pmatrix}$ x M5(x)

   b) $\begin{pmatrix} 1 & 7 \end{pmatrix}$ x M5(x)

   c) $\begin{pmatrix} 2 & 8 \end{pmatrix}$ x M5(x)

   d) $\begin{pmatrix} 3 & 9 \end{pmatrix}$ x M5(x)

   e) $\begin{pmatrix} 4 & 10 \end{pmatrix}$ x M5(x)

   f) $\begin{pmatrix} 5 & 11 \end{pmatrix}$ x M5(x)

   g) $\begin{pmatrix} 0 & 6 \end{pmatrix}$ x M7(x)

   h) $\begin{pmatrix} 1 & 7 \end{pmatrix}$ x M7(x)

   i) $\begin{pmatrix} 2 & 8 \end{pmatrix}$ x M7(x)

   j) $\begin{pmatrix} 3 & 9 \end{pmatrix}$ x M7(x)

   k) $\begin{pmatrix} 4 & 10 \end{pmatrix}$ x M7(x)

   l) $\begin{pmatrix} 5 & 11 \end{pmatrix}$ x M7(x)

6. Perform the indicated operations.

   a) $T_5M7\{1, 4, 7, 10\} = \{7+5, 4+5, 1+5, 10+5\} = \{0, 9, 6, 3\} = \{0, 3, 6, 9\}$.

   b) $T_0M5\{8, 9, 11, 3\} =$

   c) $T_3M7\{6, 8, 9, 10, 11, 1\} =$

   d) $T_6M5\{2, 4, 6, 7, 9, 11\} =$

   e) $T_2M7\{4, 5, 6, 10, 11, 0\} =$

   f) $T_{11}M5\{0, 1, 4, 5, 8, 9\} =$

NOTES

[1] More strictly speaking, a mapping is a kind of operation, and both mappings and operations are kinds of relations.

[2] This "usual understanding" applies to all mappings in this system, including also T_n, T_nI, etc.

[3] For any two pitches x and y, the ordered interval between x and y equals the ordered interval between the transposition of x and the transposition of y:

$$ip<x,y> = y-x = ip<T_n^p(x), T_n^p(y)> = T_n^p(y) - T_n^p(x) = (y+n) - (x+n) = y-x+n-n = y-x.$$

[4] $i<x,y> = y-x = i<T_n(x), T_n(y)> = T_n(y) - T_n(x) = (y+n) - (x+n) = y-x+n-n = y-x.$

How would you prove this property for $i(x,y)$?

[5] 1) $ip<x,y> = y-x$; but
2) $ip<T_n^p I(x), T_n^p I(y)> = T_n^p I(y) - T_n^p I(x) = (-y+n) - (-x+n) = -y+n+x-n = x-y = -(y-x).$

[6] We have seen that T_n^p and T_n preserve ordered interval; and $T_n^p I$ and $T_n I$ change every ordered interval into one of the *same size* but opposite sign (direction). All four operations, then, preserve *unordered* interval (distance). Musicians hear pitch structures having the same interval structure as equivalent, or even identical—for those of us without "perfect pitch," listening at widely separate times. (How often have you listened to a recording of a well-known piece, realizing only when you plunked a key or plucked a string that, say, Beethoven's Eighth Symphony, had started out in F# major?) We remember interval structures at least as well as we remember pitches. Hence the significance and usefulness of operations (such as T_p and $T_n I$) that preserve interval. Moreover, an elementary theorem of group theory proves that, out of all possible operations, *only* T_n^p and $T_n^p I$ (or, T_n and $T_n I$) preserve interval; there are no other interval-preserving operations. (See, for example, *Group Theory* by Benjamin Baumslag and Bruce Chándler, Schaum's Outline Series (McGraw-Hill, 1968), section 3.4 (pp. 64–66), "Isometries of the Line.")

[7] Inversion is often defined as follows: $I(x) \rightarrow -x$ (this is identical to our $T_0 I(x)$). However, inversion (defined this way) and T_n do not "commute" (see 3.3 for an explanation of this concept): $T_n(I(x)) \neq I(T_n(x))$. $T_n(I(x)) = T_n(-x) = -x+n$; but $I(T_n(x)) = I(x+n) = -(x+n) = -x-n$. (Reversing the order in which I and T_n are applied produces complementary transpositions.) Only one of these two orders must be used, consistently. The overwhelming weight of mathematical and music-theoretical (thanks to Milton Babbitt) usage is always to *transpose last*: $T_n I$ rather than IT_n. "Transpose last" form is the "canonical form."

This source of possible confusion gives rise to our relatively foolproof definition of $T_n I$.

[8] A line transposed by T_n starts n semitones "higher." So a naive view might see a line inverted at $T_n I$ starting n semitones "higher," too. Of course this is not generally the case, since under $T_n I$ the two starting pc (or pitches, for $T_n^p I$) must *sum* to the "n" of the $T_n I$ (see the following section), and a+b is not equal to a−b (unless b=0). Transpositionally related pc have a constant *difference*, n; $T_n I$ related pc have a constant *sum*, n.

There are alternative ways of defining inversion. Among them are definitions such that, if A is a line with starting pc A^1, $T_n I(A)$ starts with (A^1+n). These and other definitions have their virtues. They may also avoid the intuitively absurd consequence of our definition that the name of the relation between two sets related by $T_n I$ changes (the "n" of $T_n I$ changes) whenever the zero is moved, relabelling the pc but leaving them otherwise unchanged. (This is not the case for T_n.) However, the present definition ($T_n I(x) = n-x$) is current and has been standard for many years; it has been built into much theory, and has its own advantages and its own kind of elegance.

[9] See, for example, David Lewin's "Inversional Balance as an Organizing Force in Schoenberg's Music and Thought," *PNM* 6/2 (1968): 1–21.

[10] The system of T_n, $T_n I$, $T_n M5$, and $T_n M7$ is similarly closed, where $T_n M5(x) = 5x+n$ and $T_n M7(x) = 7x+n$. See section 3.4.

[11] See Milton Babbitt, *op. cit.*, and references in notes to 5.6.

[12] The formal structure of matrix B is known as a "Klein four group" and is ubiquitous.

[13] They are isomorphisms on the group (Z12,+), which consists of the integers mod 12 with the operation of addition.

[14] More formally, the interval between the images is equal to the image of the interval between the preimages. This is also true for homomorphisms such as M2, M3, M4, M6, M8, M9, and M10 on the group (Z12,+). However, the homomorphisms do not map Z12 into itself but into its subgroups and cosets. See Baumslag and Chandler, *Group Theory*, or any similar text.

[15] For examples of the compositional use of M5 and M7 and for further study of their relation to the more traditional operations, see respectively Godfrey Winham's "Composition with Arrays," in *PNM* 9/1 (1970): 43–67; and Hubert S. Howe's "Some Combinational Properties of Pitch Structures," *PNM* 4/1 (1965): 45–61.

[16] The effect of the basic operations on the subgroups and cosets of (Z12,+)—that is, its maximally symmetrical pc subsets (see later sections on "degree of symmetry")—will be of particular importance in the theory of musical "combinatoriality." Exercises 2 through 5 (3–V) contain all such maximally symmetrical subsets and their multiplicative transforms. See section 5.6 and the references in its footnotes. Robert Morris and Daniel Starr's "A General Theory of Combinatoriality and the Aggregate," *PNM* 16/1 (1977) and 16/2 (1978) is particularly apt.

ANALYSIS TWO
Schoenberg's Five Pieces for Orchestra: **Farben**, op. 16 no. 3

1. INTRODUCTION AND RETROSPECTIVE

No one could fail to notice that Schoenberg's *Five Pieces for Orchestra* are a very different kind of music from the Webern *Symphonie* of Analysis 1. According to a broad program-note type of description, the Schoenberg is robust, luxuriantly orchestrated old-style Romantic music, using lots of notes; and (if you recall) Alban Berg's opera *Wozzeck* is even more so. By comparison, the Webern is crystalline, spare, always rather delicate. None of these pieces is "tonal" (in the sense that, say, Brahms is tonal). The differences among them must lay to rest once for all any ill-informed notions that "all atonal music sounds alike," or "expresses the same emotion" (e.g., "agony"), or "has the same musical character."

Indeed even within the Webern op. 21 and Schoenberg op. 16, the various sections and movements are of markedly different character. Again permitting outselves the slightly depraved luxury of program-note type description, the music of Webern's op. 21 can be characterized as metaphysically serene (the first half of the first movement), becoming metaphysically agonized and indecisive (the second half of that movement), human but rather solitary (Thema), like a throng of people (var. I), like a captain of industry or war in action amidst his subordinates (var. II), droll (var. III), sleepy (var. IV), tense (var. V), jocose (var. VI), etc.

The music of Schoenberg's op. 16, on the other hand, can be characterized as upset and dramatically turbulent ("Premonitions," op. 16 no. 1), quietly thoughtful and reminiscent ("Yesteryears," op. 16 no. 2), like a "Summer Morning by a Lake" (op. 16 no. 3), a dialogue ("Peripetia," op. 16 no. 4), fragmented and expressively lyrical ("The Obligatory Recitative," op. 16 no. 5). You can find your own descriptions—Schoenberg had to furnish his titles at the request of his publisher—and although any such descriptions are of doubtful precision and intersubjectivity, the differences of musical character they reflect remain. You might relisten to these pieces now to bring such distinctions of character into focus.

Schoenberg's first published title for op. 16 no. 3 was *Farben,* the German word for "colors." It was this piece that started many musicians pursuing a notion that Schoenberg himself called (referring to this piece) *"Klangfarben-*

60   Basic Atonal Theory

melodie," a melody of tone colors (timbres). Certainly *Farben* (1909) is revolutionary in its sensitive structural use of orchestration, and much of the interest of the piece lies in the orchestration. The piece is in slow $\frac{4}{4}$ time; the orchestration changes every half-note or faster. Some idea of the variety, if not the structure, of the orchestration may be gathered from the fact that, in the 1922 version, as one commentator has described it, "from measure 13 to the end, no vertical alignment of five instruments repeats even for the duration of a quarter note."[1]

But *Farben* is surprisingly effective, if less so, even in Webern's arrangement of it for two pianos. The piece presents no obvious local rhythmic subtleties. Much of its interest then must inhere in its pitch structure. Since it is so complexly structured in nonpitch ways, it is free to present an unusually (for Schoenberg) *simple* pitch structure, particularly suited for our introductory listening and analysis here.

2.   EAR-TRAINING: WITHOUT SCORE

Listen to *Farben* only for its pitch structure. What remains the same? What is it that changes, and how does it change?

Play Farben.

The most obvious unifying agent is the continually present, slowly changing five-voice chord.

Play mm. 32-36.

Only for one measure (m. 29), a transition to the final section, probably heard initially as a very soft, short avalanche, is the slowly moving chord texture absent; and closer examination will integrate this measure also.

Play mm. 29-32.

The other events of the piece stand out like raisins in a tapioca pudding, set apart even by their rhythm alone. Notice the ♪♩ motive first appearing in mm. 7 and 9 of the first section.

Play mm. 7-9.

The ♩·♪♪♪ "leaping trout" motive (Schoenberg's term!) heralds the final process (m. 20) and final arrival (mm. 24-25) within the long middle section.

Play mm. 20-25.

Yet it will be seen later that even these contrasting elements derive their pitches from the underlying chord process. *Farben* would have been one splendid response to a textbook assignment of the following sort: find a set of pitches (or of pitch-classes) that you like, develop relations inherent within and among forms of this set into a "syntax," and arrange these syntactically related sounds into a beautifully coherent structure in time—a composition—paying special attention to the structural possibilities of orchestration.

One of Schoenberg's titles for this piece is "The Changing Chord." We can start by aurally identifying just what this Chord and its changes are. Assume that the piece starts with the Chord. Listen to mm. 1-13. When does the first change of pitch occur? Is there a pattern common to all change of pitch? What is the result, or goal, of all these changes?

Play 1-13.

It is hard to hear the pitches in this *ppp*, ever-changing, and probably out-of-balance-in-performance orchestration. Believe it or not, there is no change of *pitch* until m. 4, when the second-from-the-top voice moves up one semitone.

Play mm. 1-4.

What are the pitches in mm. 1-3? The *highest* pitch is an A 440 (or thereabouts). It will be very hard, but try to take down in dictation the rest of the pitches from mm. 1-3.

Play mm. 1-3. Repeat as necessary.

Ex. 1 shows the five pitches—the Chord—in mm. 1-3. If you got all the correct pitches in dictation from mm. 1-3, both you and the recording are exceptionally good. It is actually much easier to hear the pitches of the Chord as the piece goes on, by hearing them change one by one. Play Ex. 1 on the piano several times (beware of tuning differences with the recording). Listen again to mm. 1-13, ignoring the ♪♫ motives for now. Is there a pattern common to all changes of pitch? What is the result of these changes? Follow the five voices of the Chord.

Play mm. 1-13.

In fact, there is a sort of canon. Each voice in turn moves up one semitone, then down two semitones, for a net loss of one semitone. The result of the process is the same Chord transposed one semitone lower (T^p_{-1}).

EXAMPLE 1

Astounding! Having decided, for some reason, to move from the Chord (T^p_0) to its transposition a semitone lower (T^p_{-1}), one does not dully move all voices at once, nor are they moved separately simply down one semitone: rather, one moves each voice separately, canonically, through a linear motive, $<+1, -2>$ semitones, which leaves each voice one semitone lower at its end. Ex. 2 sketches this process for mm. 1-13.

62 Basic Atonal Theory

EXAMPLE 2

Whenever one voice moves down two semitones to complete its motive, the next voice moves up one semitone to begin its (overlapping) motive. If the voices are numbered from 1 to 5 upwards, the "firing order" of the canon is 4—5—2—3—1. The final Chord (T^p_{-1}) is doubled an octave lower around the fermata (mm. 10–12), and is somewhat obscured initially by the ♪♫ motive pitches (mm. 7–10), but reappears clearly alone at T^p_{-1} pitch level in m. 13 (just before the new Chord T^p_{-1} itself begins to change).

Play mm. 1-13.

Of course, the simultaneities during the canon in mm. 4–8 are not necessarily close relatives of the Chord. They depend on the firing order of the voices. A different firing order, such as the one in the final, inverted canon in mm. 31–38, would give different intermediate chords between the initial and final versions of the Chord. Play Ex. 2, very slowly, on the piano, to fix the pitch changes in your mind. Listen again to mm. 1–13, with attention to the canon.

Play mm. 1-13.

Now listen to the entire piece. Can you hear the Chord or its canonic motive in later sections? Are you hearing more than you did before?

Play Farben.

3. ANALYSIS WITH SCORE

1 The ♪♫ motive and mm. 1-11

Refer to the two piano arrangement on pp. 69–72. [2] The ♪♫ motive appears first in m. 7, F♯—E; then to emphasize the arrival at T^p_{-1} in m. 9, it appears twice in simultaneous stacked fifths (see Ex. 3):

D—C   and   F♯—E
G—F   B—A
C—B♭   E—D

EXAMPLE 3

The stacked-fifth simultaneities remind us of the stacked fourths that occupy the three highest pitches of the Chord: e.g., A/E/B for T$_8$. (They are, of course, both a (0,2,7) *type* of pitch-class set—see section 2.5 on normal form, and chapter 4, particularly section 4.21). The linear movement down two semitones imitates the last linear movement in each voice of the Chord's canon (down two semitones). The bass interval of 8 semitones in the Chord between C and G♯ is replaced by a bass interval of 8 semitones between the terminal E of the first ♩♫ motive and the Chord's C, just when the Chord's G♯ voice has reached the end of its motive on G in m. 7.

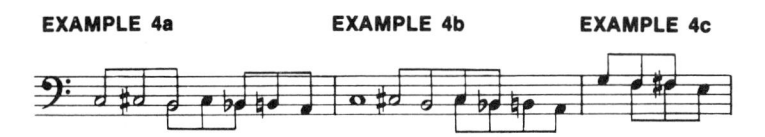

EXAMPLE 4a   **EXAMPLE 4b**   **EXAMPLE 4c**

Notice (Ex. 4a) how the canon motive—<+1, −2>—in the bass of the chord is extended by overlapping itself to produce the pattern in that register for the pitches of the ♩♫ motives of m. 9. That overlapping pattern (Ex. 4a) contains within itself another four-note overlapping pattern (Ex. 4b) that accounts for the ♩♫ pitches a fifth higher (Ex. 4c). This four-note pattern itself can be heard as an overlap of the retrograde inversion of the canon motive, that is, <−2, +1>, with the motive itself <+1, −2> (Ex. 4c).

Notice also the intricate hierarchically closural pattern of common pitches and pitch-classes within the ♩♫ motives (Ex. 5).

EXAMPLE 5

The lowest pitches of the ♩♫ motives, F♯—E—E—D, and C—B♭, start a "whole-tone scale" process of their own that is picked up with their next occurrences and completed later in the piece (see Ex. 6).

EXAMPLE 6

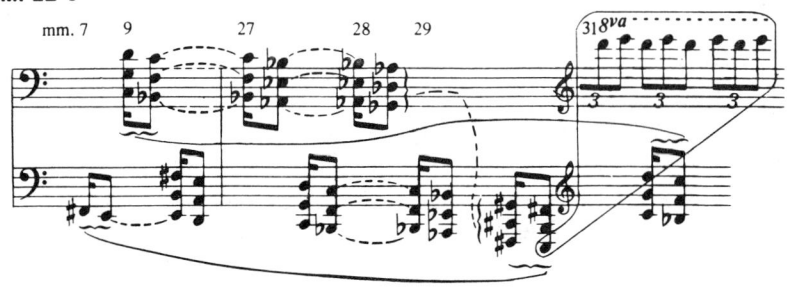

64   Basic Atonal Theory

The lowest-note pitch span F♯—D (−4 semitones) in mm. 7-9 and its analogs in mm. 27-29 (B♭—G♭, C—A♭; see Ex. 6) draw attention to the structurally crucial and syntactically unique large-scale 4-pc-semitone transposition (T₄) of the Chord, to be discussed later.

In fact, the within-motive common tones C and E in m. 9 (see Ex. 5) give the pitches for the bass of the Chord's large-scale movement T₀—T₄—T₀ (for which, look ahead briefly to Ex. 8). Finally, I cannot help hearing locally the lowest-note F♯—E and E—D as proceeding motivically in serial order from the second and third pitches of the first moving Chord voice (see Exx. 7a and 7b).

EXAMPLE 7a   **EXAMPLE 7b**

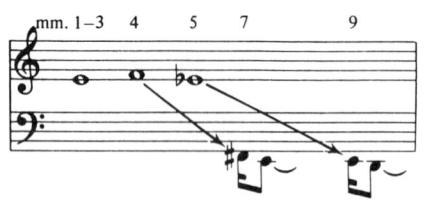

2   Large-scale Structure

Ex. 8 shows the various instances of the Chord throughout the piece. Measure numbers above give the actual timespans of each Chord. Every appearance of a canonic transition between two Chords is indicated by an arrow at the very bottom of Ex. 8. The gaps in the measure numbers (e.g., 1-3, *gap*, 9-13) are always specifically transitional measures between one Chord and the next (e.g., the canon in mm. 4-8). All canons are identical (employing <+1, −2> motives in the firing order of voices 4—5—2—3—1) except the last canon, which uses <−1, +2> (the inversion of the original motive) in firing order 4—2—5—3—1 to get up from T_0^p to T_1^p. Lines between notes indicate pitch-classes held in common. In m. 23, a canon which has been producing T_1^p fires only voices 4—5—2—3, leaving the bass (voice 1) unfired. We are encouraged to hear the resulting simultaneity as an incomplete or altered T_1^p Chord if only because of the preceding canonic process. This incomplete T_1^p (m. 23) then moves directly (no canon) to a similarly incomplete T_{-1}^p (m. 23½), in which the bass anticipates the E of the culminating T_4^p (mm. 24½-26).

EXAMPLE 8

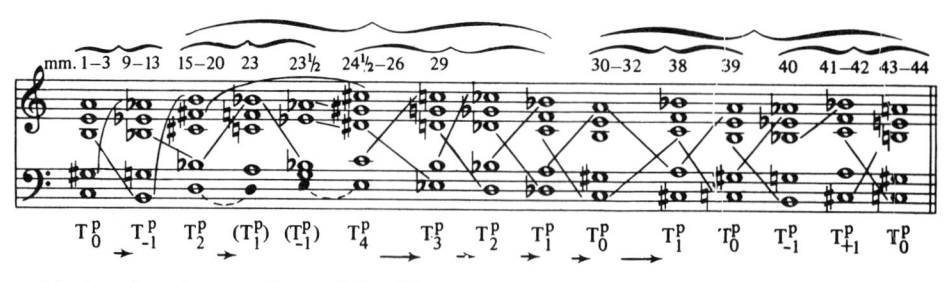

Notice that the set of pc of the Chord is always arranged in pitch the same way, so that Chords are *pitch*, not merely pc, transpositions of one another. This particular Chord is such that there are two pc in common between semitone-related transpositions. The pitch arrangement ensures that a movement down one semitone (as is produced by the canon) always results in the new Chord's *outermost* pitches being the pc in common, considerably enhancing the audibility of the common pc. Moreover (if the two incomplete Chords in m. 23 are ignored) the highest pitch of each new Chord is always a common pc with the preceding Chord, with a single exception at m. 38 after the inverse canon. (See Ex. 8 for all these common-tone relations.) The possible transpositions of the Chord producing a high-pitch common tone are T_2, T_3, T_7, and T_{11}; of these, only T_7 is not used in *Farben* (T_{11} equals T_{-1}^p).

The pc that is originally in voice 2 (second from the bottom) of the Chord alone is in every simultaneity of a canon, including the Chords at the canon's extremities (see Ex. 2). The ubiquity of G♯ in mm. 1–13 makes its demise in m. 15 quite shocking. The sense of abruption is artfully compounded by a superficial voice-leading at m. 15 of A♭ (G♯) and E♭ to G♭ and D♭ respectively (the "syntactic" voice-leading carries A♭ up to B♮ one beat later, in voice 5 of the Chord); for the G♭ and D♭ so conspicuously arrived at in m. 15 are the only two pc missing from the 10-pc chord at mm. 9½–10, and ever since. The B♮ that enters in m. 15 was not present in every simultaneity since m. 1 (as was G♯), but is the only pc in common to T_0^p, T_{-1}^p, and T_2^p and thus to the large-scale structure of mm. 1–20. This B♮ is proud of its role as sole survivor, as evidenced by the smug piccolo/celeste high B's in mm. 16–17. The entrance of the bass D of T_2^p in m. 14, one measure early, prepares us for similar shenanigans in the two incomplete Chords of m. 23.

EXAMPLE 9

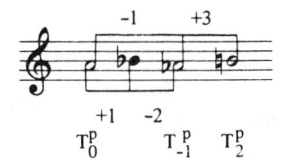

Ex. 9 uses only the highest pitches of each structure to show how the larger-scale movement $T_0^p - T_{-1}^p - T_2^p$ can be heard as developing from the smaller-scale canonic linear movement. The inversion of the canonic $<+1, -2>$ motive would be $<-1, +2>$, e.g.,

$$A \xrightarrow{-1} A♭ \xrightarrow{+2} B♭.$$

Schoenberg "expands" the second interval from 2 to 3 semitones, giving us a variant $<-1, +3>$ form of the inversion of the old $<+1, -2>$ motive. Both forms show up later, corroborating this derivation, in the "leaping trout" motives:

$$F \xrightarrow{-1} E \xrightarrow{+3} G \quad (mm. 20, 24, 25);$$

both the original and "intervallically expanded" form are presented simultaneously in

$$F \xrightarrow[+2]{-1} E \xrightarrow[+2]{+3} \genfrac{}{}{0pt}{}{G}{F♯} \quad (mm. 25, 40, 42).$$

The term "intervallic expansion" and the general concept of its motivic application are Schoenberg's.

66   Basic Atonal Theory

EXAMPLE 10

Ex. 10 again represents each Chord by its highest pitch alone. The expanded inversion <-1, +3> overlaps with itself moving from T_0^p to T_2^p to T_4^p; the problematical embedded <-2, +5> is an expansion of the expansion. Corroboration for its existence can be found in the similar "up 5" treatment of the superficial voice-leading in m. 24 and the analogous m. 15 (compare Ex. 8): G♯ to C♯ in m. 24, F♯ to B in m. 15—in both cases between the first and second beats of the measure. The final six Chords (mm. 30–44; see Exx. 8 and 10) can be heard to articulate multiple overlapping forms of the original motive <+1, -2>, its inversion <-1, +2>, and its retrograde <+2, -1>. The last four Chords (mm. 39–44) are juxtaposed without any transition. This encourages us to look favorably back on our similar motivic interpretation of longer-range relations among Chords that do have transitions (e.g., mm. 1–20).

Occasionally (mm. 16–19, 24–26) within a section designated by one Chord in Ex. 8, one or two pitches of the Chord will wiggle: see Ex. 11.

EXAMPLE 11

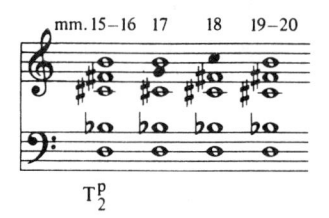

This can be heard as a "false start" to a canon that does not materialize, or as simply a "chromatic neighbor" kind of configuration, or both; the point being that the continued presence of the Chord is not seriously disturbed. The second kind of "leaping trout" motive (e.g., fourth beat of m. 20) can be accounted for in this way as a pitch-class chromatic wiggle (see Ex. 12).

EXAMPLE 12

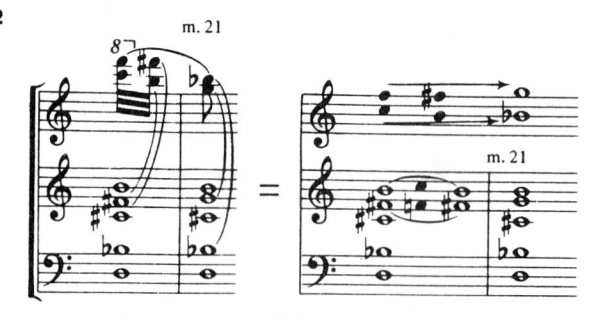

More importantly, the last six Chords (mm. 30–44) can, by extension, also be heard as a large-scale chromatic wiggle around T_0^p (see Ex. 10, Ex. 8), so that in this sense, the entire last section (mm. 30–44) is an ornamented T_0^p. The entire piece may be heard simply as $T_0^p—(T_2^p)—T_4^p—T_0^p$, or $T_0^p—T_4^p—T_0^p$. Why this rather than some other sequence of transposition?

Analysis Two 67

The answer lies in the common-tone theorem for transposition, which is treated in chapter 5. A preview here should whet your appetite.

We have noticed that common-tone relations are treated very consistently in this piece; for example, the fact that the highest pitch of each Chord was present as a pc in the previous Chord, the treatment of the demise of the ubiquitous G♯, the smug survivor B♮, etc. There is a theorem that gives the number of pc in common between a set of pc and each of the set's transpositions (see chapter 5). As a pc set, in normal form, the Chord is {8, 9, 11, 0, 4} (C = 0). Its interval content (see chapter 5) is <2, 1, 2, 3, 2, 0>. (The numbers here are not pc but "multiplicities" of intervals 1 through 6—see sections 5.1 and 5.2.) Therefore its common tones follow this table:

	T_1	T_2	T_3	T_4	T_5	T_6	
T_0	2	1	2	3	2	0	# of pc in common

T_4 gives the *unique maximum* number of pc in common with T_0 for the Chord! (T_0 and T_4 of the Chord both contain C, E, and A♭—look at Ex. 8.) Ex. 13 shows the sequence of Chords in the piece, with the number of pc in common written on the lines joining Chord names.

EXAMPLE 13

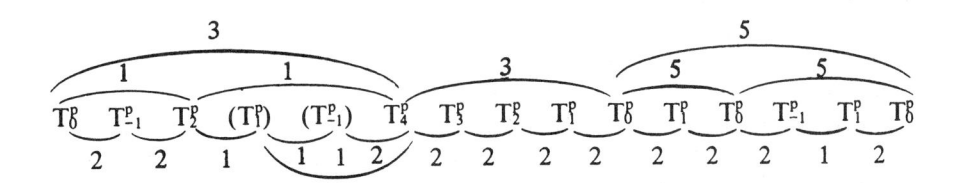

As you can see, adjacent Chords nearly always have 2 pc in common. The adjacent Chords in the larger-scale movement from T_8^p to T_2^p to T_4^p have only one pc in common, which means that it makes even more sense, having reached T_4^p, to refer back to T_8^p (with which T_4^p has 3 pc in common) rather than only back to T_2^p. The relative instability of the medium scale structure ($T_8^p - T_2^p - T_4^p$) only reinforces the apprehension of the large-scale structure ($T_8^p - T_4^p$).

3 Recapitulation and Generalization

This has by no means been a comprehensive analysis even of the pitch structure of Schoenberg's *Farben*. The compact form of presentation in the second part of the analysis could no longer ensure that you would take pains to *hear* all the relations mentioned; always go back over an analysis and relisten to the piece until everything that makes musical sense in the analysis is audible.

All pitch structure for the piece was derived from the *Chord* (a set of pitches or pc) and the <+1, −2> *motive* of the initial canon. Moreover, one particular transposition of the Chord, T_8^p, takes priority; the piece starts with T_8^p and ends with a chromatic ornamentation of T_0^0 (mm. 30-44). T_4^0 enjoys a priority second only to that of T_0^0. The structural position of T_4^0 (as the goal in the middle) is reinforced by its unique status as a provider of a maximum number of pc in common with T_0^0. In a sense, T_4^0 is the transposition syntactically "closest" to T_0^0 (only 2 pc are different).

The principle of "unity of musical space" does *not* seem to apply here. As in tonal music, certain pitch intervals in *Farben* are reserved primarily for linear motion (one and two pitch semitones) and do not appear structurally as simultaneities.

Farben centers itself syntactically around one particular pitch collection (the Chord at T_0^0). Tonal music similarly centers itself around one pitch or pc collection (its "tonic triad"). However, tonal music goes further, centering its tonic triad around one of its pitches (the "root"); a tonal piece, for instance, may be "in C." *Farben* refers to no one pc; there is no apparent hierarchy among the pitches of its Chord.

Farben's large-scale structure is a move to and from a collection (T_4^0 of the Chord) of maximal pc content intersection with its primary collection (T_0^0 of the Chord). Tonal music's large-scale structure is also often characterized by a move to and from a collection (by "modulation," to the diatonic collection of the "dominant") of maximal pc content intersection with the primary collection (the diatonic collection of the tonic) (see chapter 5).

But *Farben's* syntax lacks the hierarchical structure of tonal syntax. In tonal music, the chromatic collection (aggregate) gives birth to subsets that are diatonic collections; each diatonic collection gives birth to hierarchically ordered subsets (triads, with the tonic triad preeminent); and each of these triadic subsets structures its pitches hierarchically (so that the "root" is preeminent). In *Farben*, however, the aggregate spawns the Chord, which is internally hierarchically unstructured and only hints at giving birth to subsets of itself (the stacked fourths become the stacked fifths of the ♪ ♫ motive). *Farben's* syntax is therefore shallower, having fewer levels.

As if to make up for this, the role of the linear motive is much more structural in *Farben* than in tonal music. It would be a very unusual tonal piece indeed in which a typically linear motive (using mainly intervals of one and two semitones) is used not only for movement between structural simultaneities but also to determine large-scale transpositional relationships (modulation to various "keys") as is done in *Farben*—e.g., the transpositional levels of the last three Chords (keys?) forming the retrograde of the canonic motive.

EXERCISES

Listen, if possible, with score, to Schoenberg's Orchestral Songs op. 22, and read Schoenberg's own lecture, "Analysis of the Four Orchestral Songs Opus 22," available in a translation by Claudio Spies in *Perspectives on Schoenberg and Stravinsky*, revised edition, edited by Benjamin Boretz and Edward T. Cone (Norton, 1972).

Arnold Schoenberg *Farben* op. 16, no. 3, arranged for two pianos by Anton Webern. Copyright © 1913 by C. F. Peters. Reprinted by permission of the publisher.

70 Basic Atonal Theory

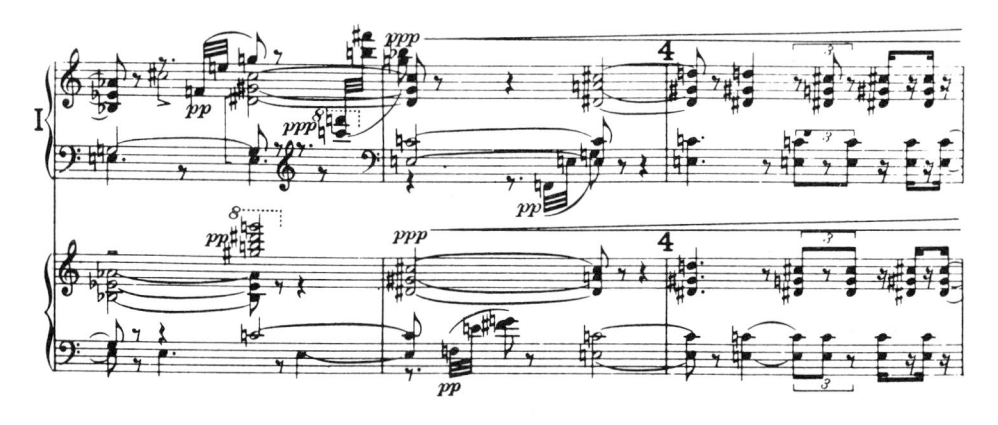

Analysis Two 71

72 Basic Atonal Theory

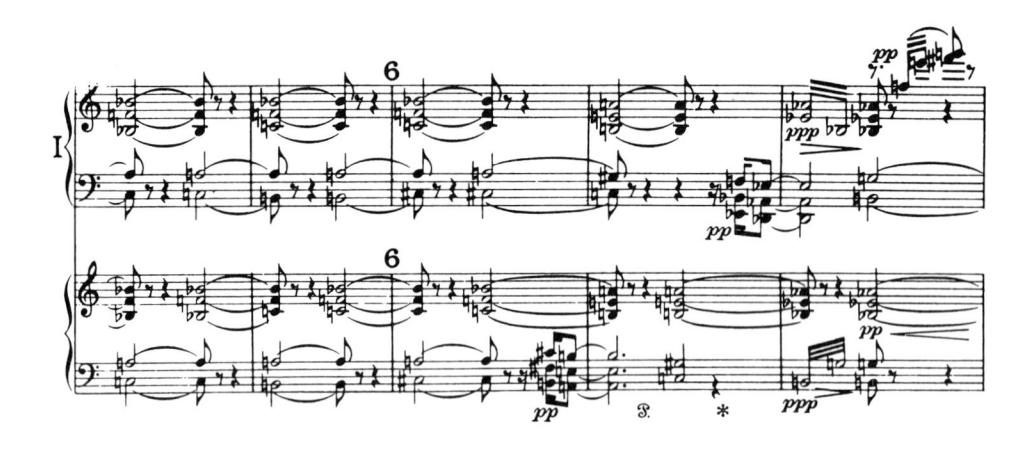

NOTES

[1] Charles Burkhart, "Schoenberg's *Farben*," *PNM* 12/1 and 12/2 (double issue, 1973-74): 141-72. There are many published analyses of *Farben*. See also (perhaps after reading chapters 3 and 4), Jane Coppock, "Ideas for a Schoenberg Piece," *PNM* 14/1 (1975): 3-85; and, not least, Allen Forte's *The Structure of Atonal Music*, pp. 166-77, which also contains a condensed score of this piece.

[2] Both Webern's arrangement and this analysis are based on the 1922 version. Schoenberg's 1949 revision for smaller orchestra is missing the G3—F3 in the ♩♫ motiv in m. 9. In this analysis, the music makes more sense with these notes than without them.

CHAPTER FOUR

SET TYPES

4.1 TYPES

Sets and lines of pitches and pc are very usefully classifiable into types. One familiar type of pc set is the "major triad"; another type, the "minor triad". One type of line is the "major scale." The following discussion centers on types of *sets of pc*, but you may easily extend the exposed concepts to sets of pitches. In addition, it should be pointed out that *all* structural properties of sets are also properties of *lines* (though not vice versa), since we can treat the elements of a line as elements of a set.

4.11 Cardinality Types

Most generally, sets may be classified by "cardinality," that is, by the number of their members. The following table gives the possible cardinalities of pc sets and the conventionally used names of the corresponding types; the starred names are most common.

cardinality	type name
0	null set
1	monad
2	dyad*
3	trichord*
4	tetrachord*
5	pentachord*
6	hexachord*
7	septachord
8	octachord
9	nonachord
10	decachord
11	undecachord
12	aggregate* (or dodecachord)

"Types" are "equivalence classes." For example, the type "dyad" is a class or set whose members are all and only those sets that have themselves just two members. Cardinality types are equivalence classes that "partition"[1] the domain of all possible pc sets. Equivalence classes, as mentioned previously, must meet two main criteria:

1. "exhaustivity" the set of equivalence classes (the "partition") must exhaust the domain (i.e., the set sum of the equivalence classes must equal the domain) and
2. "exclusivity": no two equivalence classes may have a member in common (i.e., the intersection of every pair of the equivalence classes must equal the null set).

Both conditions are fulfilled by cardinality types: all possible pc sets are of one of these types (in a 12-pc system), and (for example) there aren't any trichords that are also dyads.

Each of these cardinality types may in turn be partitioned into other kinds of equivalence classes. Dyads can be partitioned into sets of pairs of pc which form the same unordered pc interval. (In fact, this is an alternative definition of interval: listing all so-equivalent dyads for each interval. This brute-force, laborious definition—a definition by "extension" rather than "intension" or algorithm—panders to the table-look-up theory of intelligence.)

4.12 T_n-types

In particular, both T_n (for all n) and T_nI (for all n) separately and together partition each cardinality type. For example, the set {0,4,7}, with C = 0, can be transposed twelve ways; each of the resulting sets is related by T_n for some n to each of the other resulting sets, and no such set is any transposition of any set not among those resulting sets, fulfilling the two conditions for an "equivalence class" or type of set within the cardinality type "trichord."

T_0 = {0,4,7}	T_6 = {6,10,1}
T_1 = {1,5,8}	T_7 = {7,11,2}
T_2 = {2,6,9}	T_8 = {8,0,3}
T_3 = {3,7,10}	T_9 = {9,1,4}
T_4 = {4,8,11}	T_{10} = {10,2,5}
T_5 = {5,9,0}	T_{11} = {11,3,6}

These are all the "major triads" there are. All are given in "normal form." This *transpositional-type* or T_n-*type* of trichord—that is, the set of all twelve transposed sets—is *named* by the following expression: "(0,4,7)$_{Tn}$", or, more colloquially, is *represented* by "{0,4,7}".

Why was {0,4,7} chosen instead of any of the other equivalent members of the class? By convention, a type is *named* or *represented by* the one of its members which is, so to speak, in *most normal form*. If you will review the rules for normal form, you will find that in this case only the "smallest initial pc number" criterion applies, resulting in the selecting of {0,4,7} as the *representative* ("representative form") for this trichord type and "(0,4,7)$_{Tn}$" as the *name* of this trichord type.[2] The subscript "T_n" will be necessary to distinguish this name from a T_n/T_nI-type name, as we shall see.[3]

4.13 T_n/T_nI-types

The equivalence class remaining possible is that of *all sets equivalent under either T_n or T_nI (or both)*, a "T_n/T_nI" set type.

For the set {0,4,7}, T_n or T_nI together generate a total of 24 (not 12) distinct pc sets which each map into each other under T_n or T_nI, and none of which map into any set not among those 24 under T_n or T_nI, therefore forming a true equivalence class or type.

Again, the name of the type uses that equivalent set-member that is in "most normal form." Two sets start with zero, {0,4,7} and {0,3,7}, but {0,3,7} is in more normal form: the *name* of the type is then "$(0,3,7)_{Tn/TnI}$" and its *representative* is {0,3,7}.

The subscript "Tn/TnI" is a bit awkward. Let {A} be the representative form of any T_n/T_nI-type. Then "$(A)_{Tn/TnI}$" is the *name* of that type, and we can define an abbreviation:

DEF [A] = $(A)_{Tn/TnI}$

In the definition, the square brackets are used to show that the expression *names* the T_n/T_nI-type of the enclosed representative form. For example, "$(0,1,3)_{Tn/TnI}$" is abbreviated by "[0,1,3]"; and both expressions are names of the equivalence class or type of 24 pc trichords related to the pc set {0,1,3} by operations T_n or T_nI. We say, for example, that {6,7,9} and {8,10,11}, etc., are all "[0,1,3] trichords"; {6,7,9} = T_6 {0,1,3}, and {8,10,11} = $T_{11}I${0,1,3}. Both {6,7,9} and {8,10,11} are members of the equivalence class or type whose *representative form* is {0,1,3} and whose *name* is "[0,1,3]" or "$(0,1,3)_{Tn/TnI}$." "[0,1,3]" can be pronounced, "0,1,3 inversional type."

Similarly, we can define an abbreviation for the T_n-type of a set {A}:

DEF (A) = $(A)_{Tn}$

Thus parentheses can be used to show that "(0,1,3)" is an abbreviation for "$(0,1,3)_{Tn}$", and both notations name the equivalence class of twelve sets related to {0,1,3} and to each other by some T_n. (Context should make clear when parentheses are just parentheses, rather than part of a name of a T_n-type.)

All 24 members of $(0,3,7)_{Tn/TnI}$, that is, [0,3,7], are listed below; all sets are in normal form.

$$[0, 3, 7] = (0, 3, 7)_{Tn/TnI}$$

T_0 = {0, 3, 7}	T_6 = {6, 9, 1}	T_0I = {5, 9, 0}	T_6I = {11, 3, 6}
T_1 = {1, 4, 8}	T_7 = {7, 10, 2}	T_1I = {6, 10, 1}	T_7I = {0, 4, 7}
T_2 = {2, 5, 9}	T_8 = {8, 11, 3}	T_2I = {7, 11, 2}	T_8I = {1, 5, 8}
T_3 = {3, 6, 10}	T_9 = {9, 0, 4}	T_3I = {8, 0, 3}	T_9I = {2, 6, 9}
T_4 = {4, 7, 11}	T_{10} = {10, 1, 5}	T_4I = {9, 1, 4}	$T_{10}I$ = {3, 7, 10}
T_5 = {5, 8, 0}	T_{11} = {11, 2, 6}	T_5I = {10, 2, 5}	$T_{11}I$ = {4, 8, 11}

Occasionally authors blur the distinction between T_n-type and T_n/T_nI-type. When in doubt, try assuming they mean T_n/T_nI-type. The left pair of columns in the preceding chart lists $(0,3,7)_{Tn}$; the right column lists $(0,4,7)_{Tn}$. Both pairs of columns together list [0,3,7].

Of course useful equivalence classes may also be formed under T_n^p and T_n^p/T_n^pI for sets of *pitches*, and under each of T_n^p, T_n^p/T_n^pI, T_n, T_n/T_nI, for *lines*. Table I (Appendix 2) lists first in its examples the suggested notation for each of these eight kinds of equivalence classes. Abbreviations (such as "(0,1,6)" for "$(0,1,6)_{Tn}$") are listed second. Only types 1) and 5) in Table I have been discussed explicitly.

You have just been set loose in an enormous room. The major/minor triad type—the identifiable "chord" of your beloved Bach-chorale-style exercises— is only one of (as it happens) twelve different such T_n/T_nI trichord types, each of possible equivalent significance in a syntax that is waiting for your invention of it—not to mention tetrachords, etc.

The numbers of T_n/T_nI-types for each cardinality form an arch, as shown here:

cardinality:	2	3	4	5	6	7	8	9	10
number of T_n/T_nI types:	6	12	29	38	50	38	29	12	6

See Table II (Appendix 2) for a complete listing.

4.14 Set Types in Music

Anyone can "find" set types in any music. The important consideration is whether it is musically and analytically profitable to do so. In any music, sounds that are associated with each other in the analyst's hearing—perhaps because they sound simultaneously, or nearly simultaneously, or share a common register or instrument or dynamic, etc.—can have their pitch-classes abstracted (thereby discarding the very factors of timespan, instrument, register, dynamic, etc., that may have led to these sounds' association). If, further, any *order* implied by the sounds is discarded, what is left is a set of pitch-classes. And if such pc sets are only labelled as to T_n-type or T_n/T_nI-type, even distinctions of pc content and the particular interrelations of equivalent pc sets are discarded. Can anything of value remain? Can less be more, and more, less?

Cautiously, echo answers yes. Each step up the ladder of abstraction loses particular distinctions but gains generality; recall the discussion of intervals in section 2.4. Relations that may lie obscured in the thicket of the full particularity of things can be perceived clearly when a process of generalization has pruned away the underbrush of reality. A coherent structure of such abstract relations does exert its own perceptual pull, forming associations strongly in conjunction with and even in despite of the criteria of "same perceptual neighborhood" mentioned in the previous paragraph.

However, an analysis must, if it is not to lapse into an inanity of vacuous generalizations, reflect especially its most general observations (such as those about pc set type) back into the particularities from which those generalities were abstracted. A structure of pc sets should grow both out of and into particular relations of pitch (register), timespan, instrument, etc. (Analyses 1 and 2 attempt to exemplify this in a small way.) A mere compilation of set types "discovered in" a piece of music can never be a satisfactory analysis.

78   Basic Atonal Theory

Therefore it is only with a certain subdued horror that I provide "examples of pc set types in music" without setting the existence of these set types in perspective by providing also a fuller analysis of the music.

Particularly futile are analyses that employ a theory inappropriate to the music, and among these are most so-called pc set type analyses of music usually considered "tonal." But the Prelude to the opera *Tristan* by Richard Wagner is notoriously resistant to "tonal" analysis. Benjamin Boretz has produced an analysis of the Prelude that accounts elegantly for some of its most recalcitrant features; in this analysis, and to the extent that it succeeds, the Prelude is of atonal, even serial, organization.[4]

In the context of such an analysis, then, observe the pc sets that can be abstracted from the circled notes in this piano reduction of the beginning of the Prelude (see Ex. 1).

EXAMPLE 1

Langsam und schmachtend

The set types of the thirteen circled simultaneities in Ex. 1 are given below.

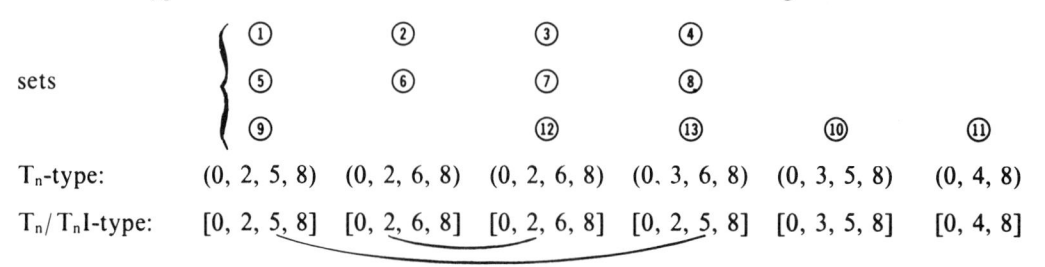

sets: ① ② ③ ④ ⑤ ⑥ ⑦ ⑧ ⑨ ⑫ ⑬ ⑩ ⑪

T_n-type: (0, 2, 5, 8) (0, 2, 6, 8) (0, 2, 6, 8) (0, 3, 6, 8) (0, 3, 5, 8) (0, 4, 8)

T_n/T_nI-type: [0, 2, 5, 8] [0, 2, 6, 8] [0, 2, 6, 8] [0, 2, 5, 8] [0, 3, 5, 8] [0, 4, 8]

The higher degree of abstraction of the T_n/T_nI-type shows the retrograde-symmetrical structures clearly. A careful listening will reveal that lines articulate pc sets similar to those of the simultaneities in a closely worked net of relations. For example, the very audible first and last highest pitches in each block of simultaneities are G♯—B   B—D   D—F♯. The pc set {G♯,B,D,F♯} is of T_n-type (0,2,5,8)—the type of the first simultaneity heard—and of T_n/T_nI-type [0,2,5,8], the type exemplified by the first and last simultaneities within each phrase. An abstract structure thus can clearly relate local events to large-scale events.

Probably, satisfactory analyses of the preserial works of Stravinsky will, when they finally appear, employ theories that graft nontonal referential collections and unique Stravinskian transformation rules into a wildly Schenkerian-derived kind of theory of pc set "prolongation" in various pitch-structural and rhythmic-structural "levels."[5] The need for such radically new or skewed theories for early Stravinsky is patent in the following excerpt (transposed to concert pitch) from the middle of "Var. E" (the fugue) of his Octet for wind instruments (1923). (See Ex. 2).

EXAMPLE 2

[musical score excerpt with simultaneities numbered ① through ⑯]

Copyright 1924 by Edition Russe de Musique. Renewed 1952. Cnpyright and renewal assigned to Boosey and Hawkes, Inc. Revised Version Copyright 1952 by Boosey and Hawkes, Inc. Reprinted by permission.

EXAMPLE 3

simultaneity:	①	②	③	④
pc set (C = O):	{5,6,10,11}	{4,0,7,5}	{4,6,7,0}	{2,6,7,1,8}
T_n-type:	(0,1,5,6)	(0,4,5,7)	(0,4,6,7)	(0,1,5,6,7)
T_n/T_nI-type:	[0,1,5,6]	[0,2,3,7]	[0,1,3,7]	[0,1,2,6,7]

⑤	⑥	⑦	⑧	⑨	⑩
{2,7,1,8}	{2,7,3,8}	{2,9,10}	{3,7,4,11}	{3,7,11}	{5,9,2,10}
(0,1,6,7)	(0,1,5,6)	(0,1,5)	(0,1,4,8)	(0,4,8)	(0,1,5,8)
[0,1,6,7]	[0,1,5,6]	[0,1,5]	[0,1,4,8]	[0,4,8]	[0,1,5,8]

⑪	⑫	⑬	⑭	⑮	⑯
{6,11,4,0}	{5,9,6,1}	{8,9,5,1}	{6,10,5,0}	{6,11,4,0}	{6,11,3,0}
(0,1,5,7)	(0,1,4,8)	(0,3,4,8)	(0,1,5,7)	(0,1,5,7)	(0,1,4,7)
[0,1,5,7]	[0,1,4,8]	[0,1,4,8]	[0,1,5,7]	[0,1,5,7]	[0,1,4,7]

80 Basic Atonal Theory

The pitch spellings of Ex. 2 alone—F against E♯, E/B♯/G/C/F/F×, D/F×/G/D♭/G♯, etc.—would make a "tonal" analysis of any kind extremely tortuous. Ex. 3 merely identifies the set type of each simultaneity.

The total network of set-type appearances does seem to support the kind of evolving, unceasing musical progression heard here. The music of this fragment migrates from [0,1,5,6]-ness (closure of a vague sort in ①-⑥); through [0,1,4,8,]-ness (⑧-⑬); to [0,1,5,7]-ness (⑪-⑮)—all glued together by subset appearances of [0,1,5]. [0,3,7], [0,4,8], and other types not chronicled here. Ex. 4 shows the flow of the music through these recurrent set types; here an appearance in parentheses is an appearance as a proper *subset* of the full simultaneity at that point.

The three basic set types—[0,1,5,6], [0,1,4,8], and [0,1,5,7]—are interrelated by their subset types. In particular, a [0,1,5] type set is always a subset of any [0,1,5,7] type set and also twice a subset of any [0,1,5,6] type set (see section 4.4). A [0,1,4,8] type set always has subsets of types [0,4,8] and [0,3,7].[6]

EXAMPLE 4

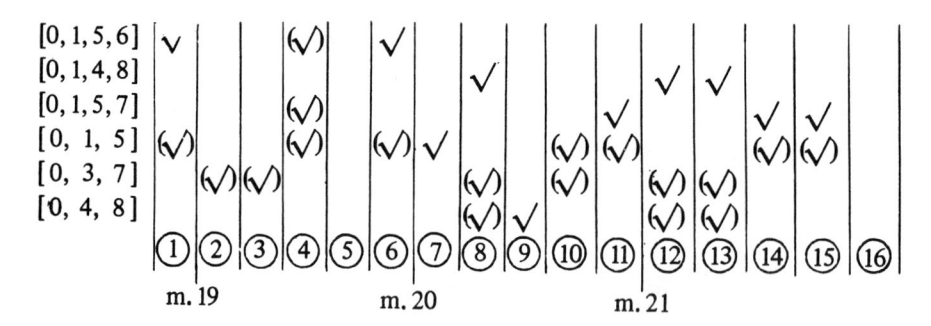

m. 19   m. 20   m. 21

Although such pc set type abstraction does bring some order from the chaos of a first impression of this music, it is at best one aspect of a satisfactory analysis, ignoring as it does the interaction of linear movement with the simultaneities, the rhythms of the various parts and their internal phrasing, the larger context from which this excerpt without beginning or end is rudely ripped, all other particularities of the sounds heard (e.g., timbres), and especially the ways in which the set types shown are specifically related to each other and manifested in particular pitch/rhythms and contrapuntal lines. Notice, for example, the disregarded web of common-tone relations from set to set.

If there is any music that does receive a mere pc-set-type analysis gratefully, it is classical and postclassical serial music. Subsequent analytical exercises in this chapter will refer to the (classically serial) *Klavierstück* op. 33a of Arnold Schoenberg.

4.2 APPLICATIONS

4.21 How to Find The Type of a Set

Given a set of pc, the following procedure will find its type. (See a and b in musical notation—under Ex. 5.)

EXAMPLE 5

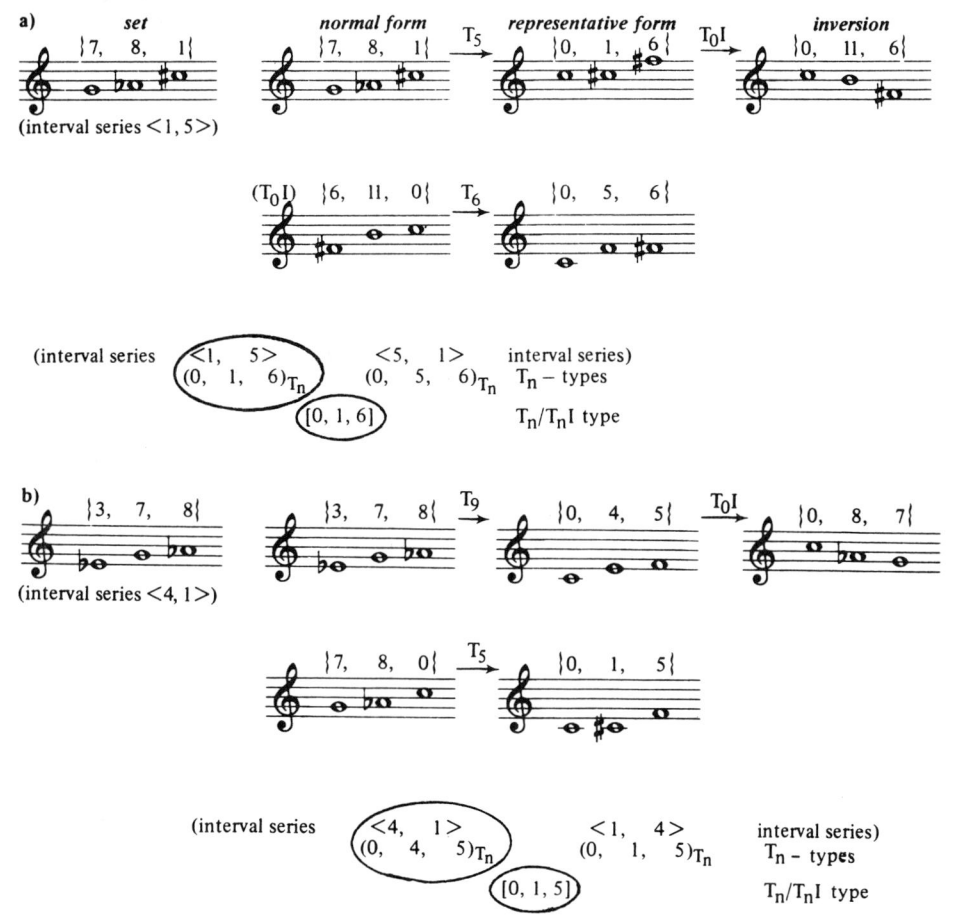

a) set: {7, 8, 1} (interval series <1, 5>)

normal form: {7, 8, 1} $\xrightarrow{T_5}$ representative form: {0, 1, 6} $\xrightarrow{T_0I}$ inversion: {0, 11, 6}

(T_0I) {6, 11, 0} $\xrightarrow{T_6}$ {0, 5, 6}

(interval series <1, 5>)   <5, 1> (interval series)
(0, 1, 6)$_{T_n}$ (0, 5, 6)$_{T_n}$ T_n – types
[0, 1, 6] T_n/T_nI type

b) {3, 7, 8} (interval series <4, 1>)

{3, 7, 8} $\xrightarrow{T_9}$ {0, 4, 5} $\xrightarrow{T_0I}$ {0, 8, 7}

{7, 8, 0} $\xrightarrow{T_5}$ {0, 1, 5}

(interval series <4, 1>)   <1, 4> (interval series)
(0, 4, 5)$_{T_n}$ (0, 1, 5)$_{T_n}$ T_n – types
[0, 1, 5] T_n/T_nI type

1. List the set in normal form.
2. Transpose the set so that the first pc is zero. (Shortcut: temporarily shift the zero to the first pc; e.g., so that G is zero in example a.)

* This is the "representative form" of the set's T_n-type.

3. Perform T_nI on the set and repeat steps 1) and 2).

* This is the "representative form" of the set's inversion's T_n-type.

4. Compare the T_n-type representative forms. The "most normal form" of the two is the representative form of the set's T_n/T_nI-type.

Shortcut to get T_n-type of the set (step 2): starting on zero, produce the same adjacency-interval series as found in the normal form of the set. For example:

$$\begin{cases} \text{normal form} & \{7, 9, 10, 0, 3\} \\ \text{interval series} & <2, 1, 2, 3> \\ T_n\text{-type} & (0, 2, 3, 5, 8) \end{cases}$$

82 Basic Atonal Theory

Shortcut to get T_n-type of the inversion (step 3): the following shortcut works with exceptions (see "Summary: Invariance of Normal Form" in section 3.22). Starting on zero, produce the adjacency-interval series of the previous T_n-type *in reverse:* first move up the interval between the last two pc of the previous T_n-type, then move up the interval between the third-from-last and the second-from-last pc, etc. For example:

$$\begin{cases} \text{intervals} & 3 \quad 1 \quad 2 \quad 1 \\ T_n\text{-type} & (0, 3, 4, 6, 7) \end{cases}$$

$$\begin{cases} \text{intervals} & 1 \quad 2 \quad 1 \quad 3 \\ T_n\text{-type of inversion} & (0, 1, 3, 4, 7) \end{cases}$$

The interval series of the T_n-type is the retrograde of the interval series of the T_n-type of the inversion: $<3,1,2,1>$ is the retrograde of $<1,2,1,3>$.

See and check Ex. 6. Write out the steps for (a) through (f) in musical notation.

With a little practice, using the shortcuts, you will soon find yourself doing this quickly in your head. For example, learn to identify {7,8,1} as "up 1, up 5" in normal form ({7,$^{+1}$8,$^{+5}$1}) which, starting on zero, produces {0,$^{+1}$1,$^{+5}$6}. The inversion will be "down 1, down 5," and the *reverse* of this upwards will be "up 5, up 1" for normal form, which, starting on zero, gives {0,$^{+5}$5,$^{+1}$6}. Obviously {0,1,6} is "more normal" than {0,5,6} so the T_n/T_nI-type is [0,1,6].

EXAMPLE 6

a)	{4, 5, 8, 10}	(0, 1, 4, 6)$_{Tn}$	[0, 1, 4, 6]
b)	{11, 3, 5, 6}	(0, 4, 6, 7)$_{Tn}$	[0, 1, 3, 7]
c)	{10, 0, 2, 3, 4, 5}	(0, 2, 4, 5, 6, 7)$_{Tn}$	[0, 1, 2, 3, 5, 7]
d)	{7, 9, 10, 11, 0, 2}	(0, 2, 3, 4, 5, 7)$_{Tn}$	[0, 2, 3, 4, 5, 7]
e)	{9, 1, 2, 3}	(0, 4, 5, 6)$_{Tn}$	[0, 1, 2, 6]
f)	{3, 5, 6, 8}	(0, 2, 3, 5)$_{Tn}$	[0, 2, 3, 5]

EXERCISES 4-I: Set Types

The musical excerpt (the first nine measures of Schoenberg's *Klavierstück* op. 33a) has certain pitches circled. Treat each circled set of pitches as a set of pc. For each set (numbered ① through ⑳), list:

1. the normal form of the actual pc set (e.g., "{2, 6, 9}");
2. the name of its T_n-type (e.g., "(0, 4, 7)$_{Tn}$");
3. the name of its T_n/T_nI-type (e.g., "[0, 3, 7]").
   List the normal forms in pitch notation (musical notation) as well as in numbers. For these exercises, B♭ **equals** *zero.*

Set Types 83

KLAVIERSTÜCK

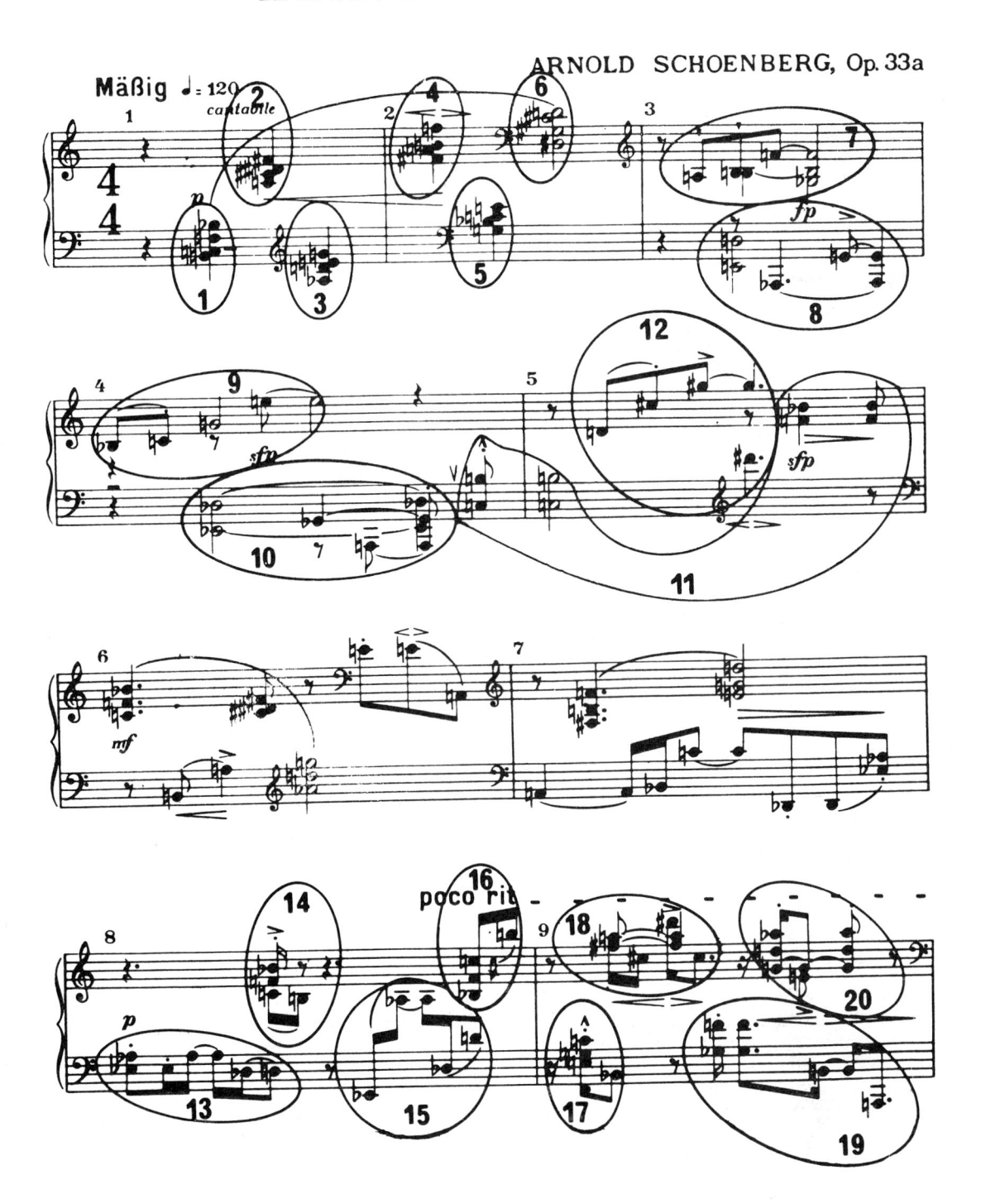

ARNOLD SCHOENBERG, Op. 33a

84 *Basic Atonal Theory*

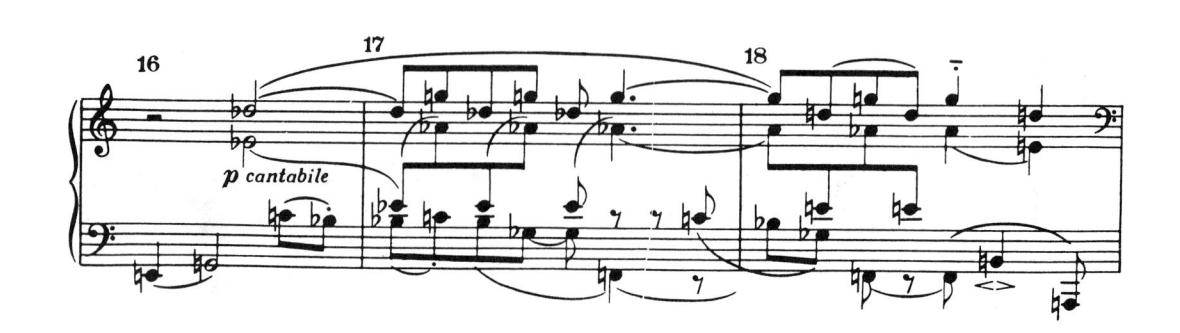

Set Types 85

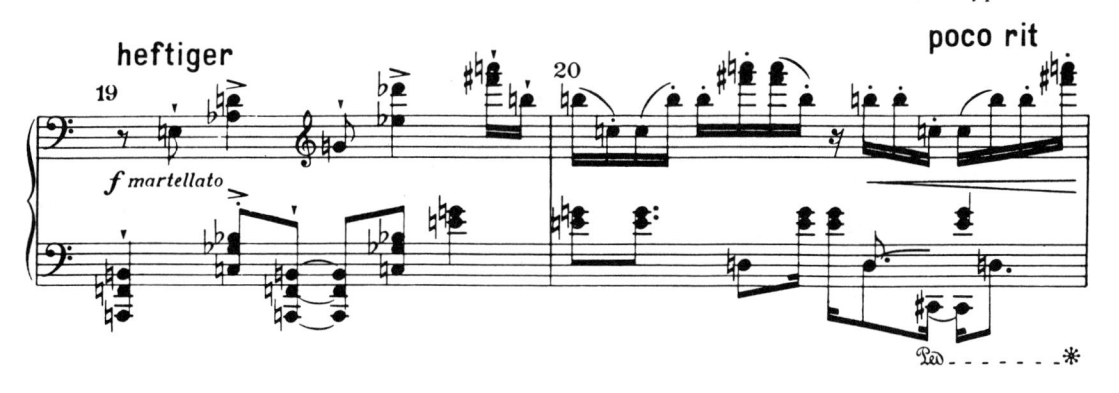

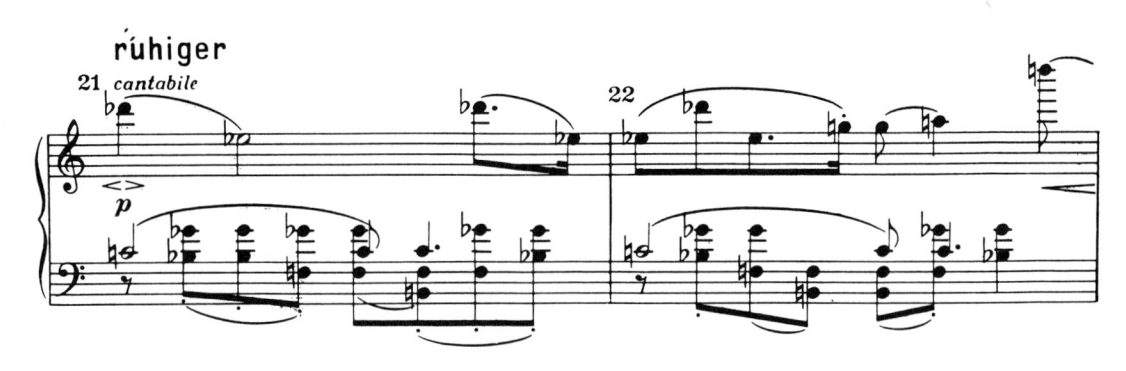

86 Basic Atonal Theory

Arnold Schoenberg *Klavierstück* op. 33a. Used by permission of Belmont Music Publishers, Los Angeles, California 90049.

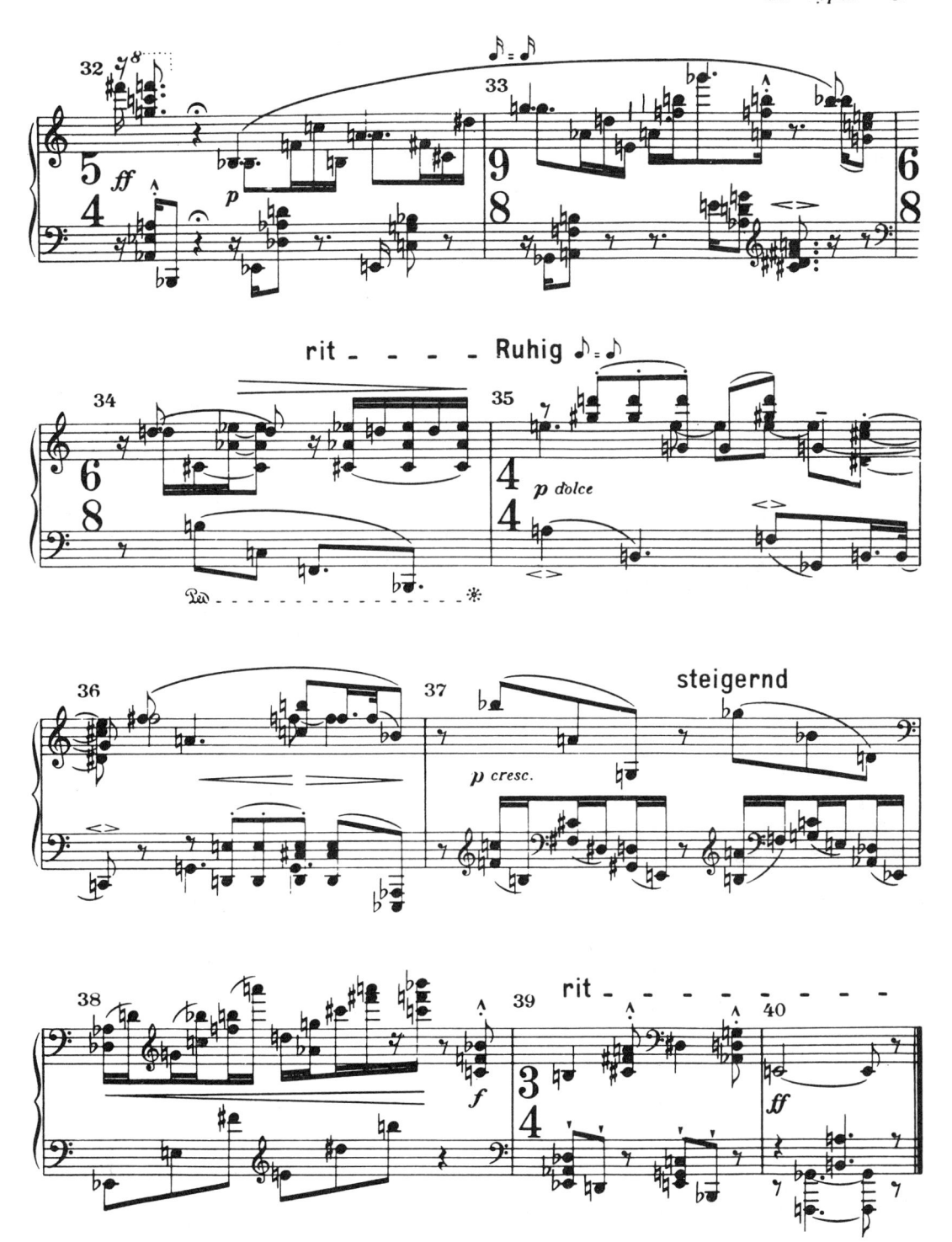

88   Basic Atonal Theory

4.22   Recognizing Sets Related by T_n

Two sets are transpositionally related if and only if their normal forms have the same adjacency-interval series.

Let "A1" and "B1" denote respectively the first pitch-classes in the normal forms of sets A and B. Then specifically, $T_{(B1-A1)}(A) \rightarrow B$ and $T_{(A1-B1)}(B) \rightarrow A$.

Example 1: let A = {0, 1, 3, 6} and B = {5, 6, 8, 11}. They are both in normal form and their adjacency-interval series are the same: <1, 2, 3>. Therefore they *are* transpositionally related. Specifically, $T_{(B1-A1)} = T_{(5-0)} = T_5$, so $T_5(A) \rightarrow B$; and $T_{(A1-B1)} = T_{(0-5)} = T_7$, so $T_7(B) \rightarrow A$.

Example 2: let A = {0, 1, 3, 6} and B = {7, 9, 0, 3}. Both are in normal form. The interval series of A is <1, 2, 3> but the interval series of B is <2, 3, 3>. Therefore these two sets are *not* transpositionally related.

Example 3: let A = {0, 1, 3, 6} and B = {4, 6, 9, 10}. Both are in normal form. The interval series of B is <2, 3, 1>, which is *not* the same as the interval series of A, <1, 2, 3>. These sets are *not* transpositionally related.

4.23   Recognizing Sets Related by T_nI

Two sets are related by T_nI if and only if they each can be written in a "canonical ordering with respect to each other." A "canonical ordering" is an "ascending" ordering such that the adjacency-interval series of the canonical orderings of both sets are mutually retrograde.

Canonical ordering is almost always normal form. Try normal form first. If both sets are "inversionally symmetrical" (see section 4.3) and are also transpositionally related, then they are T_nI-related.

Specifically, if "A1" and "B1" denote the *first* pc in the canonical orderings of sets A and B, and "AL" and "BL" denote the *last* pc in those orderings, then (A1 + BL) = (AL + B1) = the inversional index (section 3.23) and sets A and B map into each other under $T_{(A1+BL)}I$.

The pc members of any two T_nI-related sets can always be paired so that the sums of the pairs are the inversional index n = (A1+BL) = (B1+AL).

Example 1: let A = {11, 0, 3, 5} and B = {4, 6, 9, 10}. Both are in normal form. Their interval series <1, 3, 2> and <2, 3, 1> are mutually retrograde, so the two sets *are* inversionally related. The normal forms are the canonical orderings.

Specifically, the index equals (A1+BL) = (11+10) = 9, so sets A and B map into each other under T_9I:

T_9I {11, 0, 3, 5} → {10, 9, 6, 4} = B

T_9I {4, 6, 9, 10} → {5, 3, 0, 11} = A

$$A \xleftarrow{T_9I} B$$

The pc in the two sets can be paired so the pairs sum to the index 9.

{11, 0, 3, 5}
 + + + +   sums = 9
{10, 9, 6, 4}

Example 2: let A = {0, 2, 7} and B = {11, 1, 6}. Both are in normal form. Both interval series are <2,5>, so they are transpositionally related. But B can be rewritten in a canonical ordering {6,11,1} whose interval series <5,2> is mutually retrograde with the <2,5> of {0,2,7}. So the two sets *are* inversionally related. Specifically, the index equals (A1 + BL) = (0 + 1) = 1, so the sets map into each other under T_1I:

T_1I {0,2,7}→{1,11,6} = B

T_1I {11,1,6}→{2, 0,7} = A

$$T_1I$$
$$A \longleftrightarrow B$$

The pc in the two sets can be paired so the pairs sum to the index 1:

{0, 2, 7}

+ + +   sums = 1

{1, 11, 6}

{0,2,7} is inversionally symmetrical—see section 4.32.

4.24 Names of Operations, Sets, and Lines

The notation "T_n^p" refers to or names the *operation* of pitch transposition in general; "T_{+4}^p", for example, refers to (names) the particular operation of pitch transposition up four semitones. But "$T_n^p(x)$" refers to (names) the *result* of transposing any given pitch x by n semitones; "$T_{+4}^p(2)$" is just another name for the pitch whose number is "6" (since pitch 6 is the *result* of transposing pitch 2 up 4 semitones). So when we write "$T_{+4}^p(2) = 6$", the equals sign connects two different names for the same pitch (6).

Similarly, "T_n", "T_n^pI", and "T_nI" name the general operations of pc transposition, pitch inversion, and pc inversion, respectively; "$T_4^pI(3)$" is another name for the result of inverting pitch 3 and transposing up 4 semitones— "$T_4^pI(3)$" is another name for the pitch called "(−3+4)" or most simply "1". "$T_3I(7)$" is another name for the pc number "(−7+3)" or "8" (−4 = 8).

The principle extends to names of sets and lines of elements. Thus, "T_7 {0,4,7}" names the pc set {7,11,2}; "$T_{11}I$ <3, 10, 2, 5, 4, 0>" names the pc line <−3+11, −10+11, −2+11, −5+11, −4+11, −0+11> = <8, 1, 9, 6, 7, 11>.

Often during the analysis or composition of a piece of music one particular set or line may be "referential" (e.g., an "E♭ major triad" in the Eroica Symphony's first movement). In this case other sets or lines are named by their relation to the referential set or line; e.g. {7,11,2} might be named "T_7{0,4,7}". (Of course, in this case, E♭ = 0.) If there is absolutely no ambiguity about exactly what is the referential norm, the name of the norm can be omitted; {7,11,2} is then named by "T_7".

Notations vary. Much literature uses the notation "I_n" (or, "I-n") for "T_nI". A set or line may be given a label such as "S" or "P". Then "P_n" notates "$T_n(P)$" and "$I_n(P)$" or simply "I_n" notates "$T_nI(P)$".

90 Basic Atonal Theory

EXERCISES 4-II: Recognizing Set Relations

Refer to the excerpt from Schoenberg's *Klavierstück* op. 33a and the exercises for set types (4-I). Using circled sets ①, ②, and ③ as referential, express each set from ⑤ through ⑳ as a T_n or T_nI of ①, ②, or ③, with B♭ equal to zero. (Warning: set ① is special (see 4.3); there may be two "right" answers involving ①, but which is more consistent?)

Example:

$$\begin{array}{c} \quad\quad 1 \ \ 3 \ \ 2 \quad \text{(intervals)} \\ ④ = \{8,11,1,7\} = \{7, 8, 11, 1\} \end{array}$$

$$\begin{array}{c} \quad\quad 2 \ \ 3 \ \ 1 \\ ③ = \{4, 6, 9, 10\} \quad T_{(1+4)}I\{4,6,9,10\} = \\ \{7, 8, 11, 1\} \end{array}$$

so, ④ = T_5I (③).

1. ⑤ =
2. ⑥ =
3. ⑦ =
4. ⑧ =
5. ⑨ =
6. ⑩ =
7. ⑪ =
8. ⑫ =
9. ⑬ =
10. ⑭ =
11. ⑮ =
12. ⑯ =
13. ⑰ =
14. ⑱ =
15. ⑲ =
16. ⑳ =

4.3 SYMMETRY

4.31 Degree of Symmetry

The degree of symmetry of a structure is the number of distinct operations in the system that map that structure into itself.[7] Our system[8] so far includes

24 distinct operations: T_n and T_nI for n = 0...11 each. Every pc structure maps into itself under the identity operation, T_0. So every pc structure has at least "one degree of symmetry."

A structure that maps into itself under T_n (where n ≠ 0) is called "transpositionally symmetrical." A structure that maps into itself under T_nI is called "inversionally symmetrical." All pc sets of the same T_n-type or T_n/T_nI-type have the same degree of symmetry, so we can (loosely) speak of the degree of symmetry of the type.

THEOREM
>The number of distinct members of a T_n/T_nI equivalence class of sets in our system equals 24 divided by the degree of symmetry of the set.

Example 1: {0,4,8} maps into itself under T_0, T_4, and T_8. (T_4 {0,4,8} = {4,8,0} = {0,4,8}; T_8 {0,4,8} = {8,0,4} = {0,4,8}.) Thus {0,4,8} has three degrees of *transpositional* symmetry. {0,4,8} also maps into itself under T_0I, T_4I, and T_8I. Thus {0,4,8} has three degrees of *inversional* symmetry. Altogether, then, {0,4,8} has six degrees of symmetry, and the number of sets in [0,4,8] = 24/6 = 4. Check this and find that [0,4,8] = { {0,4,8}, {1,5,9}, {2,6,10}, {3,7,11} }; [0,4,8] indeed has these 4 members.

Example 2: {0,1,3,4} maps into itself under T_0 and T_4I. (T_4I {0,1,3,4} = {4,3,1,0} = {0,1,3,4}.) With two degrees of symmetry, [0,1,3,4] has 24/2 = 12 members. The 12 members are its twelve transpositions, since every inversion equals some transposition.

Example 3: {0,3,7} maps into itself only under T_0. [0,3,7] has 24/1 = 24 members (listed in section 4.13).

4.32   Inversional Symmetry

THEOREM
>An inversionally symmetrical set always has a "canonical ordering" whose interval series is its *own* retrograde (retrograde-symmetrical). For each such canonical ordering it may have, it will map into itself under T_xI, where the inversional index x equals the sum of the first and last members of that canonical ordering.

In Example 1 in 4.31, {0,4,8} had three canonical orderings— {0,4,8}, {4,8,0}, and {8,0,4}—each with the same retrograde-symmetrical interval series, <4,4>, and with indices 0 + 8 = 8, 4 + 0 = 4, and 8 + 4 = 0.

In Example 2 in 4.31, {0,1,3,4} had one canonical ordering—{0,1,3,4}—with retrograde-symmetrical interval series <1,2,1>, and index 0 + 4 = 4. (It maps into itself under T_4I.)

Example 4: {0,2,4,5,7,9} is in canonical ordering, with interval series <2,2,1,2,2>. It maps into itself under T_9I.

92   *Basic Atonal Theory*

Example 5: {0,2,7}. A canonical ordering is {7,0,2,7}, with retrograde-symmetrical interval series <5,2,5>. The index is 7 + 7 = 2. The set maps into itself under T_2I. Note that {0,7,2}, which has a retrograde-symmetrical series <7,7> and is therefore another canonical ordering, has the same index 0 + 2 = 2.

Due to the retrograde-symmetry of its interval series, an inversionally symmetrical set in canonical ordering always makes a pretty nested structure of the paired pc that sum to the index. In the following examples, curved lines connect the pc in the canonical orderings that add up to the index.

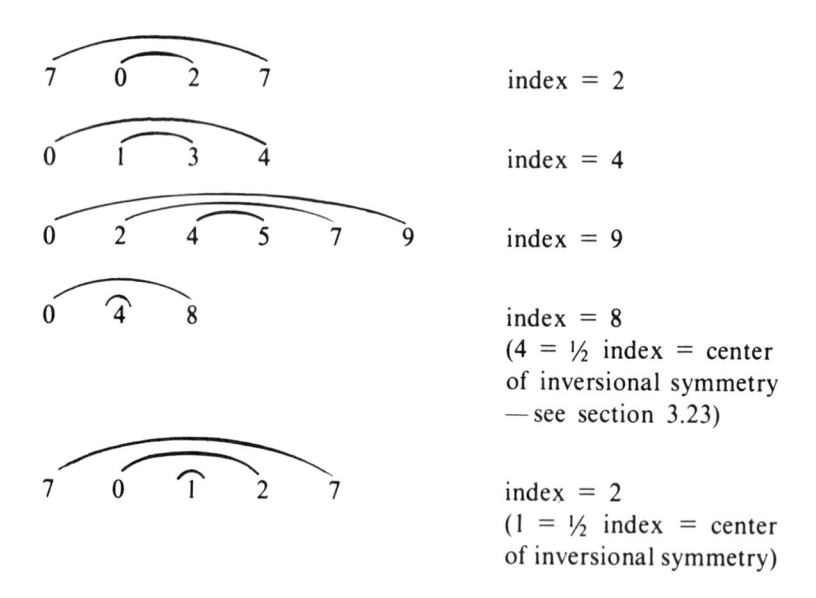

7 0 2 7   index = 2

0 1 3 4   index = 4

0 2 4 5 7 9   index = 9

0 4 8   index = 8
(4 = ½ index = center of inversional symmetry — see section 3.23)

7 0 1 2 7   index = 2
(1 = ½ index = center of inversional symmetry)

4.33   Transpositional Symmetry

A set is "transpositionally symmetrical" if and only if its normal form can be partitioned into segments such that under some particular nonzero "n", T_n maps each m-th segment into each (m + 1)-th segment cyclically (the last segment maps into the first). For example, T_6 {0,1,2,6,7,8}→{6,7,8,0,1,2}. The first segment, 012, maps into the second, 678, and 678 maps around into 012. Another example: {0,1,4,5,8,9} can be partitioned into three segments 4 semitones apart:

         T4   T4   T4
    0,1 ─────► 4,5 ─────► 8,9 ─────► 0,1.

So   T4{0,1,4,5,8,9}→{4,5,8,9,0,1}   and

        T8{0,1,4,5,8,9}→{8,9,0,1,4,5}.

4.34   Relation to Common-Tone Theorems

It may relieve you to know that there is a more systematic and completely comprehensive way to learn the specific operations that map a set into itself:

Set Types 93

the common-tone theorems given in chapter 5. A set B with m members maps into itself under some operation Z if and only if B and Z (B) have all m members in common. The specific T_n and T_nI that accomplish this are easily read off using the common-tone theorems. The more informal methods in 4.3 are most useful for quick comprehension of the properties of smaller sets.

EXERCISES 4-III: Symmetry

For each set below: A) list exactly which operations map the sets into themselves (including T_0); B) write each inversionally symmetrical set in canonical ordering and show the pretty nested structure of paired pc that sum to the index; C) tell how many sets are in the T_n/T_nI equivalence class of the set shown.

1. {0, 1, 2, 7}
2. {0, 1, 3, 6, 7, 9}
3. {2, 4, 5, 6, 7, 8}
4. {5, 6, 7, 8, 9, 10}
5. {8, 10, 11, 0, 2}
6. {6, 8, 9, 10, 0, 3}
7. {2, 3, 8, 9}
8. {1, 3, 5, 7, 9, 11}

4.4 UNION AND DISUNION OF INVERSIONALLY SYMMETRICAL SETS

The union of any two inversionally related sets is an inversionally symmetrical set. Conversely, an inversionally symmetrical set may always be "disunited" into at least one pair of inversionally related subsets.

Example 1: {0,2,5} ∪ T_2I{0,2,5} = {0,2,5} ∪ {2,0,9} = {0,2,5,9} = {9,0,2,5} in normal form = canonical ordering (interval series <3,2,3>).

{9,0,2,5} maps into itself under $T_{(9 + 5)}I$ or T_2I.

Example 2: {1,7,9} ∪ T_1I{1,7,9} = {1,7,9} ∪ {0,6,4} = {1,7,9,0,6,4} = {0,1,4,6,7,9} in normal form, {0,4,6,7,9,1} in canonical ordering (interval series <4,2,1,2,4>).

$T_{(0 + 1)}I$ = T_1I maps {0,1,4,6,7,9} into itself.

As you can see, in the case of a union of T_nI-related sets, the resulting set maps into itself at the same T_nI that related its components.

94   Basic Atonal Theory

Example 3: {0,1,3,4} maps into itself at T_4I. It may be disunited into many pairs of T_4I-related subsets:

0 1 3 4   {0,1,4} ∪ {0,3,4} =
                 {0,1,4} ∪ T_4I{0,1,4}

0 1 3 4   {0,1,3} ∪ {1,3,4} =
                 {0,1,3} ∪ T_4I{0,1,3}

0 1 3 4   {0,1} ∪ {3,4} =
                 {0,1} ∪ T_4I{0,1}

0 1 3 4   {0,3} ∪ {1,4} =
                 {0,3} ∪ T_4I{0,3}

Especially interesting are *partitioning subsets* that are disunions of a larger set; such subsets have no pc in common.[9]

Example 4: {1,2,4,6,8,9} is in canonical ordering = normal form with interval series <1,2,2,2,1>. It maps into itself under $T_{(1+9)}I$. Its partitioning T_nI-related trichords of disunion are:

	trichord type
{1,2,4} ∪ {6,8,9} = {1,2,4} ∪ $T_{10}I${1,2,4}	[0,1,3]
{1,2,6} ∪ {4,8,9} = {1,2,6} ∪ $T_{10}I${1,2,6}	[0,1,5]
{1,4,8} ∪ {9,6,2} = {1,4,8} ∪ $T_{10}I${1,4,8}	[0,3,7]
{1,6,8} ∪ {2,4,9} = {1,6,8} ∪ $T_{10}I${1,6,8}	[0,2,7]

EXERCISES 4-IV: Union/Disunion of Inversionally Symmetrical Sets

1. List all T_nI-related pairs of partitioning trichords. Give the T_n/T_nI-type of each such subset. You may find it helpful to work with musical notation in these examples (C = 0). See also section 5.5, "Subset Content."

    The hexachords in 1a through 1f each belong to one of the six "all-combinatorial" hexachords (see section 5.6) so important to serial theory,[10] as are the types of trichords that partition them—this exercise (especially) has future relevance.

    a) {3,4,5,6,7,8}

    b) {10,0,1,2,3,5}

    c) {6,8,10,11,1,3}

    d) {8,9,10,2,3,4}

    e) {2,3,6,7,10,11}

    f) {1,3,5,7,9,11}

Set Types 95

2. List all T_nI-related pairs of subsets of the given size subsets (*not* necessarily partitioning) whose union is the given set. Give the T_n/T_nI-type for each such pair.

   a) {4,5,6,11}   (trichords)

   b) {0,2,4,7,9}   (tetrachords, trichords)

   c) {10,11,2,5,6}   (tetrachords, trichords)

   d) {6,7,8,9,0,3}   (tetrachords, trichords)

   e) {2,4,5,6,7,8,9,11}   (partitioning tetrachords only)

ASSIGNMENTS

Analysis

Analyze mm. 1-9 of the Schoenberg *Klavierstück* op. 33a. The tetrachordal identification in exercises for sections 4.21 and 4.22/4.23/4.24 is a mere beginning. An analysis should include more than the answers to the following questions.

How are these tetrachords made separately audible? What is the structure audibly revealed within each presented tetrachord and how do these "intratetrachord" structures audibly relate to each other and to the "intertetrachord" structures among the variously presented different tetrachords? What are the contributions to musical coherence of octave placement, dynamics, articulation? How are "phrases" made audibly unified entities, and how do their intra and inter structures relate to structures of pitch-class (tetrachords, etc.), pitch, dynamics, articulation, duration, etc.? What is the "rhythm," and in what senses? Look ahead to the rest of op. 33a, superficially at least. How does the music of mm. 1-9 grow into the music of the entire piece? But concentrate on mm. 1-9.

Composition

Compose a short piece of music with a clearly coherent (but not boring!) underlying structure of related sets of pitch-classes. Section 4.4 may be particularly helpful. Remember, for any "precomposed" structure of pitch-classes, that pitch placement, instrumentation, dynamics, articulation, texture, and most especially, rhythm, are ways in which music can be created or in which even the bare, scanty coherence of the precomposed pc structure can be effectively destroyed—made inaudible or all too audible. A pc structure is a structure of very bare bones indeed. But, in favor of pc structure, regard the jellyfish.

NOTES

[1] Formally, a "partition" is a set of equivalence classes.

[2] Many authors use the *representative* as the name, speaking of a "{0,4,7} trichord" or "{0,4,7} type trichord." *But there is only one "{0,4,7} trichord,"* namely, {0,4,7}; and the formulation "{0,4,7} type trichord" cannot in some instances specify the criterion by which the type is formed: T_n^p, T_n, T_n^pI, T_nI, T_n^p/T_n^pI, T_n/T_nI, and $T_n/T_nI/T_nM5/T_nM7$ (see 3.4) are all criteria which form different sets of equivalence classes.

[3] If then "$(0,4,7)_{Tn}$" is the name for the class of all trichords equivalent to {0,4,7} and to each other under the operation T_n, "$(0,4,7)_{TnI}$" might be a name for the class of twelve trichords that are transposed inversions of {0,4,7}, i.e., all the "minor triads." However, this does not work in a parallel fashion; for while the compound of any number of T_n operations is still a T_n for some n, on the contrary, every T_nI of a T_nI returns you to a T_n for some n:

$$T_j(T_k(x)) = T_j(x+k) = (x+k) + j = x+j+k = T_{(j+k)}(x) = T_n(x) \text{ for n}$$
$$= (j+k), \text{ but}$$

$$T_jI(T_kI(x)) = T_jI(-x+k) = -(-x+k) + j = x+j-k = T_{(j-k)}(x) = T_n(x) \text{ for n} = (j-k).$$

Consequently the class of all T_nI of the members of $(0,4,7)_{Tn}$ itself contains members related by T_n, *not* by T_nI: $T_nI\{0,4,7\} = \{0+n,-4+n,-7+n\}$ for n from 0 through 11. For example, for n = 0, $\{0,-4,-7\} = \{0,8,5\} = \{5,8,0\}$ in normal form; for n = 2, $\{2,-2,-5\} = \{2,10,7\} = \{7,10,2\}$ in normal form; and $T_2\{5,8,0\} = \{7,10,2\}$.

[4] See Benjamin Boretz, "Meta-Variations, Part IV: Analytic Fallout (I)," *PNM* 11/1 (1972): 146-223.

[5] See, for example, William Benjamin's "Tonality Without Fifths: Remarks on the First Movement of Stravinsky's Concerto for Piano and Winds," *In Theory Only* 2/11 and 2/12 (double issue, Feb.-March 1977): 53-70, and *In Theory Only* 3/2 (May 1977): 9-31.

[6] A syntax of possible subset relations among set types is developed in Allen Forte's *The Structure of Atonal Music*.

[7] This group-theoretical definition corresponds with "intuitive" notions of what "symmetry" is.

[8] "Our system" being T_n and T_nI on the 12 pc; mathematically, the group $(Z12,+)$. "Our system" can be extended to include T_n, T_nI, T_nM5, and T_nM7 on $(Z12,+)$ (see section 3.4). This increases the number of distinct operations to 48, with "n" varying from 0 through 11 for each of T_n, T_nI, T_nM5, and T_nM7. The number of ways a set can map into itself is increased. For example, {0,1,7} maps into itself under T_0 and T_0M7; {0,2,3,4,5,7} maps into itself under T_0, T_7I, T_3M7, and T_4M5. In general:

THEOREM: **The number of members of an equivalence class of sets equals the number of distinct operations in the system (48 now) divided by the degree of symmetry of the set.**

(This theorem is easily proven in group theory.) The system can be extended even further by the addition to the system of operations on *order,* such as retrograde, rotation, etc.

[9] Subsets of the aggregate — not necessarily T_nI-related — are defined by segments of 12-tone rows. For compositional examples and further theory, see David Lewin, "A Theory of Segmental Association in Twelve-Tone Music," *PNM* 1/1 (1962): 89-116. Conversely, new rows may be "generated" by such segmental content; see Milton Babbitt, "Since Schoenberg," *PNM* 12/1 and 12/2 (double issue, 1973-74): 3-28.

[10] See Milton Babbitt's pioneering article, "Some Aspects of Twelve-Tone Composition," *The Score and IMA Magazine* 12 (June 1955): 53-61, and Donald Martino's "The Source Set and its Aggregate Formations," *JMT* 5/2 (1961): 224-273.

CHAPTER FIVE
COMMON-TONE THEOREMS

The "common-tone" theorems relate the structure of a set of pc to the number of pc in common between that set and each of its transformations. The preceding analysis of Schoenberg's *Farben* showed how such common-tone relations participate in one musical structure. In the broadest sense, common-tone relations exemplify one of the basic principles of musical construction in general: varied repetition, or variation. Later events in a composition grow out of earlier ones. In order to do this a later event must be similar in some respect to an earlier event, yet different from it in some other respect. A set of pc may be followed by a transformation (T_n, T_nI) of that set. The transformation is similar to the set in that it *is* a transposition or inversion of the set—thus, for these two kinds of transformations, having identical "interval content" (section 5.1). Beyond this similarity of interval content there exists a basis for hierarchizable differentiation—the number of pc in common between the old and new forms of the set, and thus the number of new pc that arrive only with the later form of the set may vary from all pc in common (for identical sets) to none in common. The tonal system of Beethoven and Brahms has built into it a great care in introducing "new" pc, combined with a maximum degree of hierarchization. Modulation by a fifth (7 semitones) introduces just one new pc into the resulting diatonic collection (6 pc in common)—the minimum pc content variation; while each transposition, to within unordered pc interval, of a diatonic collection has a distinct number of common-tones, resulting in the maximum possible hierarchization. These matters are directly inferable from the interval content of the diatonic collection, given the common-tone theorem for T_n (section 5.2), and this theorem is even more useful in systems using other types of pc sets. Moreover, the notion of interval content alone is a valuable tool for uncovering the compositional possibilities inherent in one set of pc (see section 5.22).

Just as the common-tone theorem for T_n is based on the notion of interval, the common-tone theorem for T_nI is based on the notion of index (section 3.23). The musical relevance of the sum of two pc number-names is less patent than that of their difference (interval), but, indirectly at least, the two concepts are equally useful. Certainly the number of pc in common between a set and its inversion is a very audible kind of relation. Beyond this, though, many composers (including Schoenberg, Berg, and Webern) have used center of symmetry

98 Basic Atonal Theory

relations to structure their work audibly; and some modern composers—notably George Perle and Paul Lansky—have developed from Berg's uses of index and center of symmetry a highly sophisticated systematic syntax for composing music. (See Lansky (1) and Perle (8) and (9) in the Bibliography.)

5.1 MULTIPLICITY; INTERVAL CONTENT; INTERVAL VECTOR

5.11 Multiplicity

The notions of interval multiplicity and interval content of a pc set are valuable in many ways, perhaps the most immediately germane of which is their use as a basis for the common-tone theorem for transposition (5.2). It is true that it is possible to "look up" the interval content of any T_n/T_nI-type in various published tables. But learning yourself how to find interval content from the set alone not only short-circuits the aridity of table-looking-up and provides a deeper understanding of what interval content is and means, but actually can be more convenient—especially in case the table is across the room, across the hall, across the campus, or across town. It will also build skills toward approaching concepts—like TICS (5.3) and "subset content" (5.5)—whose results are not generally look-up-able in tables.

DEF   **Given a set of pc and a particular unordered pc interval, the "multiplicity" of that interval in that set equals the number of different pairs of pc from that set which form that interval.**

For example, in the set $\{0,2,4,5,7,9,11\}$ the interval 4 is formed just three times:

$i(0, 4) = 4$

$i(5, 9) = 4$

$i(7,11) = 4$

Therefore the "multiplicity" of 4 in that set is 3. In symbols, the "multiplicity in set B of interval K" is written, "$M_B(K)$". If we label $\{0,2,4,5,7,9,11\}$ as set "D", then $M_D(4) = 3$, or "the multiplicity in set D of interval 4 equals 3."

5.12 Interval Content

DEF   **A list of the multiplicities in a set of pc of *each* unordered pc interval 1 through 6 is called the "interval content" of that pc set.**

The interval content of a set takes into account every possible pair of pc from that set. There is a simple procedure which will insure that you do include every possible pair in your interval content:

1. List the pc of the set from left to right (in any order).

2. Find the unordered pc interval of every pair that includes the left-hand-most member, from left to right.

3. Find the unordered pc interval of every pair that includes the next-to-left-hand-most member, from left to right.
4. Continue until the process ends with the pair consisting of the next-to-the-last and the last members.

A convenient form for tabulation is to list the possible unordered pc intervals 1-6 and place a mark or tally beneath the appropriate interval every time you calculate the interval between a new pair of pc. We shall follow such a process here for {0 2 4 5 7 9 11}.

		possible i(x,y) intervals:	1	2	3	4	5	6
0 11 5 9 4 2 7	(any order)							
i(0,11) = 1	0 11 5 9 4 2 7		I					
i(0, 5) = 5							I	
i(0, 9) = 3					I			
i(0, 4) = 4						I		
i(0, 2) = 2				I				
i(0, 7) = 5							I	
i(11, 5) = 6	11 5 9 4 2 7							I
i(11, 9) = 2				I				
i(11, 4) = 5							I	
i(11, 2) = 3					I			
i(11, 7) = 4						I		
i(5, 9) = 4	5 9 4 2 7					I		
i(5, 4) = 1			I					
i(5, 2) = 3					I			
i(5, 7) = 2				I				
i(9, 4) = 5	9 4 2 7						I	
i(9, 2) = 5							I	
i(9, 7) = 2				I				
i(4, 2) = 2	4 2 7			I				
i(4, 7) = 3					I			
i(2, 7) = 5	2 7						I	
		totals:	2	5	4	3	6	1

100 Basic Atonal Theory

That is, if {0,2,4,5,7,9,11} = D:

$M_D(1) = 2$

$M_D(2) = 5$

$M_D(3) = 4$

$M_D(4) = 3$

$M_D(5) = 6$

$M_D(6) = 1$

In practice, rather than rewriting each segment and making such a pretty pattern with one mark per line, it's easier to tally with strokes, so that the final totals as tallied would look like this:

intervals:	1	2	3	4	5	6
	//	/////	////	///	///// /	/
totals:	2	5	4	3	6	1

5.13 Interval Vector

If it is assumed that the multiplicities are listed in order of increasing size of interval 1 through 6, the interval content can be given by an ordered 6-tuple <2,5,4,3,6,1>. Interval content given in this way is called an "interval vector."[1]

DEF   **An "interval vector" of a pc set is an ordered 6-tuple of the multiplicities of intervals 1,2,3,4,5,6 in that order.**

Therefore the interval vector of {0,2,4,5,7,9,11} is <2,5,4,3,6,1>.[2]

This interval vector <2,5,4,3,6,1> is unusual in that every interval appears at least once and appears a different number of times than any other interval—each interval has a "unique multiplicity." There are only two "types" of pc sets which have unique nonzero interval multiplicity, and they are the diatonic collection {0,2,4,5,7,9,11} and the 7/12 chromatic scale {0,1,2,3,4,5,6}. The T_n common-tone theorem (section 5.2) will show that "unique interval multiplicity" ensures that for each unordered pc interval, sets related by intervals of transposition corresponding to that unordered interval have a unique number of pc in common, so that the transpositional relation can be identified to within unordered interval from the common-tone relation.

One more example for practice: the initially attacked pitch simultaneity of Schoenberg's *Suite* op. 29 (see Ex. 1).

EXAMPLE 1

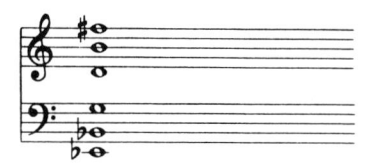

[musical notation showing six pitches on grand staff]

This example gives a chord or simultaneity of six pitches, which will be treated as a set of six pc, and its interval content found. Calling the lowest note E♭ = 0, the pitches represent the pc set {E♭, B♭, G, D, B, F♯} or {0,7,4,11,8,3}. We now proceed as we did before:

```
0 7 4 11 8 3                        1  2  3  4  5  6
i(0,7)  = 5     0 7 4 11 8 3                    1
i(0,4)  = 4                               1
i(0,11) = 1           1
i(0,8)  = 4                               1
i(0,3)  = 3                 1
i(7,4)  = 3      7 4 11 8 3    1
i(7,11) = 4                               1
i(7,8)  = 1           1
i(7,3)  = 4                               1
i(4,11) = 5      4 11 8 3                       1
i(4,8)  = 4                               1
i(4,3)  = 1           1
i(11,8) = 3      11 8 3     1
i(11,3) = 4                               1
i(8,3)  = 5      8 3                            1
                      totals:  3  0  3  6  3  0
```

The interval vector is <3,0,3,6,3,0>; that is, there are three of interval 1, zero of interval 2, three of interval 3, six of interval 4, three of interval 5, and zero of interval 6.

102 Basic Atonal Theory

To illustrate the fact that the order in which the pc are listed does not affect the interval content, let us work on the same set {0,7,4,11,8,3} but list it in another order: 11 7 3 4 0 8.

		1	2	3	4	5	6
11 7 3 4 0 8							
i(11,7) = 4	11 7 3 4 0 8				1		
i(11,3) = 4					1		
i(11,4) = 5						1	
i(11,0) = 1		1					
i(11,8) = 3				1			
i(7,3) = 4	7 3 4 0 8				1		
i(7,4) = 3				1			
i(7,0) = 5						1	
i(7,8) = 1		1					
i(3,4) = 1	3 4 0 8	1					
i(3,0) = 3				1			
i(3,8) = 5						1	
i(4,0) = 4	4 0 8				1		
i(4,8) = 4					1		
i(0,8) = 4	0 8				1		
totals:		3	0	3	6	3	0

The interval vector is <3,0,3,6,3,0> again.

5.14 Invariance of Interval Content; Z-Related Sets

The interval content or interval vector of a pc set is invariant under T_n and T_nI. (Transposing or inverting a set preserves unordered pc interval.) All sets in one T_n-type or T_n/T_nI-type will have the same interval content.

However, the converse does not hold. Some sets that have the same interval content are of different T_n-type and T_n/T_nI-type. Such sets are called (after Allen Forte) "Z-related."[3] For example, {0,1,4,6} and {0,1,3,7} are the representative forms of their separate T_n/T_nI-types, and therefore are *not* transpositionally or inversionally related. But they do have same interval vector, <1,1,1,1,1,1>, and are then called "Z-related."

To be "Z-related," two sets must both (1) belong to different T_n/T_nI-types, and (2) have the same interval content.

Common Tone Theorems 103

EXERCISES 5-I

Ex. 2 of Analysis 2 shows the five simultaneities produced by the canon between T_0^0 and T_{-1}^0 of the Chord of Schoenberg's *Farben* op. 16 no. 3. Treat each of those five intermediate simultaneities as a set of pc (with C = 0). List it in normal form and find its T_n-type, T_n/T_nI-type, and interval vector without using Table II (Appendix 2).

	normal form	T_n-type	T_n/T_nI-type	interval vector
1.	(m.4)			
2.	(m.5)			
3.	(m.6)			
4.	(m.7)			
5.	(m.8)			

*5.15 Interval Content Under Multiplicative Operations

Section 3.4 indicated that all multiplicative operations are homomorphisms (M11, M7, M5, and M1 are, in addition, isomorphisms). Therefore, when you operate multiplicatively on two pc you operate identically on their ordered pc interval; the interval between the images is equal to the image of the interval between the preimages. What effect, then, does each multiplicative operation on a set of pc have on the multiplicities of the unordered pc intervals of that set — its interval content?

M1, the identity operation on pc, is then the identity operation also on their ordered pc interval and therefore on their unordered pc interval. The multiplicity of each unordered interval remains the same, as does (therefore) the interval content.

M11, which equals T_0I, is the following mapping on $i\langle x,y\rangle$:

$$\begin{array}{cc} x & \begin{pmatrix} 1 & 2 & 3 & 4 & 5 & 6 & 7 & 8 & 9 & 10 & 11 \\ 11 & 10 & 9 & 8 & 7 & 6 & 5 & 4 & 3 & 2 & 1 \end{pmatrix} \\ M11(x) & \end{array}$$

and is therefore an identity operation on $i(x,y)$, so that unordered pc interval content remains unchanged under inversion. (A pair of pc that forms ordered interval 7 forms unordered interval 5; a pair forming ordered interval 8 forms unordered interval 4; ordered interval 9 forms unordered interval 3; ordered interval 10 forms unordered interval 2; and ordered interval 11 forms unordered interval 1. Under M11, these pairs of intervals map into each other— 7↔5, 8↔4, 9↔3, 10↔2, 11↔1 — and intervals 6 and 0 map into themselves, so that no change of *un*ordered interval occurs.)

M5 is this mapping on ordered pc interval:

$$\begin{array}{cc} x & \begin{pmatrix} 1 & 2 & 3 & 4 & 5 & 6 & 7 & 8 & 9 & 10 & 11 \\ 5 & 10 & 3 & 8 & 1 & 6 & 11 & 4 & 9 & 2 & 7 \end{pmatrix} \\ M5(x) & \end{array}$$

Intervals 1 and 5 map into each other, as do intervals 7 and 11. The unordered pc intervals of pc pairs producing intervals 7 and 11 are respectively 5 and 1. So

104 Basic Atonal Theory

unordered pc intervals 1 and 5 map into each other, and *their multiplicities are exchanged*. All the other multiplicities remain unchanged: ordered intervals 2↔10, 3↔3, 4↔8, and 9↔9, so that unordered intervals 2,3,4, and 6 map into themselves.

M7 is this mapping on i<x,y>:

$$\begin{matrix} x \\ M7(x) \end{matrix} \begin{pmatrix} 1 & 2 & 3 & 4 & 5 & 6 & 7 & 8 & 9 & 10 & 11 \\ 7 & 2 & 9 & 4 & 11 & 6 & 1 & 8 & 3 & 10 & 5 \end{pmatrix}$$

The multiplicities of unordered intervals 2,3,4, and 6 again remain unchanged: ordered intervals 2↔2, 3↔9, 4↔4, 6↔6, 8↔8, and 10↔10. But unordered intervals 1 and 5 map into each other (ordered intervals 1↔7 and 5↔11) so that the multiplicities of unordered intervals 1 and 5 are exchanged.

THEOREM M5 and M7 have exactly the same effect on interval content: the multiplicities of unordered intervals 1 and 5 are exchanged and all other multiplicities remain unchanged.

That the effect of the two operations is identical should not be surprising, since M5 and M7 are related by M11, and M11 preserves unordered interval. T_nM5 and T_nM7 may be substituted for M5 and M7 in the theorem, since T_n preserves ordered interval and thus (*a fortiriori*) unordered interval.[4]

In 5.14 the tetrachord types [0,1,4,6] and [0,1,3,7] were given as examples of Z-related sets. These are the *only* tetrachord types that are Z-related. The interval vector of each type is <1,1,1,1,1,1>. In this vector 1 and 5 have the same multiplicity, so that if their multiplicities are exchanged the vector is unchanged. This tells us that one of two situations obtains: either each set of each type maps into itself under T_nM5 or T_nM7 for some value of "n" (in this case the type is called "M5-symmetrical"), or the sets of each type map into each other under these operations. In fact, T_7M5 {0,1,4,6} = {7,0,3,1} = {0,1,3,7} so T_1M5 {0,1,3,7} = {0,1,4,6} (the inverse operation of T_7M5 is T_1M5—see section 3.4, Exercises 3–V, item 1). The two sets map not into themselves but into each other. Thus if we add T_nM5 and T_nM7 to T_nI and T_n in our system of basic operations, the already closely related sets (Z-related) {0,1,4,6} and {0,1,3,7} are no longer of separate types but are "*M5-equivalent*," belonging to the type $[0,1,4,6]_{M5}$ of $T_n/T_nI/T_nM5/T_nM7$-equivalent sets. (See number 9 of Table 1, Appendix 2, and section 3.4 and footnote 8 in section 4.31.)

Under T_nM5 and T_nM7, segments of the chromatic scale and circle of fifths map into each other. For example, two of the three "first-order all-combinatorial hexachords" (section 5.6) are such segments.

$$\begin{matrix} & T_4M5 \\ & T_5M7 \\ \{0,1,2,3,4,5\} & \rightleftarrows & \{0,2,4,5,7,9\} \\ & T_1M7 \\ & T_4M5 \end{matrix}$$

The remaining first-order, all-combinatorial hexachord type, [0,2,3,4,5,7], is M5-symmetrical; its representative form maps into itself under T_3M7 and T_4M5.

(See section 3.4, Exercises 3–V, especially item 6, and section 5.6 ahead.) The interval vector of {0,2,3,4,5,7} is <3,4,3,2,3,0>; intervals 1 and 5 both have multiplicity 3, so their exchange results in an unchanged vector. The vectors of {0,1,2,3,4,5} and {0,2,4,5,7,9} are respectively <5,4,3,2,1,0> and <1,4,3,2,5,0>; only the multiplicities of intervals 1 and 5 are exchanged.

EXERCISES 5-II

1. Is every pair of Z-related sets equivalent under T_nM5 or T_nM7? Give reasons.

2. Is a set necessarily M5-symmetrical if its interval vector has identical multiplicities for intervals 1 and 5? Give reasons.

3. Are two sets necessarily M5-equivalent if their interval vectors are the same except for exchanged multiplicities for intervals 1 and 5? Give reasons.

4. If two sets are M5-equivalent, are their interval vectors necessarily the same except for exchange of the multiplicities of intervals 1 and 5? Give reasons.

5. Table II (Appendix 2) lists all T_n/T_nI types, that is, all equivalence classes of pc sets under T_n or T_nI. Some types that are distinct T_n/T_nI types merge into a single $T_n/T_nI/T_nM5/T_nM7$-type (e.g., $[0,1,4,6]_{M5}$ as discussed in 5.15). Make a table listing only $T_n/T_nI/T_nM5/T_nM7$-types of pc pentachords and hexachords.

6. List the degree of symmetry of each $T_n/T_nI/T_nM5/T_nM7$-type of pc trichord. (For example, the representative form of $[0,2,4]_{M5}$ maps into itself under T_0, T_4I, T_0M7, and T_4M5, so the degree of symmetry of all sets in $[0,2,4]_{M5}$ is 4.)

7. Repeat 6 for tetrachords, pentachords, and hexachords.

8. Do M5-equivalent T_n/T_nI-types always have M5-equivalent set-complement types?

9. Does every set type have the same degree of symmetry as its set-complement type?

*5.16 The Hexachord Theorem

The various forms of what is known as "the hexachord theorem" quantitatively relate the multiplicity of an interval in a set to the multiplicity of that interval in the set complement of the former set with respect to the aggregate. The theorem exists in several levels of generality. In its simplest form, for an aggregate of 12 pc, it states that

THEOREM (1)
> **The unordered pc interval content of any two complementary hexachords is identical.**

106 Basic Atonal Theory

This is not as obvious as it might seem, given the invariance of interval under T_n and T_nI—remember "Z-related" sets. Quite a few complementary hexachords are "Z-related": for example, the two hexachords in the *Jakobsleiter* example (item 49 in Exercises 2-III).

More generally, for an aggregate of 12 pc with complementary sets A and B (not necessarily of equal size—see Table II) and unordered pc interval $n \neq 0$ and $n \neq 6$:

THEOREM (2)
$$M_B(n) = 12 - 2 \cdot |A| + M_A(n)$$

If A and B are complementary pc sets, and the interval n is neither 0 nor 6, the multiplicity of interval n in B equals 12 minus twice the cardinality of A plus the multiplicity of interval n in A.

COROLLARY (2)
$$\text{For } n = 6, M_B(n) = 6 - |A| + M_A(n)$$

If A and B are complementary pc sets, and the interval n equals 6, the multiplicity of interval n in B equals 6 minus the cardinality of A plus the multiplicity of interval n in A. (In any set, the multiplicity of the unison interval 0 equals the cardinality of that set.)

For example, let A = {0,1,4,6} and B equal the set complement of {0,1,4,6}, namely B = {2,3,5,7,8,9,10,11}. In this particular case, $M_A(1) = M_A(2) = M_A(3) = M_A(4) = M_A(5) = M_A(6)$, since the interval vector of {0,1,4,6} is <1,1,1,1,1,1>. Then, to find the interval vector of B, for $n \neq 6$ the multiplicities are:

$$M_B(n) = 12 - 2 \cdot |\{0,1,4,6\}| + M_A(n) =$$
$$12 - 2 \cdot 4 + 1 =$$
$$12 - 8 + 1 =$$
$$5$$

and for n = 6:

$$M_B(n) = 6 - |\{0,1,4,6\}| + M_A(6) =$$
$$6 - 4 + 1 =$$
$$3$$

So the interval vector of B = {2,3,5,7,8,9,10,11}, the set complement of A = {0,1,4,6}, is <5,5,5,5,5,3>.

Theorem (1) is obviously a particular case of theorem (2) and corollary (2). If $|A| = 6$ then $|B| = 6$, and for $n \neq 6$:

$$M_B(n) = 12 - 2 \cdot 6 + M_A(n)$$
$$\text{so } M_B(n) = 12 - 12 + M_A(n)$$
$$\text{or } M_B(n) = M_A(n) \text{ for complementary hexachords.}$$

For $n = 6$ and $|A| = 6$:

$$M_B(n) = 6 - 6 + M_A(n)$$

or $M_B(n) = M_A(n)$ again, for complementary hexachords.

Yet more generally, if S is the set of all pitch-classes defined in any equal-tempered system (perhaps $|S| = 19$ or $|S| = 31$, both promising "microtonal" possibilities), then for any two sets A and B complementary with respect to S (that is, $A = S \sim B$), this theorem would apply:

THEOREM (3)
> For $n \neq 0$ and $n \neq \frac{1}{2} \cdot |S|$, $A = S \sim B$, $M_B(n) = M_S(n) - 2 \cdot |A| + M_A(n)$.

For intervals n not equal to 0 or to one-half the cardinality of the aggregate S, if A and B are complementary sets with respect to S, the multiplicity of interval n in B equals the multiplicity of interval n in S minus twice the cardinality of A plus the multiplicity of interval n in A. In case S is even, the corollary is needed:

COROLLARY (3)
> For $n = \frac{1}{2} \cdot |S|$, $A = S \sim B$, $M_B(n) = M_S(n) - |A| + M_A(n)$.

For the interval n when n equals one-half the cardinality of the aggregate S, if A and B are complementary sets with respect to S, the multiplicity of interval n in B equals the multiplicity of interval n in S minus the cardinality of A plus the multiplicity of interval n in A.

Since for $|S| = 12$, $M_S(n) = 12$ for all $n \neq 6$ and $M_S(6) = 6$, theorem (2) and corollary (2) are obviously special cases of theorem (3) and corollary (3).

EXERCISE 5-III

The proofs of these theorems and corollaries, being both instructive and laborious, are left to the reader.

5.2 COMMON-TONE THEOREMS FOR TRANSPOSITION

5.21 The Theorems

Given two sets of pc, A and B, one of the most immediately audible relations between them is the pc they have in common, that is, the set intersection of A and B, $A \cap B$. For example, if $A = \{0,2,4,5,7,9,11\}$ and $B = T_7(A) = \{7,9,11,0,2,4,6\}$, the pc in common between the diatonic collection A and the diatonic collection of its dominant, B, form the set

$$A \cap B = \{0,2,4,5,7,9,11\} \cap \{7,9,11,0,2,4,6\} = \{7,9,11,0,2,4\}.[5]$$

The usual form of the common-tone theorem does not give the exact set of pc in common between A and B, $A \cap B$, but rather the number of pc in common between A and B, $|A \cap B|$. Thus if A is a diatonic collection and $B = T_7(A)$, then $|A \cap B| = 6$ as shown above.

108   Basic Atonal Theory

The common-tone theorem for T_n states that the *number of pc in common between any set A and any nontritone transposition of A, $T_m(A)$, equals the multiplicity of the interval of transposition "m" in the set A*. In symbols it is more succinct:

THEOREM
>For any pc set A and any ordered pc interval m except 6, $|A \cap T_m(A)| = M_A(n)$, where n is the unordered pc interval equivalent of ordered interval m.

The theorem has this exception:

>**if m = 6, $|A \cap T_6(A)| = 2 \cdot M_A(6)$**

That is, interval 6's "count double."[6]

"$M_A(n)$", as stated earlier, means "the multiplicity in set A of interval n." The unordered pc interval equivalents of ordered intervals m are given below, from the definition of "i(x,y)":

ordered pc interval: 0 1 2 3 4 5 6 7 8 9 10 11

unordered equivalent: 0 1 2 3 4 5 6 5 4 3   2   1

Thus, knowing the interval vector of a set will quickly give the number of pc in common between that set and each of its transpositions. If A = {0,2,4,5,7,9,11} then its interval vector is <2,5,4,3,6,1> and the following table gives the number of pc in common between A and $T_m(A)$ for each m from 0 through 11:

$|A \cap T_1(A)| = M_A(1) = 2$

$|A \cap T_2(A)| = M_A(2) = 5$

$|A \cap T_3(A)| = M_A(3) = 4$

$|A \cap T_4(A)| = M_A(4) = 3$

$|A \cap T_5(A)| = M_A(5) = 6$

$|A \cap T_6(A)| = 2 \cdot M_A(6) = 2 \cdot 1 = 2$

$|A \cap T_7(A)| = M_A(5) = 6$

$|A \cap T_8(A)| = M_A(4) = 3$

$|A \cap T_9(A)| = M_A(3) = 4$

$|A \cap T_{10}(A)| = M_A(2) = 5$

$|A \cap T_{11}(A)| = M_A(1) = 2$

interval of   11 10 9 8 7 6
transposition: 1   2 3 4 5 6

vector: < 2, 5, 4, 3, 6, 1>
number of pc
in common: 2   5 4 3 6 2

As this table shows, transposing the diatonic collection "up" or "down" 5 pc semitones gets 6 pc in common; transposing "up" or "down" 4 semitones gets 3 pc in common; etc. The greatest change in pc content (2 pc in common, 5 new pc) is by T_6 or T_1 or T_{11}.

How does this theorem work? Take, for example, the set of Schoenberg's *Farben* op. 16 no. 3:

EXAMPLE 2

What pairs of pc form ordered pc interval 1 in this set? Just {C,B} and {G♯,A}; therefore the multiplicity of interval 1 is two. If the set is transposed by T₁, B → C and G♯ → A, so that only C and A will be in common with the transposed set. If the set is transposed by T$_{-1}^p$ or T₁₁, C → B and A → G♯, so that only B and G♯ are in common between T₀ and T₁₁ of this set:

EXAMPLE 3

Notice how Schoenberg has cleverly arranged that the pc in common between these first two large-scale sets, B and G♯, are the lowest and highest in the pitch arrangement of the new set.

Thus a list of the pairs of pc forming each interval enables a prediction of precisely which pc will be in common, while the mere number of pairs forming each interval—the interval content—predicts the number of pc in common.

In the case of the tritone, a pair of pc 6 apart map into each other under T₆, so that both pc will remain in common for such pairs.[7]

The common-tone theorem for *pitches*, that is, for T$_n^p$(A), does not contain the exception for tritones.[8]

THEOREM

For any pitch set A and any ordered pitch interval m, $|A \cap T_m^p(A)| = M_A(n)$, where n = the absolute value of m.

5.22 Example: A Compositional Structure

Suppose you liked the sound of pc hexachord H = {0,2,3,4,5,6} and wished to construct a composition using this hexachord. The interval vector of H is <4,4,3,2,1,1>. Quite a lot of music could be invented using only the pc in {0,2,3,4,5,6} in various octaves, rhythms, lines, simultaneities, and instrumentations. The interval vector tells you that, in a two-part counterpoint or for lines or simultaneities of only two pc, 4 different pairs of pc from H form unordered pc interval 1; 4 pairs form interval 2; 3 pairs form interval 3; 2 pairs form interval 4; 1 pair forms interval interval 5; and 1 pair forms interval 6. This information alone suggests certain compositional strategies, such as sparing and circumspect use of interval 5 and interval 6 (to avoid the boredom of an often-repeated single pair of pc for these intervals), perhaps even using their rarity value by saving them for "rare" moments in the music. Also, intervals 1 and 2 might be most freely used. One variation technique might be to generate a new section by exchanging intervals of equal multiplicity; for instance, systematically substitute the 2's for the 1's and vice versa, or the 5's for the 6's.

110 Basic Atonal Theory

But sooner or later your ear—your mind's ear—might get tired of hearing only single pc, dyads, trichords, tetrachords, pentachords, and (the) hexachord whose members are members of {0,2,3,4,5,6}. You might, for example, get a yen for a C♯ (if C = 0). But you still like to hear something closely related to {0,2,3,4,5,6}; or perhaps you feel that to move immediately to something only distantly related to {0,2,3,4,5,6} would emperil the coherence of the piece too greatly.

If you are *very* cautious (like Stravinsky) about introducing "new" pc, the common-tone theorem suggests a structure in which *adjacent* transpositions of {0,2,3,4,5,6} will have *fewest* new pc (4 in common, 2 new):

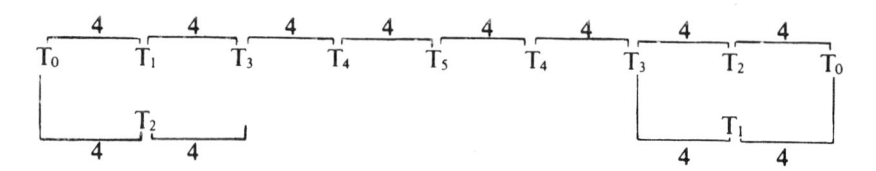

```
   4     4     4     4     4     4     4     4
T₀    T₁    T₃    T₄    T₅    T₄    T₃    T₂    T₀
      │                                │
      T₂                               T₁
        4   4                        4   4
```

but which will gradually move to and return from a form of {0,2,3,4,5,6}—that is, T₅ of it—which has the *most* "new" pc relative to the initial and final T₀ {0,2,3,4,5,6}. The numbers over the arches indicate pc in common; the number of new pc equals 6 minus the number in common.

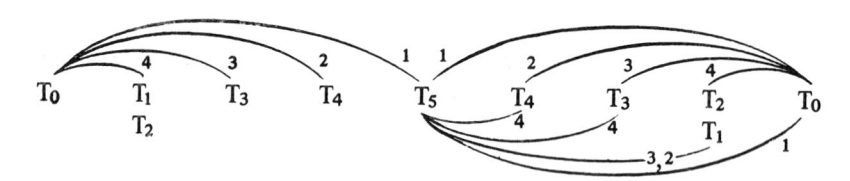

```
         4      3     2    1  1    2      3      4
      T₀    T₁    T₃    T₄    T₅    T₄    T₃    T₂    T₀
            T₂                        4     4    T₁
                                          3,2         1
```

The second half of the structure shows common tones relative to the midway arrival point, T₅, which would function as secondarily referential set after its arrival.

(Note that the absence in this structure of *any* two hexachords that are "complementary"—have *no* pc in common—suggests that the relation of set complementation be employed in extending your piece, with this structure included only as its first element.)

The construction of *any* such structure is made enormously more easy by the common-tone theorem.

EXERCISES 5-IV

1. Find the interval vectors of the following hexachord types (a-f). (These are the six "all-combinatorial" hexachords. See Exercises 4-IV, item 1, and section 5.6 ahead.)

    a) (0,1,2,3,4,5)

    b) (0,2,3,4,5,7)

    c) (0,2,4,5,7,9)

d) (0,1,2,6,7,8)

e) (0,1,4,5,8,9)

f) (0,2,4,6,8,10)

Form a structure of transpositions (using the common-tone theorem) for each of any *three* of the above (separately). Explain why you chose the three you did.

2. Choose any pc set of any size, construct a structure of its transpositions (using the common-tone theorem), and explain the advantages of your structure and how the particular pc set chosen helps determine that structure. (Review Analysis 2 on *Farben*.) A glance through Table II (Appendix 2) will provide many possible interval vectors for your common-tone structure.

5.3 COMMON-TONE THEOREM FOR T_nI; TICS VECTORS

The multiplicity of an interval in a set was defined as the number of different pairs of pc from that set which form that interval (see 5.11).

DEF Let "$M_A^+(n)$" denote "the multiplicity of the sum n of pairs of pc from set A," that is, the number of pairs of different pc from set A that add up to n.

DEF Let "$Q_A^+(n)$" denote the number (quantity) of pc in a set A which add to themselves to make the index n; their numbers (names) can be (½ · n) or (½ · n + 6).

$Q_A^+(n)$ will be, at most, two. It counts the centers of symmetry in A with respect to T_nI. Then the common-tone theorem for T_nI is:

THEOREM
The number of pc in common between A and $T_nI(A)$ equals twice the multiplicity of the pair sum, n, in set A plus the number of pc in A that add to themselves to make the index n.

$$|A \cap T_nI(A)| = 2 \cdot M_A^+(n) + Q_A^+(n)$$

The multiplicities of the sums may be obtained by the same procedure used to find the multiplicity of the differences (see "interval content"), and we can define the common-tone T_nI structure of any set by listing $M_A^+(n)$ and $Q_A^+(n)$ for that set for each of the 12 values of the index, n. (This "common-tone T_nI structure" is analogous to the "interval content" or "interval vector" defined and used in the common-tone theorem for T_n. It would be slightly misleading to call it the "index content" or "index vector," here though, because "common-tone T_nI structure" includes the $Q_A^+(n)$ term.) We will abbreviate "T_nI-common-tone structure" as "TICS," and define it as follows:

DEF The T_nI-common-tone structure of A equals the number of pc in common between A and $T_nI(A)$ for each of the 12 indices n = 0,1,2,3,4,5,6,7,8,9,10,11.

$$TICS_A = |A \cap T_nI(A)| = 2 \cdot M_A^+(n) + Q_A^+(n) \text{ for } n = 0,1,\ldots 11$$

112 Basic Atonal Theory

An ordered list (12-tuple) of the number of common tones for each index from 0 through 11 in that order will be called a "TICS vector."

Example 1: How to get the TICS of $\{0,1,4,5,8,9\} = A$.

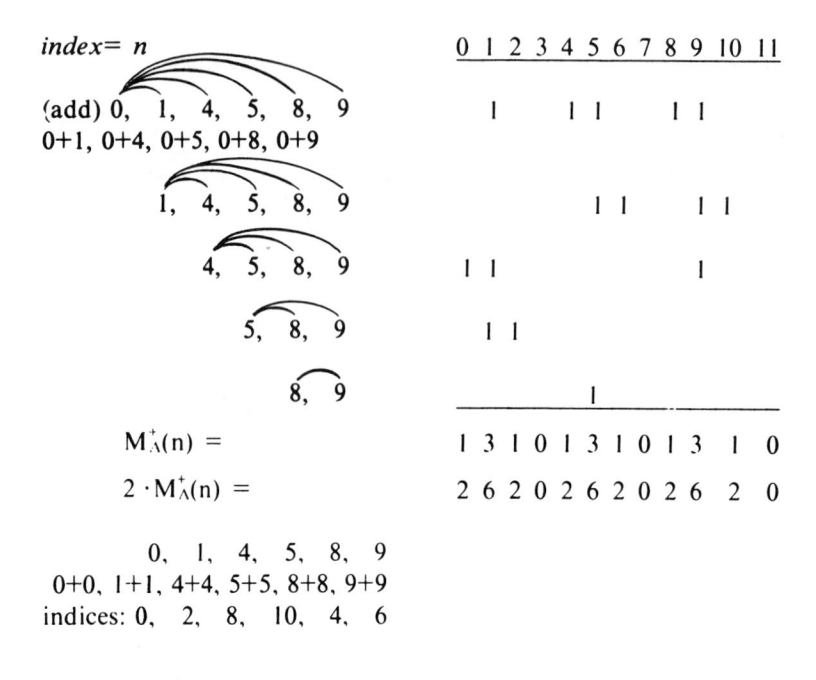

```
index = n                          0  1  2  3  4  5  6  7  8  9  10  11
(add) 0, 1, 4, 5, 8, 9             1     1  1        1  1
0+1, 0+4, 0+5, 0+8, 0+9
      1, 4, 5, 8, 9                         1  1        1  1
         4, 5, 8, 9                1  1              1
            5, 8, 9                1  1
               8, 9                      1
```

$M_A^+(n) =$ 1 3 1 0 1 3 1 0 1 3 1 0

$2 \cdot M_A^+(n) =$ 2 6 2 0 2 6 2 0 2 6 2 0

```
   0,   1,   4,   5,   8,   9
0+0, 1+1, 4+4, 5+5, 8+8, 9+9
indices: 0, 2, 8, 10, 4, 6
```

$Q_A^+(n) =$ 1 0 1 0 1 0 1 0 1 0 1 0

$2 \cdot M_A^+(n) + Q_A^+(n) =$ 3 6 3 0 3 6 3 0 3 6 3 0

The TICS vector of $\{0,1,4,5,8,9\}$ is $\langle 3,6,3,0,3,6,3,0,3,6,3,0 \rangle$.

To summarize *Example 1*:

index = n	0 1 2 3 4 5 6 7 8 9 10 11
$2 \cdot M_A^+(n) =$	2 6 2 0 2 6 2 0 2 6 2 0
$Q_A^+(n) =$	1 0 1 0 1 0 1 0 1 0 1 0
TICS$_A = |A \cap T_nI(A)| =$	3 6 3 0 3 6 3 0 3 6 3 0

Therefore, as the preceding summary clearly shows, this hexachord must map into itself (6pc in common) under T_1I, T_5I, and T_9I. It must map into its set complement—the remaining 6 pc—when there are no pc in common, under T_3I, T_7I, and $T_{11}I$. At all other T_nI—T_0I, T_2I, T_4I, T_6I, T_8I, and $T_{10}I$—it must map into a hexachord having 3 pc in common with it.

Example 2: How to get the TICS of $\{5,6,10,11\} = A$.

```
index = n                          0  1  2  3  4  5  6  7  8  9  10  11
         5, 6, 10, 11                       1  1              1
5+6, 5+10, 5+11
```

indices: 11, 3, 4

$\overparen{6, 10, 11}$

$\overparen{10, 11}$

	1 1
	1
$M_A^+(n) =$	0 0 0 1 2 1 0 0 0 1 0 1
$2 \cdot M_A^+(n) =$	0 0 0 2 4 2 0 0 0 2 0 2

5, 6, 10, 11

5+5, 6+6, 10+10, 11+11

indices: 10, 0, 8, 10

$Q_A^+(n) =$	1 0 0 0 0 0 0 0 1 0 2 0
$2 \cdot M_A^+(n) + Q_A^+(n) =$	1 0 0 2 4 2 0 0 1 2 2 2

The TICS vector of {5,6,10,11} is <1,0,0,2,4,2,0,0,1,2,2,2>. The set must map into itself at T_4I (4 in common for index = 4). There will be no pc in common with T_1I, T_2I, T_6I, or T_7I; one pc in common with T_0I or T_8I; and 2 pc in common with T_3I, T_5I, T_9I, $T_{10}I$, and $T_{11}I$ of {5,6,10,11}.

5.4 THEOREMS ABOUT TICS VECTORS OF T_n AND T_nI-RELATED SETS

Let "$VTICS_A$" denote "the vector of the T_nI common-tone structure of A" or "the $TICS_A$ vector." Unlike interval vector, $VTICS_A$ is *not* invariant for transpositions or inversions of A. That is, the interval vector for A equals the interval vector for $T_n(A)$ or $T_nI(A)$ for any n, since unordered pc interval is invariant under transposition and inversion. But *sum,* of course, is not invariant under T_n or T_nI.[9] So in general:

$$VTICS_A \neq VTICS_{T_n(A)} \quad \text{and}$$

$$VTICS_A \neq VTICS_{T_nI(A)}$$

Nevertheless, some useful generalizations can be made. If X is an n-tuple (such as an interval vector, line of pc, or TICS vector), then let "$r_n(X)$" denote the n-th *rotation* of X. This move requires a more specific definition of the rotation operation "r_n".

If the members of an n-tuple, X, are numbered from left to right with integers $0, 1, \ldots (n-1)$ in increasing order, e.g.,

$$\begin{matrix} 0, & 1, & 2, & 3 \\ <a, & b, & c, & d> \end{matrix}$$

these integers are called the *order numbers* mod. n of the associated members. The operation r_n maps each order number x into the order number $(x + n)$, mod n; e.g., for n-tuples, mod 4:

$$r_1 \begin{pmatrix} 0, 1, 2, 3 \\ a, b, c, d \end{pmatrix} = \begin{pmatrix} 0, 1, 2, 3 \\ d, a, b, c \end{pmatrix} \quad \text{each element moved one place to the right, cyclically}$$

$$r_2 \begin{pmatrix} 0, 1, 2, 3 \\ a, b, c, d \end{pmatrix} = \begin{pmatrix} 0, 1, 2, 3 \\ c, d, a, b \end{pmatrix} \quad \text{each element moved two places to the right, cyclically, etc.}$$

114 Basic Atonal Theory

THEOREM
> The TICS vector of $T_m(A)$ equals the 2 · m-th rotation of the TICS vector of A.
> $$\text{VTICS}_{T_m(A)} = r_{2 \cdot m}(\text{VTICS}_A)$$

COROLLARY
> The TICS vectors of sets a tritone apart are identical.
> $$\text{VTICS}_{T_m(A)} = \text{VTICS}_{T_{(m+6)}(A)}$$

Since taking a TICS vector is so tedious, these are very useful theorems.[10] For example, the TICS vector of $\{0,2,3,4,5,7\}$ is (by tedious toil) $<3,0,3,2,3,4,3,6,3,4,3,2>$. What is the TICS vector of $\{10,0,1,2,3,5\}$, that is, $T_{10}\{0,2,3,4,5,7\}$? By the above theorem, easily, $r_{2 \cdot 10} <3,0,3,2,3,4,3,6,3,4,3,2> = r_{20} = r_{(20-12)} = r_8 <3,0,3,2,3,4,3,6,3,4,3,2> = <3,4,3,6,3,4,3,2,3,0,3,2>$. Every multiplicity has been moved 8 places to the right, or, equivalently mod 12, 4 places to the left.

What about the TICS vectors of T_nI-related sets?

THEOREM
> The TICS vector of $T_mI(A)$ equals the $(2m + 1)$-th rotation of the retrograde of the TICS vector of A.
> $$\text{VTICS}_{T_mI(A)} = r_{2m+1}R(\text{VTICS}_A)$$

(Of course, one always retrogrades *before* rotating.)

The preceding is yet another labor-saving theorem.[11] For example, $\{10,0,1,2,3,5\} = T_5I\{0,2,3,4,5,7\}$. The TICS vector of $\{0,2,3,4,5,7\}$ is $<3,0,3,2,3,4,3,6,3,4,3,2>$. Then the TICS vector of $T_5I\{0,2,3,4,5,7\}$ is $r_{(2 \cdot 5 + 1)}R<3,0,3,2,3,4,3,6,3,4,3,2> = r_{11}R<3,0,3,2,3,4,3,6,3,4,3,2> = <3,4,3,6,3,4,3,2,3,0,3,2>$; that is, the retrograde rotated forward 11 places or (equivalently mod 12) back 1 place:

$$R<3,0,3,2,3,4,3,6,3,4,3,2> = <2,3,4,3,6,3,4,3,2,3,0,3>;$$
$$r_{11}<2,3,4,3,6,3,4,3,2,3,0,3> = <3,4,3,6,3,4,3,2,3,0,3,2>$$

as above. Of course, for this particular set ($\{0,2,3,4,5,7\}$), due to its symmetry, $T_{10} = T_5I$; but the two theorems give the same resulting TICS vector for $T_{10} = T_5I$ by different processes.

EXERCISES 5-V

1. Find the TICS vectors for the following all-combinatorial hexachords:

   a) $\{0,1,2,3,4,5\}$ g) T_2I $\{0,1,2,3,4,5\}$

   b) $\{0,2,3,5,10,1\}$ h) T_2 $\{0,2,3,5,10,1\}$

   c) $\{0,2,4,5,7,9\}$ i) T_5I $\{0,2,4,5,7,9\}$

   d) $\{0,1,2,6,7,8\}$ j) T_6 $\{0,1,2,6,7,8\}$

   e) $\{3,6,7,10,11,2\}$ k) $T_{11}I$ $\{3,6,7,10,11,2\}$

   f) $\{0,2,4,6,8,10\}$ l) T_7I $\{0,2,4,6,8,10\}$

2. Construct an exciting common-tone compositional structure using both the interval vector and the TICS vector of {0,2,3,4,5,6}. (See section 5.22.)

3. Explore the T_n and T_nI common-tone structure of the first three tetrachords (m. 1) of Schoenberg's op. 33a.

4. Use the common-tone theorems to find exactly which operations map the following sets, first, into themselves and, second, into their set complements. (See item 1 in this set of exercises and item 1 in Exercises 5-IV.)

   a) {9,11,0,1,2,4}

   b) {4,6,8,9,11,1}

   c) {3,4,5,6,7,8}

   d) {2,3,4,8,9,10}

   e) {1,2,5,6,9,10}

   f) {7,9,11,1,3,5}

*5.5 SUBSET CONTENT

In finding the interval content of a set we inspected every possible dyad-subset of the set and classified that dyad according to its T_n-type (interval). This process may be extended to subsets of every possible size, yielding a comprehensive list of every possible subset of a set,[12] with subsets categorized according to both T_n-type and T_n/T_nI-type. Such a categorized list will be called the "subset content" of a set.

Example 1: {0,1,4,6} has altogether ($2^4 - 1$) or 15 subsets. We ignore the four monadic subsets {0}, {1}, {4}, and {6}. Its T_n-type dyad content is $(0,1)_0$, $(0,2)_4$, $(0,3)_1$, $(0,4)_0$, $(0,5)_1$, $(0,6)_0$, where the handy notation "$(0,2)_4$" (for example) means that T_n-type $(0,2)_{T_n}$ is present as $T_4\{0,2\} = \{4,6\}$. Each dyad-type has here just one subscript, so each is present at just one transpositional level. The trichord-type content of {0,1,4,6} is

0 1 4 6	$(0,1,4)_0$	(the set without 6)
0 1 4 6	$(0,1,6)_0$	(the set without 4)
0 1 4 6	$(0,4,6)_0$	(the set without 1)
0 1 4 6	$(0,3,5)_1$	(the set without 0)

and it contains only one tetrachord-subset, itself.

Example 2: the Schoenberg *Farben* Chord {8,9,11,0,4}. Dyad subsets are listed first.[13] The trichord subset process follows.

(0,1)$_{8,11}$	(= T$_8${0,1} and T$_{11}${0,1})
(0,2)$_9$	(= T$_9${0,2})
(0,3)$_{8,9}$	(= T$_8${0,3} and T$_9${0,3})
(0,4)$_{0,4,8}$	(= T$_0${0,4} and T$_4${0,4} and T$_8${0,4})
(0,5)$_{4,11}$	(= T$_4${0,5} and T$_{11}${0,5})

Dyad and trichordal subsets of {8,9,11,0,4} are shown in the following table. The easiest method of determining the trichords will be to *exclude* each possible *dyad*; the residues will be each possible trichord.

Dyads						Trichords	
(0,1)$_8$	8	9	11	0	4	{11, 0, 4} =	(0,1,5)$_{11}$
(0,3)$_8$	8	9	11	0	4	{ 9, 0, 4} =	(0,3,7)$_9$
(0,4)$_8$	8	9	11	0	4	{ 9,11, 4} =	(0,2,7)$_9$
(0,4)$_4$	8	9	11	0	4	{ 9,11, 0} =	(0,2,3)$_9$
(0,2)$_9$	8	9	11	0	4	{ 8, 0, 4} =	(0,4,8)$_0$
(0,3)$_9$	8	9	11	0	4	{ 8,11, 4} =	(0,4,7)$_4$
(0,5)$_4$	8 ,9	11	0	4		{ 8,11, 0} =	(0,3,4)$_8$
(0,1)$_{11}$	8	9	11	0	4	{ 8, 9, 4} =	(0,4,5)$_4$
(0,5)$_{11}$	8	9	11	0	4	{ 8, 9, 0} =	(0,1,4)$_8$
(0,4)$_0$	8	9	11	0	4	{ 8, 9,11} =	(0,1,3)$_8$

Brackets connect T$_n$I-related trichord T$_n$-types. The T$_n$-type trichord content is given in the right-hand column; the T$_n$/T$_n$I content is [0,1,5]^2, [0,3,7]^2, [0,2,7]^1, [0,1,3]^2, [0,4,8]^1, [0,1,4]^2 — a listing in which superscripts do not indicate transpositional level but merely number of occurrences of type (multiplicity).

Tetrachordal subsets of {8,9,11,0,4} are shown in the following table. Eliminate each single pc in turn:

✗	9	11	0	4	{9,11, 0,4} =	(0,2,3,7)$_9$
8	✗	11	0	4	{8,11, 0,4} =	(0,3,4,8)$_8$
8	9	✗	0	4	{8, 9, 0,4} =	(0,1,4,8)$_8$
8	9	11	✗	4	{8, 9,11,4} =	(0,4,5,7)$_4$
8	9	11	0	✗	{8, 9,11,0} =	(0,1,3,4)$_8$

The one pentachordal subset of {8,9,11,0,4} is itself. The total subset content may be displayed as follows:

dyadic	T$_n$-type	(0,1)$_{8,11}$	(0,2)$_9$	(0,3)$_{8,9}$	(0,4)$_{0,4,8}$	(0,5)$_{4,11}$
	T$_n$/T$_n$I-type	[0,1]^2	[0,2]^1	[0,3]^2	[0,4]^3	[0,5]^2

trichordal

T_n-type $(0,1,5)_{11}(0,4,5)_4$ $(0,3,7)_9(0,4,7)_4$ $(0,2,7)_9$

T_n/T_nI-type $[0,1,5]^2$ $[0,3,7]^2$ $[0,2,7]^1$

$(0,2,3)_9(0,1,3)_8$ $(0,4,8)_0$ $(0,3,4)_8(0,1,4)_8$

$[0,1,3]^2$ $[0,4,8]^1$ $[0,1,4]^2$

tetrachordal

T_n-type $(0,4,5,7)_4(0,2,3,7)_9$ $(0,3,4,8)_8(0,1,4,8)_8$

T_n/T_nI-type $[0,2,3,7]^2$ $[0,1,4,8]^2$

$(0,1,3,4)_8$

$[0,1,3,4]^1$

pentachordal

T_n-type $(0,1,3,4,8)_8$

T_n/T_nI-type $[0,1,3,4,8]^1$

T_n-type content is invariant under T_n only; T_n/T_nI-type content is invariant under both T_n and T_nI.

EXERCISES 5-VI

Find the total subset content for the following sets.

1. {0,2,3,4}
2. {0,1,2,3,4,5}
3. {0,1,6,7}
4. {0,1,2,6,7,8}
5. {0,1,4,5,8,9}
6. {0,2,3,4,5,6}

*5.6 HEXACHORDAL COMBINATORIALITY: AN INTRODUCTION

The "all-combinatorial" hexachords fulfill each of the four criteria for the four kinds of hexachordal combinatoriality. They must

1. map into themselves under T_n ("retrograde combinatoriality");
2. map into themselves under T_nI ("retrograde inversional combinatoriality");

3. map into their complements under T_n ("prime combinatoriality");
4. map into their complements under T_nI ("inversional combinatoriality").

The first two criteria mean transpositional and inversional symmetry. (Conditions 3 and 4 entail that the hexachord and its complement cannot be "Z-related".) Every hexachord satisfied 1), under T_0. To discover which of the four kinds of combinatoriality some given hexachord possesses, and for which operations, you need only apply the common-tone theorems. (A hexachord maps into itself with 6 pc in common; it maps into its complement with 0 pc in common.)

Only six hexachord types satisfy all four criteria. Three hexachord types satisfy all criteria for *one* value of "n" each; these are called (following Milton Babbitt) "first-order all-combinatorial." The "second-order all-combinatorial hexachord type" satisfies all four criteria for *two* values of "n" each; the "third-order" for *three* values of "n" each; and the "sixth-order" (sometimes called "fourth-order") for *six* values of "n" each. They are:

All-combinatorial Hexachords

first-order	a.	[0,1,2,3,4,5]
	b.	[0,2,3,4,5,7]
	c.	[0,2,4,5,7,9]
second-order	d.	[0,1,2,6,7,8]
third-order	e.	[0,1,4,5,8,9]
sixth-order	f.	[0,2,4,6,8,10]

Some hexachords have only "retrograde combinatoriality" (under T_0). Others have various combinations of combinatorialities. Again, the common-tone theorems tell all.

Although the hexachord/complement pairs remain *invariant as sets*, if the hexachords are ordered (as segments of a row), the *ordering changes* while the content remains the same. This change/no-change relation, common to every "combinatorial" strategy (for sets of any sizes), is one of the foundations of serial composition.

Schoenberg's serial works almost invariably exhibit hexachordal combinatoriality.

The general idea of "combinatoriality" is an extension of the "unity of musical space" principle. It is to create aggregates (or some other predetermined reference set) both as successions and as simultaneities,[14] horizontalities or verticalities. The abstract situation—before time interpretation—can be modelled as a "combinatorial matrix" (abbreviated "CM"). The m-th entry (in the m-th column) in the n-th row of such a matrix contains some m-th ordered segment of the ordering that is the entire n-th matrix row. Each such segment is then treated as a *set* of its pc. The union of all segment-sets in each matrix row must equal the aggregate (or reference set), and the union of all segment-sets in each matrix column must equal that same aggregate (reference set).[15]

Common Tone Theorems 119

For hexachordal aggregate combinatoriality, the model is simple. Let "P" denote some permutation of the aggregate (a "twelve-tone row"). Let P^1 and P^2 denote the first and second hexachordal segments of the row. If P is *any* ordering, a "retrograde combinatorial" CM can be set up as follows:

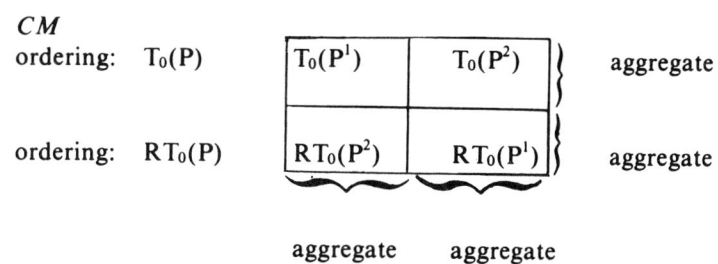

CM

ordering: $T_0(P)$	$T_0(P^1)$	$T_0(P^2)$	} aggregate
ordering: $RT_0(P)$	$RT_0(P^2)$	$RT_0(P^1)$	} aggregate

aggregate   aggregate

Example: the orderings discovered in Analysis 1 in the clarinet and non-clarinet parts. Call the clarinet ordering "P". The nonclarinet pc are then ordered in $RT_0(P)$.

CM

$T_0(P)$	F—A♭—G—F♯—B♭—A— $T_0(P^1)$	E♭—E—C—C♯—D—B $T_0(P^2)$
$RT_0(P)$	$RT_0(P^2)$ B—D—C♯—C—E—E♭—	$RT_0(P^1)$ A—B♭—F♯—G—A♭—F

Similar CM's can be set up for hexachordal combinatoriality of types 2), 3), or 4) for appropriate hexachords (see list at beginning of section 5.6). For these types, in general, only the hexachord/complement *content* remains invariant, while the reordering within hexachords depends on the particular row-ordering and operation used. For example, take the famous inversionally combinatorial row from Schoenberg's Fourth String Quartet:[16]

CM

$T_0(P)$	0—11—7—8—3—1—	2—10—6—5—4—9
$T_5I(P)$	5—6—10—9—2—4—	3—7—11—0—1—8

5.7 VALEDICTORY: FURTHER READINGS

Having come to the end of this study of basic atonal theory, you may expect your further sustenance in the field to spring from two founts: your own listening and analysis of music, and the professional literature—published articles and books on atonal music, music theory, and analysis. Beyond the short Select Bibliography at the beginning of the book, the Bibliography which follows contains many—by no means all!—of the more competent, interesting, or historically important works in the professional literature. Your examination of this literature should go hand in hand with your own analysis of pieces of music that are of particular interest to you.

Further work in this field will probably require some knowledge of serial theory not provided by this text—at the minimum, some skill and experience at "12-counting" (identifying each pitch as to its order function in one or more particular identified row-forms.) I will suggest, as a first course, a more or less concurrent reading of the chapters on serialism in the Perle text and/or the Wuorinen text (see Select Bibliography), along with Babbitt (4) and Westergaard (2) (see Bibliography).

A second course of readings from the Bibliography might include Babbitt (5), (6), (9), (11), (12), (13), and (15); Barkin (1), (2); Clifton (3); Howe; Lewin (3), (4), (6), (7), (8), (11), (12), (13), (14), (15); Rahn (2), (4); Rothgeb; Swift (2); Westergaard (1), (3), (4); and Zuckerman.

After reading these, you might choose among more specialized topics: *advanced serialism and combinatoriality*— Babbitt (14), (16), (17); Bazelow and Brickle (1), (2); Martino; Morris and Starr (1), (2), (3); *recent serial polyphony*— Batstone; Lewin (5); Lewin, Babbitt, Browne, and Morris; Westergaard (4); Winham; Wintle (1); *recent Stravinsky and semiserial matrix systems*— Babbitt (9); Rogers (1), (3); Spies (1), (2), (3); *methodology and theory-construction*— Babbitt (5), (11), (15); Boretz (2), (9), (10), (11), (12), (13); Clifton (1); Kassler (1), (2), (3), (4); Rahn (1); and so on.

Many topics will cut across other lists; for example, *serialization of rhythm*— Arnold and Hair (1); Babbitt (7); Batstone; DeYoung; Lewin, Babbitt, Browne, Morris; Ligeti (1); Rahn (2); Stockhausen (1), (2); Swift (2); Westergaard (3); Wintle (1). Further topics may be self-evident from the titles of the works cited in the Bibliography, or very comprehensive, or both: analysis of Berg (Perle is eminent here); of Schoenberg; of Webern; of Babbitt; analysis of early preserial Viennese music (Forte is eminent here); of preserial Stravinsky (includes Benjamin, Berger, Cone, Pousseur); etc. These analysis topics also go well with the "second course" of readings. Some topics are slighted here, for example, theory of alternate scale systems and their music. Please view the Bibliography only as providing a few starting suggestions. It is meant to be stimulative, not limiting.

NOTES

[1] The term "interval vector" is Allen Forte's (see *The Structure of Atonal Music*). Related concepts are summarized, contrasted, and developed in David Lewin's article "Forte's Interval Vector, My Interval Function, and Regener's Common-Note Function," *JMT* 21/2 (1977): 194-237. See also David Lewin's "Intervallic Relations between Two Collections of Notes," *JMT* 3/2 (1959): 298-301, and "The Intervallic Content of a Collection of Notes." *JMT* 4/1 (1960): 98-101; Allen Forte's "A Theory of Set Complexes for Music," *JMT* 8/2 (1964): 136-183; and Eric Regener's "On Allen Forte's Theory of Chords." *PNM* 13/1 (1974): 191-212.

[2] The sum of the multiplicities should equal the total number of possible pairs of pc (each pair forms an interval) in the set of pc given. There is a general formula giving "the number of combinations of n things taken m at a time" or "C(n,m)":

$$C(n,m) = \frac{n!}{m!(n-m)!}$$

In this case, the number of possible pairs of pc from the set $\{0,2,4,5,7,9,11\}$ is the number of combinations of 7 things taken 2 at a time:

$$C(7,2) = \frac{7!}{2!(7-2)!} = \frac{7 \cdot 6 \cdot 5 \cdot 4 \cdot 3 \cdot 2 \cdot 1}{(2 \cdot 1) \cdot (5 \cdot 4 \cdot 3 \cdot 2 \cdot 1)} = 7 \cdot 3 = 21$$

Indeed, 21 is the sum of the multiplicities above (2+5+4+3+6+1) for this 7 pc collection $\{0,2,4,5,7,9,11\}$.

[3] Oddly enough, the "Z-relation" only *pairs* types of sets. No *three* or more sets belonging to (three or more) different $T_n/T_n I$-types share the same interval content.

[4] The effects on interval content of the less used homomorphisms M2, M3, M4, M6, M8, M9, and M10 are found similarly. For example, for M2:

$$\begin{matrix} x \\ M2(x) \end{matrix} \begin{pmatrix} 1 & 2 & 3 & 4 & 5 & 6 & 7 & 8 & 9 & 10 & 11 \\ 2 & 4 & 6 & 8 & 10 & 0 & 2 & 4 & 6 & 8 & 10 \end{pmatrix}$$

intervals 1 and 7 become interval 2, 2 and 8 become 4, 3 and 9 become 6, 4 and 10 become 8, 5 and 11 become 10, and 6 becomes 0. The effect on interval content is that the multiplicities of all odd intervals (1,3,5) become 0; the multiplicity of 2 in the image set is the sum of the multiplicities of 1 and 5 in the preimage set; the multiplicity of 4 in the image set is the sum of the multiplicities of 2 and 4 in the preimage set; and the multiplicity of 6 becomes the multiplicity of the unison, 0, which is always equal to the cardinality of the set.

[5] This may also be described as the set of new pc; that is, the set of pc that are in B but are not in A:

$$B \sim A = \{7,9,11,0,2,4,6\} \sim \{0,2,4,5,7,9,11\} = \{6\}$$
$$A \sim B = \{0,2,4,5,7,9,11\} \sim \{7,9,11,0,2,4,6\} = \{5\}$$

Sets A and B have six pc in common. If C = 0, the new "leading tone" F♯ = 6 is the only pc in B that is not also in A, and the pc F = 5 is the only pc in A that is not also in B. "B ~ A" denotes this set difference between B and A, B minus A.

[6] In the case of pc interval 6, $x \xleftarrow{T6} x+6$; for all $n \neq 6$ $x \xrightarrow{Tn} x+n$ and *not* $x+n \xrightarrow{Tn} x$.

[7] The sets of pc in common for complementary intervals of transposition from the original set are (the sets) themselves always transpositionally related:

THEOREM: $A \cap Tm(A) \xrightarrow{T(-m)} A \cap T_{(-m)}(A)$

For example, the intersection of the *Farben* set with its T_{11} is $\{B,G\sharp\}$, which is mapped by $T_{(-11)} = T_1$ into the intersection of the first set with its T_1, $\{C,A\}$.

[8] Because for pitches, $x \neq x + 12$.

[9] In general, the sum of x and y is not equal to the sum of the transposition (or inversion) of x and the transposition (or inversion) of y; for all values of x, y, and n:

$$T_n(x) + T_n(y) = (x+n) + (y+n) = (x+y+2n) \neq x+y;$$
$$T_n I(x) + T_n I(y) = (-x+n) + (-y+n) = -(x+y) + 2n \neq x+y.$$

122 *Basic Atonal Theory*

[10] Informal proof of the theorem for T_m:
For every pair of pc $\{a,b\}$, $T_m\{a,b\} \to \{a + m, b + m\}$. Then for every sum $(a + b)$ from set A ($a \in A$, $b \in A$), there corresponds a sum $((a + m) + (b + m))$ from set $T_m(A)$ $((a + m) \in T_m(A), (b + m) \in T_m(A))$. Now $((a + m) + (b + m)) = 2m + (a + b)$, so that the multiplicity in A of index $(a + b)$ is mapped into (becomes) the multiplicity in $T_m(A)$ of index $(2m + (a + b))$, for every index, $n = a + b$. What mapping maps $n \to 2m + n$, where n is any index multiplicity in an index vector from 0 through 11? $r_{2 \cdot m}$. Every multiplicity is moved along to the right 2m places in the vector. VTICS$_A$ becomes r_{2m}(VTICS$_A$) for $T_m(A)$; or

$$VTICS_{T_m(A)} = r_{2m}(VTICS_A).$$

The Q_A^+ factor is taken care of similarly:

$$T_m \langle a,a \rangle \to \langle a+m, a+m \rangle, (a+m) + (a+m) = 2m + 2a, \text{ etc.}$$

[11] Informal proof of theorem for $T_m I$:
$T_m I \{a,b\} \to \{-a + m, -b + m\}$ so for every sum $(a + b)$ from set A ($a \in A$, $b \in A$), there corresponds a sum $((-a + m) + (-b + m))$ from $T_m I(A) ((-a + m) \in T_m I(A), (-b + m) \in T_m I(A))$. Therefore the multiplicity in A of every index, n (where $n = a + b$), becomes the multiplicity of index $(2m - n)$ in $T_m I(A)$, and the mapping to be described is $n \to -n + 2m$. Taken (as a compound operation) in two stages—first $n \to -n$, then $-n \to -n + 2m$—it is obvious that the second stage is (again) r_{2m} of the first stage's result. The following mapping:

$$\begin{pmatrix} 0 & 1 & 2 & 3 & 4 & 5 & 6 & 7 & 8 & 9 & 10 & 11 \\ 0 & 11 & 10 & 9 & 8 & 7 & 6 & 5 & 4 & 3 & 2 & 1 \end{pmatrix}$$

is the desired mapping of the first stage, $n \to -n$ (mod 12). But

$$\langle 0,11,10,9,8,7,6,5,4,3,2,1 \rangle = r_1 R \langle 0,1,2,3,4,5,6,7,8,9,10,11 \rangle.$$

Then $n \to -n + 2m$ is described by $r_{2m}(r_1 R)$, which equals $r_{2m + 1} R$.

[12] If a set has n members, it has $(2^n - 1)$ nonempty subsets altogether.

[13] Do we have every possible dyad? The number of m-sized subsets of an n-sized set is given by

$$\frac{n!}{m!(n - m)!} \; ; \; \frac{5!}{2!\,3!} = \frac{5 \cdot 4}{2 \cdot 1} = 5 \cdot 2 = 10;$$

we have all 10 dyads above. There will be

$$\frac{5!}{3!(5 - 3)!} \text{ or } \frac{5!}{3!2!} = 10$$

trichord subsets; and

$$\frac{5!}{4!(5 - 4)!} = \frac{5!}{4!1!} = 5$$

tetrachord subsets; and, of course,

$$\frac{5!}{5!(5 - 5)!} = \frac{5!}{5!0!} = 1$$

pentachord subset (0! is defined to equal 1).

[14] More precisely, it is to create reference sets on the one hand as "partial-order" interpretations in time of abstract syntactical orderings of pc, and on the other hand as sets of the pc of sounds attacked within some particular time "neighborhood."

[15] For detailed treatment of aspects of that part of aggregate combinatorial theory which can be applied to any row (as opposed to the theory of "special" combinatoriality of rows constructed to have certain properties), see Robert Morris and Daniel Starr, "A General Theory of Combinatoriality and the Aggregate," in two parts in *PNM* 16/1 (1977): 3-35 and 16/2 (1978). The seminal articles on special and general combinatoriality are among Milton Babbitt's; see list in *PNM* 14/2 and 15/1 (double issue, 1976) and Bibliography in this text. See also various articles by David Lewin, Donald Martino, Peter Westergaard, and Frank Brickle/Alex Bazelow in the Bibliography. These will all be difficult reading, but at least within your grasp as you complete this text.

[16] See Milton Babbitt's "Set Structure as a Compositional Determinant," *JMT* 5/2 (1961): 72-94.

BIBLIOGRAPHY

Abbreviations:
JMT = Journal of Music Theory
PNM = Perspectives of New Music

Archibald, Bruce. "Some Thoughts on Symmetry in Early Webern: Op. 5, No. 2." *PNM* 10/2 (1972): 159–163.

Arnold, S., and Hair, G. (1) "An Introduction and a Study: String Quartet No. 3." *PNM* 14/2 and 15/1 (double issue, 1976): 155–86.

———. (2) "A List of Works by Milton Babbitt." *PNM* 14/2 and 15/1 double issue, 1976): 24–25.

Babbitt, Milton. (1) "The String Quartets of Bela Bartok." *Musical Quarterly* 35 (1949): 377–85.

———. (2) Review of *Schoenberg et son école* and *Qu'est ce que la musique de douze sons?* by René Leibowitz. *Journal of the American Musicological Society* 3/1 (1950): 57–60.

———. (3) "Some Aspects of Twelve-Tone Composition." *The Score and I.M.A. Magazine* 12 (1955): 53–61.

———. (4) "Twelve-Tone Invariants as Compositional Determinants." *Musical Quarterly* 46 (1960): 246–59. Reprinted in Lang, ed. (1).

———. (5) "Past and Present Concepts of the Nature and Limits of Music." *Congress Report of the International Music Scoiety, 1961:* 398–403. Reprinted in Boretz and Cone, eds. (2).

———. (6) "Set Structure as a Compositional Determinant." *JMT* 5/2 (1961): 72–94. Reprinted in Boretz and Cone, eds. (2).

———. (7) "Twelve-Tone Rhythmic Structure and the Electronic Medium." *PNM* 1/1 (1962): 49–79. Reprinted in Boretz and Cone, eds. (2).

———. (8) "Mr. Babbitt Answers." *PNM* 2/1 (1963): 127–32. See Perle (3).

———. (9) "Remarks on the Recent Stravinsky." *PNM* 2/2 (1964): 35–55. Reprinted in Boretz and Cone, eds. (3).

———. (10) "The Synthesis, Perception, and Specification of Musical Time." *Journal of the International Folk Music Council* 16 (1964): 92–95.

———. (11) "The Structure and Function of Musical Theory." *College Music Symposium* 5 (1965): 49–60. Reprinted in Boretz and Cone, eds. (2).

---. (12) "Edgard Varèse: A Few Observations of His Music." *PNM* 4/2 (1966): 14-22. Reprinted in Boretz and Cone, eds. (1).

---. (13) "Three Essays on Schoenberg: Concerto for Violin and Orchestra, *Das Buch der hängenden Gärten, Moses and Aaron*." In Boretz and Cone, eds. (3).

---. (14) "On *Relata I*." In *The Orchestral Composer's Point of View*, edited by Robert S. Hines, pp. 11-38. Norman: University of Oklahoma Press, 1970. Reprinted in *PNM* 9/1 (1970): 1-22.

---. (15) "Contemporary Music Composition and Music Theory as Contemporary Intellectual History." In *Perspectives in Musicology*, edited by Barry S. Brook, Edward O.D. Downes, and Sherman Van Solkema, pp. 151-84. New York: W.W. Norton, 1971.

---. (16) "Since Schoenberg." *PNM* 12/1 and 12/2 (double issue, 1973-74): 3-28.

---. (17) "Responses: A First Approximation." *PNM* 14/2 and 15/1 (double issue, 1976): 3-23.

Barkin, Elaine. (1) "A View of Schoenberg's Op. 23/1." *PNM* 12/1 and 12/2 (double issue, 1973-74): 99-127.

---. (2) "Analysis Symposium: Webern, Orchestra Pieces (1913): Movement I (*'Bewegt'*)." *JMT* 19/1 (1975): 47-65. See Forte (8); and Travis.

Batstone, Philip. "Multiple Order Functions in Twelve-Tone Music." *PNM* 10/2 (1972): 60-71, and *PNM* 11/1 (1972): 92-111. See Lewin (5); Lewin, Babbitt, Browne, and Morris; Morris; and Wintle (1).

Bazelow, A., and Brickle, F. (1) "A Partition Problem Posed by Milton Babbitt (Part I)." *PNM* 14/2 and 15/1 (double issue, 1976): 280-93.

---. (2) "A Combinatorial Problem Arising out of Twelve-Tone Theory." *In Theory Only* 3/4 (July 1977): 12-13.

Benjamin, William. (1) "*The Structure of Atonal Music* by Allen Forte." *PNM* 13/1 (1974): 170-90.

---. (2) "Towards a Typology for Pitch Equivalence." *In Theory Only* 1/6 (September 1975): 3-8.

---. (3) "Tonality Without Fifths: Remarks on the First Movement of Stravinsky's Concerto for Piano and Winds." *In Theory Only* 2/11 and 2/12 (double issue, February-March 1977): 53-70, and *In Theory Only* 3/2 (May 1977): 9-31.

Berger, Arthur. (1) "Problems of Pitch Organization in Stravinsky." *PNM* 2/1 (1963): 11-42. Reprinted in Boretz and Cone, eds. (3).

---. (2) "New Linguistic Modes and the New Theory." *PNM* 3/1 (1964): 1-9. Reprinted in Boretz and Cone, eds. (2).

Berry, Wallace. "Apostrophe: A Letter from Ann Arbor." *PNM* 14/2 and 15/1 (double issue, 1976): 187-99.

Boretz, Benjamin. (1) Review of *Serial Composition and Atonality* by George Perle. *PNM* 1/2 (1963): 125-36.

---. (2) "Meta-Variations: Studies in the Foundations of Musical Thought." Ph.D. dissertation, Princeton University, 1970. Partially published in serial form, revised, in *PNM* as Boretz (3), (4), (5), (6), (7), and (8).

---. (3) "Meta-Variations: Studies in the Foundations of Musical Thought (I)." *PNM* 8/1 (1969): 1-75.

———. (4) "Sketch of a Musical System (Meta-Variations, Part II)." *PNM* 8/2 (1970): 49–112.

———. (5) "The Construction of Musical Syntax (I)." *PNM* 9/1 (1970): 23–42.

———. (6) "Musical Syntax (II)." *PNM* 9/2 and 10/1 (double issue, 1971): 232–70.

———. (7) "Meta-Variations, Part IV: Analytic Fallout (I)." *PNM* 11/1 (1972): 146–223.

———. (8) "Meta-Variations, Part IV: Analytic Fallout (II)." *PNM* 11/2 (1973): 156–203.

———. (9) "In Quest of the Rhythmic Genius." *PNM* 9/2 and 10/1 (double issue, 1971): 149–55.

———. (10) "Nelson Goodman's *Languages of Art* from a Musical Point of View." In Boretz and Cone, eds. (2): 31–44.

———. (11) "A World of Times." *PNM* 12/1 and 12/2 (double issue, 1973–74): 315–18.

———. (12) "Musical Cosmology." *PNM* 15/2 (1977): 122–32.

———. (13) "What Lingers On (‚When The Song Is Ended)." *PNM* 16/1 (1977): 102–9.

Boretz, Benjamin, and Cone, Edward, eds. (1) *Perspectives on American Composers*. New York: W.W. Norton, 1971.

———. (2) *Perspectives on Contemporary Music Theory*. New York: W.W. Norton, 1972.

———. (3) *Perspectives on Schoenberg and Stravinsky*. Rev. ed. New York: W.W. Norton, 1972.

Brody, Martin. "Sensibility Defined: Set Projection in Stephan Wolpe's *FORM for piano*." *PNM* 15/2 (1977): 3–22.

Browne, Richmond. Review of *The Structure of Atonal Music* by Allen Forte. *JMT* 18/2 (1974): 390–409.

Browne, Richmond, ed. *Index of Music Theory in the United States: 1955–1970*. Ann Arbor: *In Theory Only* 3/7 through 3/11 (October 1977 through February 1978), 1977–78.

Burkhart, Charles. "Schoenberg's *Farben*." *PNM* 12/1 and 12/2 (double issue, 1973–74): 141–72. See Coppock.

Burrows, David. "Music and the Biology of Time." *PNM* 11/1 (1972): 241–49.

Cage, John. "Lecture." *Die Reihe* 5 (1961): 84–114.

Childs, Barney. "Time and Music: A Composer's View." *PNM* 15/2 (1977): 194–219.

Clifton, Thomas. (1) "An Application of Goethe's Concept of *Steigerung* to the Morphology of Diminution." *JMT* 14/2 (1970): 165–90.

———. (2) "Types of Symmetrical Relations in Stravinsky's *A Sermon, A Narrative, and a Prayer*." *PNM* 9/1 (1970): 96–112.

———. (3) "On Listening to *Herzgewächse*." *PNM* 11/2 (1973): 87–102.

Clough, John. "Pitch-Set Equivalence and Inclusion (A Comment on Forte's Theory of Set-Complexes)." *JMT* 9/1 (1965): 163–71. See Forte (3) and (4).

Cohen, David. "Anton Webern and the Magic Square." *PNM* 13/1 (1974): 213–15.

Cone, Edward. (1) "Music: A View from Delft." *Musical Quarterly* 47/4 1961: 439–53. Reprinted in Boretz and Cone, eds. (2).

———. (2) "Stravinsky: the Progress of a Method." *PNM* 1/1 (1962): 18–26. Reprinted in Boretz and Cone, eds. (3).

———. (3) "Beyond Analysis." *PNM* 6/1 (1967): 33–51. Reprinted in Boretz and Cone, eds. (2). See Lewin (10).

———. (4) "Editorial Responsibility and Schoenberg's Troublesome 'Misprints'." *PNM* 11/1 (1972): 65–76.

———. (5) "Sound and Syntax: An Introduction to Schoenberg's Harmony." *PNM* 13/1 (1974): 21–40.

———. (6) "'Yet Once More, O Ye Laurels'." *PNM* 14/2 and 15/1 (double issue, 1976): 294–307.

Coons, Edgar, and Kraehenbuehl, David. "Information as a Measure of Structure in Music." *JMT* 2/2 (1958): 127–61.

Coppock, Jane. "Ideas for a Schoenberg Piece." *PNM* 14/1 (1975): 3–85. See Burkhart.

Craft, Robert. "Schoenberg's Five Pieces for Orchestra." In Boretz and Cone, eds. (3): 3–24. See Burkhart, Coppock.

Dean, Jerry. "Schoenberg's Vertical-Linear Relationships in 1908." *PNM* 12/1 and 12/2 (double issue, 1973–74): 173–80.

DeYoung, Lynden. "Pitch Order and Duration Order in Boulez' *Structure IA*." *PNM* 16/2 (1978), in press. See Ligeti (1).

Fennelly, Brian. "Structure and Process in Webern's Opus 22." *JMT* 10/2 (1966): 300–328.

Flynn, George. "Listening to Berio's Music." *Musical Quarterly* 61/3 (1975): 388–421.

Forte, Allen. (1) "Bartok's "Serial" Composition." *Musical Quarterly* 46/2 (1960): 233–45.

———. (2) "Context and Continuity in an Atonal Work." *PNM* 1/2 (1963): 72–82.

———. (3) "A Theory of Set-Complexes for Music." *JMT* 8/2 (1964): 136–83. See Clough; and Forte (7).

———. (4) "The Domain and Relations of Set-Complex Theory." *JMT* 9/1 (1965): 173–80. See Clough.

———. (5) "Sets and Nonsets in Schoenberg's Atonal Music." *PNM* 11/1 (1972): 43–64.

———. (6) "The Basic Interval Patterns." *JMT* 17/2 (1973): 234–73. See Forte (7).

———. (7) *The Structure of Atonal Music*. New Haven: Yale University Press, 1973. See Benjamin (1); Browne; Lewin (14); and Regener.

———. (8) "Analysis Symposium: Webern, Orchestra Pieces (1913): Movement I ('*Bewegt*')." *JMT* 18/1 (1974): 13–43. See Barkin (2); and Travis.

———. (9) "Schoenberg's Creative Evolution: The Path to Atonality." *Musical Quarterly* 64/2 (1978): 133–76.

Fuller, Ramon. "A Study of Interval and Trichord Progressions." *JMT* 16/1 and 16/2 (double issue, 1972): 102–41.

Gamer, Carlton. (1) "Deep Scales and Difference Sets in Equal-Tempered Systems." *Proceedings of the American Society of University Composers* 2 (1967): 113–22.

———. (2) "Some Combinational Resources of Equal-Tempered Systems." *JMT* 11/1 (1967): 32–59.

———. (3) "Piano Raga Music." *PNM* 12/1 and 12/1 (double issue, 1973–74): 191–230.

Gamer, Carlton, and Lansky, Paul. "Fanfares for the Common Tone." *PNM* 14/2 and 15/1 (double issue, 1976): 229–35.

Gilbert, Steven. "An Introduction to Trichordal Analysis." *JMT* 18/2 (1974): 338–62.

Graebner, Eric. "An Analysis of Schoenberg's *Klavierstück*, Op. 33a." *PNM* 12/1 and 12/2 (double issue, 1973–74): 128–40.

Hiller, Lejaren, and Fuller, Ramon. "Structure and Information in Webern's *Symphonie*, Op. 21." *JMT* 11/1 (1967): 60–115.

Hollander, John. "Notes on the Text of *Philomel*." *PNM* 6/1 (1967): 134–41.

Howe, Hubert S., Jr. "Some Combinational Properties of Pitch Structures." *PNM* 4/1 (1965): 45–61.

Jarman, Douglas. (1) "Dr. Schön's Five-Strophe Aria: Some Notes on Tonality and Pitch Association in Berg's *Lulu*." *PNM* 8/2 (1970): 23–48.

———. (2) "Some Rhythmic and Metric Techniques in Alban Berg's *Lulu*." *Musical Quarterly* 56/3 (1970): 349–66.

Kagel, Mauricio. "Translation-Rotation." *Die Reihe* 7 (1965): 32–60.

Kassler, Michael. (1) "A Sketch of the Use of Formalized Languages for the Assertion of Music." *PNM* 1/2 (1963): 83–94.

———. (2) "Toward a Theory That Is the Twelve-Note-Class System." *PNM* 5/2 (1967): 1–80. Also in Kassler (3).

———. (3) "A Trinity of Essays." Ph.D. dissertation, Princeton University, 1970.

———. (4) "Toward Development of a Constructive Tonality Theory Based on Writings by Heinrich Schenker." In Kassler (3).

———. (5) "Toward a Simple Programming Language for Musical Information Retrieval." In Kassler (3).

Klammer, Armin. "Webern's Piano Variations, Op. 27, 3rd Movement." *Die Reihe* 2 (1958): 81–92.

Kolneder, Walter. *Anton Webern: An Introduction to his Works*. Translated by Humphrey Searle. Berkeley: University of California Press, 1968.

Kraft, Leo. "The Music of George Perle." *Musical Quarterly* 57/3 (1971): 444–65.

Kramer, Jonathan. "The Row as Structural Background and Audible Foreground: The First Movement of Webern's First Cantata." *JMT* 15/1 and 15/2 (double issue, 1971): 158–81.

Lang, Paul Henry, ed. (1) *Problems of Modern Music*. New York: W.W. Norton, 1962.

———. (2) *Contemporary Music in Europe*. New York: W.W. Norton, 1966.

Lansky, Paul. (1) "Affine Music." Ph.D. dissertation, Princeton University, 1973. See Perle (9).

———. (2) "Pitch-Class Consciousness." *PNM* 13/2 (1975): 30–56.

Lester, Joel. "Pitch Structure Articulation in the Variations of Schoenberg's Serenade." *PNM* 6/2 (1968): 22–34.

Lewin, David. (1) "Intervallic Relations Between Two Collections of Notes." *JMT* 3/2 (1959): 298–301.

———. (2) "The Intervallic Content of a Collection of Notes." *JMT* 4/1 (1960): 98–101.

———. (3) "A Metrical Problem in Webern's Op. 27." *JMT* 6/1 (1962): 124–32.

———. (4) "A Theory of Segmental Association in Twelve-Tone Music." *PNM* 1/1 (1962): 89–116. Reprinted in Boretz and Cone, eds. (2).

———. (5) "On Certain Techniques of Re-Ordering in Serial Music." *JMT* 10/2 (1966): 276–87. See Batstone; Lewin, Babbitt, Browne, and Morris; and Morris.

———. (6) "*Moses und Aaron:* Some General Remarks, and Analytic Notes for Act I, Scene 1." *PNM* 6/1 (1967): 1–17. Reprinted in Boretz and Cone, eds. (3).

———. (7) "A Study of Hexachord Levels in Schoenberg's Violin Fantasy." *PNM* 6/1 (1967): 18–32. Reprinted in Boretz and Cone, eds. (3).

———. (8) "Inversional Balance as an Organizing Force in Schoenberg's Music and Thought." *PNM* 6/2 (1968): 1–21.

———. (9) "Some Applications of Communication Theory to the Study of Twelve-Tone Music." *JMT* 12/1 (1968): 50–84.

———. (10) "Behind the Beyond: A Response to Edward T. Cone." *PNM* 7/2 (1969): 59–69. See Cone (3).

———. (11) "Toward the Analysis of a Schoenberg Song (Op. 15, no. XI)." *PNM* 12/1 and 12/2 (double issue, 1973–74): 43–86.

———. (12) "On Partial Ordering." *PNM* 14/2 and 15/1 (double issue, 1976): 252–59.

———. (13) "A Label-Free Development for 12-Pitch-Class Systems." *JMT* 21/1 (1977): 29–48.

———. (14) "Forte's Interval Vector, My Interval Function, and Regener's Common-Note Function." *JMT* 21/2 (1977): 194–237. See Forte (7); Lewin (1), (2); Regener.

———. (15) "Some Notes on Schoenberg's Opus 11." *In Theory Only* 3/1 (April 1977): 3–7.

Lewin, D.; Babbitt, M.; Browne, R.; and Morris, R. "Maximally Scrambled 12-Tone Sets: A Serial Forum." *In Theory Only* 2/5 (August 1976): 13–26. See Batstone; Lewin (5); Morris.

Ligeti, György. (1) "Pierre Boulez." *Die Reihe* 4 (1960): 36–62. See DeYoung.

———. (2) "Metamorphoses of Musical Form." *Die Reihe* 7 (1965): 5–19.

MacDonald, Calum. "Luigi Dallapiccola: The Complete Works: A Catalogue." *Tempo* no. 116 (1976): 2–19.

Martin, Henry. "A Structural Model for Schoenberg's '*Der Verlorene Haufen,* Op. 12/2." *In Theory Only* 3/3 (June 1977): 4–22.

Martino, Donald. "The Source Set and its Aggregate Formations." *JMT* 5/2 (1961): 224–73. Addendum in *JMT* 6/2 (1962): 322–23.

Moldenhauer, Hans, compiler. *Anton von Webern: Perspectives.* Edited by Demar Irvine. Seattle: University of Washington Press, 1966.

Morgan, Robert P. "Stockhausen's Writings on Music." *Musical Quarterly* 61/1 (1975): 1–16.

Morris, Robert. "On the Generation of Multiple Order-Function Twelve-Tone Rows." *JMT* 21/2 (1977): 238–63. See Batstone; Lewin (5); Lewin, Babbitt, Browne, and Morris.

Morris, Robert, and Starr, Daniel. (1) "The Structure of All-Interval Series." *JMT* 18/2 (1974): 364–89.

O'Connell, Walter. "Tone Spaces." *Die Reihe* 8 (1968): 34–67.

Pazur, Robert. "A Babbitt Bibliography." *PNM* 14/2 and 15/1 (double issue, 1976): 26–28.

Peel, John. "On Some Celebrated Measures of the Schoenberg String Trio." *PNM* 14/2 and 15/1 (double issue, 1976): 260–79.

Perle, George. (1) "The Music of *Lulu*: A New Analysis." *Journal of the American Musicological Society* 12/2 and 12/3 (1959): 185–200.

———. (2) *Serial Composition and Atonality: An Introduction to the Music of Schoenberg, Berg, and Webern*. Berkeley: University of California Press, 1962. See Boretz (1).

———. (3) "Babbitt, Lewin, and Schoenberg: A Critique." *PNM* 2/1 (1963): 120–27. See Babbitt (13) and Lewin (4); reply in Babbitt (8).

———. (4) "An Approach to Simultaneity in Twelve-Tone Music." *PNM* 3/1 (1964): 91–101.

———. (5) "*Lulu*: The Formal Design." *Journal of the American Musicological Society* 17/2 (1964): 179–92.

———. (6) "The Musical Language of *Wozzeck*." *Music Forum* 1 (1967): 204–59.

———. (7) "Webern's Twelve-Tone Sketches." *Musical Quarterly* 57/1 (1971): 1–25.

———. (8) "Berg's Master Array of Interval Cycles." *Musical Quarterly* 63/1 (1977): 1–30. See Perle (9).

———. (9) *Twelve-Tone Tonality*. Berkeley: University of California Press, 1977. See Lansky (1).

Philippot, Michel. "Ear, Heart, Brain." *PNM* 14/2 and 15/1 (double issue, 1976): 45–60.

Pousseur, Henri. (1) "Outline of a Method." *Die Reihe* 3 (1959): 44–88.

———. (2) "The Question of Order in New Music." *PNM* 5/1 (1966): 93–111.

———. (3) "Stravinsky by Way of Webern: The Consistency of a Syntax." *PNM* 10/2 (1972): 13–51, and *PNM* 11/1 (1972): 112–45.

Rahn, John. (1) "Lines (Of and About Music)." Ph.D. dissertation, Princeton University, 1974.

———. (2) "On Pitch or Rhythm: Interpretations of Orderings Of and In Pitch and Time." *PNM* 13/2 (1975): 182–203.

———. (3) "Gentle Reminder #1: Two Common-Tone Theorems." *In Theory Only* 1/2 (May 1975): 10–11.

———. (4) "How Do You *Du* (by Milton Babbitt)?" *PNM* 14/2 and 15/1 (double issue, 1976): 61–80.

Randall, J.K. "Three Lectures to Scientists." *PNM* 5/2 (1967): 124–40. Reprinted as three separate articles in Boretz and Cone, eds. (2).

Regener, Eric. "On Allen Forte's Theory of Chords." *PNM* 13/1 (1974): 191–212. See Forte (7); Benjamin (1); Browne; Lewin (14).

Rogers, John. (1) "Toward a System of Rotational Arrays." *Proceedings of the American Society of University Composers* 2 (1967): 61–84.

———. (2) "Some Experiments with Contextually Defined 'Octaves'." *Proceedings of the American Society of University Composers* 3 (1968): 109–22.

---------. (3) "Some Properties of Non-Duplicating Rotational Arrays." *PNM* 7/1 (1968): 80–102. See Spies (1), (2), and (3).

Rothgeb, John. "Some Ordering Relationships in the Twelve-Tone System." *JMT* 11/2 (1967): 176–97.

Rufer, Joseph. *Composition with Twelve Notes Related Only to One Another*. Translated by Humphrey Searle. London: Barrie and Rockliff, The Cresset Press, 1969.

Schoenberg, Arnold. (1) "Analysis of the Four Orchestral Songs Opus 22." Translated by Claudio Spies. In Boretz and Cone, eds. (3): 25–45.

---------. (2) *Style and Idea: Selected Writings of Arnold Schoenberg*. Edited by Leonard Stein. New York: St. Martins, 1975. See Shifrin.

Shifrin, Seymour. "*Style and Idea* by Arnold Schoenberg." *PNM* 14/1 (1975): 174–81.

Smalley, Roger. (1) "Webern's Sketches (I)." *Tempo* no. 112 (1975): 1–12.

---------. (2) "Webern's Sketches (II)." *Tempo* no. 113 (1975): 29–40.

---------. (3) "Webern's Sketches (III)." *Tempo* no. 114 (1975): 14–22.

Smith, Charles. "Notes on "Voice-Leading" in Schoenberg." *In Theory Only* 2/10 (January 1977): 23–28.

Spies, Claudio. (1) "Notes on Stravinsky's *Abraham and Isaac*." *PNM* 3/2 (1965): 104–26. Reprinted in Boretz and Cone, eds. (3). See Rogers (1) and (3).

---------. (2) "Notes on Stravinsky's Variations." *PNM* 4/1 (1965): 62–74. Reprinted in Boretz and Cone, eds. (3). See Rogers (1) and (3).

---------. (3) "Some Notes on Stravinsky's Requiem Settings." *PNM* 5/2 (1967): 98–123. Reprinted in Boretz and Cone, eds. (3). See Rogers (1) and (3).

Starr, Daniel, and Morris, Robert. (1) "A General Theory of Combinatoriality and the Aggregate (Part I)." *PNM* 16/1 (1977): 3–35.

---------. (2) "A General Theory of Combinatoriality and the Aggregate (II)." *PNM* 16/2 (1978), in press.

Stockhausen, Karlheinz. (1) "Structure and Experiential Time." *Die Reihe* 2 (1958): 64–74.

---------. (2) "..... how time passes ......" *Die Reihe* 3 (1959): 10–40.

---------. (3) "The Concept of Unity in Electronic Music." *PNM* 1/1 (1962): 39–48.

---------. (4) "Music and Speech." *Die Reihe* 6 (1964): 40–64.

Swift, Richard. (1) "The *Demonstrations* of J.K. Randall." *PNM* 2/2 (1964): 77–86.

---------. (2) "Some Aspects of Aggregate Composition." *PNM* 14/2 and 15/1 (double issue, 1976): 236–48.

Teitelbaum, Richard. "Intervallic Relations in Atonal Music." *JMT* 9/1 (1965): 72–127.

Travis, Roy. "Analysis Symposium: Webern, Orchestra Pieces (1913): Movement I (*'Bewegt'*)." *JMT* 18/1 (1974): 2–12. See Barkin (2); Forte (8).

Unger, Udo. "Luigi Nono." *Die Reihe* 4 (1960): 5–13.

Webern, Anton. *The Path to the New Music*. Translated by Leo Black. Bryn Mawr: Theodore Presser, 1963.

Weinberg, Henry. "Donald Martino: Trio (1959): *PNM* 2/1 (1963): 82–90.

Westergaard, Peter. (1) "Some Problems in Rhythmic Theory and Analysis." *PNM* 1/1 (1962): 180–91. Reprinted in Boretz and Cone, eds. (2).

———. (2) "Webern and "Total Organization": An Analysis of the Second Movement of the Piano Variations, Op. 27." *PNM* 1/2 (1963): 107–20.

———. (3) "Some Problems Raised by the Rhythmic Procedures in Milton Babbitt's Composition for Twelve Instruments." *PNM* 4/1 (1965): 109–18.

———. (4) "Toward a Twelve-Tone Polyphony." *PNM* 4/2 (1966): 90–112. Reprinted in Boretz and Cone, eds. (2).

———. (5) "On the Problems of "Reconstruction from a Sketch": Webern's *Kunfttag III* and *Leise Düfte*." *PNM* 11/2 (1973): 104–21.

Winham, Godfrey. "Composition with Arrays." *PNM* 9/1 (1970): 43–67.

Wintle, Christopher. (1) "Multiple Order Functions in Twelve-Tone Music: an Informal Addendum." *PNM* 12/1 and 12/2 (double issue, 1973–74): 386–89. See Batstone.

———. (2) "Milton Babbitt's *Semi-Simple Variations*." *PNM* 14/2 and 15/1 (double issue, 1976): 111–54.

Wittlich, Gary. "Interval Set Structure in Schoenberg's Op. 11, No. 1." *PNM* 13/1 (1974): 41–55.

Zuckerman, Mark. "On Milton Babbitt's String Quartet No. 2." *PNM* 14/2 and 15/1 (double issue, 1976): 85–110.

APPENDICES

Appendix 1: INFORMAL EXPLANATIONS OF ASSUMED NOTATIONS AND CONCEPTS

Some of the concepts informally explained here are more rigorously defined in the text itself, but at least an informal understanding of all of them (such as that supplied here) is assumed throughout. Most should be familiar from elementary school or high school courses.

Ap 1.1   Symbols

$\neq$ means "not equal"

$<$ means "less than"

$\leq$ means "less than or equal to"

$>$ means "greater than"

$\geq$ means "greater than or equal to"

IFF abbreviates "if and only if." "IFF" is used to connect two statements that are together either both true or both false (usually, both true). For example, "It rains IFF it rains," or "$2 + 2 = 4$ IFF $1 + 3 = 4$."

$\rightarrow$ translates as the verb "maps." An "operation" or "mapping" "maps" or changes one thing into another. For example, "$T_2(5) \rightarrow 7$" is read, "transposition by 2 maps 5 into 7." See section Ap 1.6 and chapter 3, section 3.11.

$|x|$ If "x" is a number, this is read "the absolute value of x." If the enclosed number is negative, its "absolute value" is a positive number of the same magnitude; otherwise no effect. For example, $|-2| = 2; |3| = 3$. (If the enclosed is a *set,* see section Ap 1.5.)

$x \in A$ "x *is an element of* set A," or "x is a member of set A." See section Ap 1.3.

$A \sim B$ "set A - set B"; set subtraction.

133

134   Basic Atonal Theory

In general, lowercase English letters such as "b" or "x" stand for *elements* of sets or lines, while capital letters such as "B" or "X" stand for sets, lines, and operations. Capitals A through G are also used as the familiar letter names for pitch-classes; e.g., a "C major triad contains C, E, and G."

Ap 1.2   Orderings

<0,1,6>	0-1-6	0 1 6
n-tuple	string	ordered list

In these equivalent notations the objects are *ordered* from *left to right,* as in a musical *line* or syntactical *row.* (Angles "< >" always indicate such an ordering.) For example:

$$<0,1,6> \neq <1,0,6>,$$
$$<C,C\sharp,F\sharp> \neq <C\sharp,C,F\sharp>,$$
but $<C,C\sharp,F\sharp> = <C,C\sharp,F\sharp>.$

Ap 1.3   Sets

{0,1,6}	0,1,6
set	unordered list

In these notations the order in which the objects are listed is irrelevant. The curly braces "{ }" and the list they enclose notate a set. Only the *content* is significant, not the order in which the objects contained are listed:

$$\{0,1,6\} = \{1,0,6\} = \{6,0,1\} = \ldots$$
but $\{0,1,6\} \neq \{0,2,6\}.$

The "elements" or "members" of {0,1,6} are 0, 1, and 6. $0 \in \{0,1,6\}$, $1 \in \{0,1,6\}$, and $6 \in \{0,1,6\}$.

Ap 1.4   Order Operations

Any ordering (n-tuple, string, ordered list, line, row) may be transformed into an equivalent (but not identical) ordering. The two basic transformations are *retrograde* and *rotation.* To retrograde an ordering, list it *backwards.* For example, B♭—A—C—B and B—C—A—B♭ are retrograde-equivalent orderings.

To rotate an ordering once, put its *last member first,* leaving all other members unchanged in order. For example:

B♭—A—C—B is rotated once to B—B♭—A—C;

B—B♭—A—C is rotated once to C—B—B♭—A;

C—B—B♭—A is rotated once to A—C—B—B♭;

A—C—B—B♭ is rotated once to B♭—A—C—B.

As seen above, you can *repeat* the process until you reach the original ordering B♭—A—C—B. *All* the above four orderings are rotationally equivalent. (An n-tuple always has n rotations: each of its n members can serve as the first member of one of its rotations.)

It may help to think of the ordering arranged in a circle, as on a clock face. Read clockwise from noon:

$$\begin{matrix} & B\flat & \\ B & & A \\ & C & \end{matrix} \quad = \quad B\flat - A - C - B$$

Then to find the rotations, *rotate* the entire circle clockwise so that some new object is in the starting position at the top:

$$\begin{matrix} & B\flat & \\ B & & A \\ & C & \end{matrix} \quad \begin{matrix} & B & \searrow \\ C & & B\flat \\ & A & \end{matrix} \quad \begin{matrix} & C & \\ A & & B \\ & B\flat & \nearrow \end{matrix} \quad \begin{matrix} & A & \\ B\flat & & C \\ & \nwarrow B & \end{matrix}$$

B♭—A—C—B   B—B♭—A—C   C—B—B♭—A   A—C—B—B♭

In performing both retrograde and rotation on the same ordering, always perform the retrograde first, then the rotation. For example:

B♭—A—C—B is retrograded to B—C—A—B♭;

B—C—A—B♭ may then be rotated (in two steps) to A—B♭—B—C;

B♭—A—C—B and A—B♭—B—C are retrograde/rotationally equivalent.

Ap 1.5 Set Operations and Relations

The *union* of two sets is a set that contains their combined contents. A large "∪" is the symbol for set union.

$$\{C,E,G\} \cup \{G,B,D\} = \{C,E,G,B,D\}$$

The union of the set {C,E,G} and the set {G,B,D} is the set {C,E,G,B,D}. Although the G is in both sets, it is listed only once in their union. No set needs to list the same symbol more than once because, since the *order* of the listing is irrelevant, there is in principle *no way to tell two instances of the same symbol apart:*

$$\{G,G\} = \{G\} = \{G,G,G,G,G,G,G,G,G\} = \text{etc.}$$

(One cannot tell the "first" G from the "second" G because there is no firstness or secondness. One can only say that there is a G there.)

The *intersection* of two sets is the set containing only those elements the two sets *have in common*. The symbol for intersection is "∩":

$$\{C,E,G\} \cap \{G,B,D\} = \{G\}$$

The intersection of {C,E,G} and {G,B,D} is the set {G}. If we want *any* two sets to have an intersection, we have to invent "the empty set" or "null set," whose symbol is "∅", to serve as the intersection of two sets that have no elements in common:

$$\{C,E,G\} \cap \{D,F\sharp,A\} = \emptyset$$

The *number of members* in a set is notated by enclosing the set in upright lines: "|{G,B,D}|" means "the number of members in {G,B,D}"; |{G,B,D}| = 3. The number of members in a set is called the "cardinality" of the set:

|∅| = 0

|{C,E,G}∩{G,B,D}| = |{G}| = 1

A set is a *subset* of another set if every member of the subset is also a member of the other set; a subset is totally contained by its "superset." The symbol for subset is "⊆". Every set is a subset of itself. A "proper subset" must be smaller than the set it is a subset of. The symbol for "proper subset is "⊂":

{C,G}⊂{C,E,G}

Thus {C,G} is a (proper) subset of {C,E,G}. More formally:

A⊆B IFF A∪B = B, and |A| ⩽ |B|

A⊂B IFF A⊆B and A ≠ B

Take the set of all notes in the C major scale: {C,D,E,F,G,A,B}. Call this a *reference set*. Take any subset of the reference set, e.g., {C,D,E}. Then the *set complement* of {C,D,E} (with respect to {C,D,E,F,G,A,B}) is {F,G,A,B}. In general, two subsets X and Y (of reference set Z) are set complements (with respect to Z) if they have no element in common, but together they contain everything in Z. That is, X and Y are complements with respect to Z if and only if X∩Y = ∅ and X∪Y = Z.

Usually in atonal theory set complementation is with respect to the reference set of all twelve pitch classes.

Ap 1.6 Mappings

A mapping is a special kind of relation between two sets. A mapping assigns to each element of a set D (called the "domain") at most one element from a set R (called the counterdomain or "range"). The elements of the domain are called "preimages," and the elements of the range that are assigned to them are their "images" under a particular mapping. A particular mapping can be defined as a set of ordered pairs, such that the first member of each ordered pair is a preimage and the second member of that ordered pair is the image of the first. For example, if

D = {a,b}

R = {x,y,z}

one particular mapping M = { <a,x>, <b,z> }. We say that "M maps a into x" and "M maps b into z," written as "M(a)→ x" and "M(b)→ z." In this case, y ∈ R was left out, making M an "into" ("injective") type of mapping. M maps D "into" R. If R is smaller than D, a mapping can be an "onto" ("surjective") type, in which all members of R are assigned; and some one image is assigned to more than one preimage:

$D = \{a,b\}$

$R = \{x\}$

$M = \{<a,x>, <b,x>\}$

$M(a) \to x, M(b) \to x$

M maps D "onto" R.

If D and R have equal cardinality and if all elements of R are assigned as images, the mapping is called a "one-to-one" mapping or "one-to-one correspondence."

$D = \{a,b\}$

$R = \{x,y\}$

$M = \{<a,y>, <b,x>\}$

$M(a) \to y, M(b) \to x$

M is a "one-to-one correspondence."

If D and R are the same set, a one-to-one correspondence is called a "permutation."

$D = \{a,b\}$

$R = \{a,b\}$

$M = \{<a,b>, <b,a>\}$

$M(a) \to b, M(b) \to a$

M is a "permutation" of $\{a,b\}$.

Any "12-tone row" can be considered a permutation of the set consisting of the integers modulo 12. Transposition and inversion will be defined as permutations of the 12 pitch-classes.

Mappings are often notated by listing the elements of the domain in some order and listing directly below each element of the domain its image under the mapping. Thus the set of elements in the top line is the domain and the set of elements in the bottom line is the range. The two lines are enclosed with large parentheses. For example, the mapping $\{<a,b>, <b,a>, <c,c>, <d,a>\}$ can be notated simply

$$\begin{pmatrix} a & b & c & d \\ b & a & c & a \end{pmatrix}$$

with domain $\{a,b,c,d\}$ and range $\{a,b,c\}$.

Ap. 1.7 When Sets are Rows

A twelve-tone row is an ordering or *ordered collection*—a 12-tuple (section Ap 1.2)—of the twelve "pitch-classes" (C,C♯,D,D♯,E,F,F♯,G,G♯,A,A♯,B— see section 2.3). A set is an *unordered* collection (section Ap 1.3). Yet Milton Babbitt and others prefer the term "set" for a twelve-tone row. In set theory,

138   Basic Atonal Theory

orderings are defined in terms of sets. For example, under one set-theoretical definition, an ordered pair <a,b> becomes the set {{a}, {a,b}}. In particular, any "permutation" (section Ap 1.6) of a set of integers is an ordering of those integers. One permutation of the integers 0 through 11 is shown below:

$$\begin{pmatrix} 0 & 1 & 2 & 3 & 4 & 5 & 6 & 7 & 8 & 9 & 10 & 11 \\ 0 & 11 & 7 & 8 & 3 & 1 & 2 & 10 & 6 & 5 & 4 & 9 \end{pmatrix}$$

This permutation is defined as the set of ordered pairs whose second members are the images of their first members:

{<0,0>, <1,11>, <2,7>, <3,8>, <4,3>, <5,1>, <6,2>, <7,10>, <8,6>, <9,5>, <10,4>, <11,9>}.

If the images (second members of each ordered pair) are interpreted as naming the twelve pitch-classes (section 2.3), this *set* becomes an *ordering* of all twelve pitch-classes. The preimages are called the "order numbers" of their images.[1] In fact, this is the famous twelve-tone row of the Schoenberg Fourth String Quartet.[2] (If C = 0, this ordering equals the string C— B— G— Ab— Eb— Db— D— Bb— Gb— F— E— A.)

NOTES

[1] See Milton Babbitt, "Twelve-Tone Invariants as Compositional Determinants," *Musical Quarterly* 46 (1960): 246-59.

[2] See Milton Babbitt, "Set Structure as a Compositional Determinant," *JMT* 5/2 (1961): 72-94.

Appendices 139

APPENDIX 2: TABLES

TABLE I: Suggested Equivalence Class Notations

Notations		*Definitions by Example*
1. $(0,1,6)_{T_n}$	$(0,1,6)$	The class of all sets equivalent to $\{0,1,6\}$ under T_n.
2. $(19,1,50)_{T_n^p}$		The class of all sets (of *pitches*) equivalent to $\{19,1,50\}$ under T_n^p.
3. $(0-1-6)_{T_n}$	$(0-1-6)$	The class of all *lines* equivalent to $0-1-6$ under T_n.
4. $(19-1-50)_{T_n^p}$		The class of all *lines* (of *pitches*) equivalent to $19-1-50$ under T_n^p.
5. $(0,1,6)_{T_n/T_nI}$	$[0,1,6]$	The class of all sets equivalent to $\{0,1,6\}$ under T_n or T_nI or both.
6. $(19,1,50)_{T_n^p/T_n^pI}$		The class of all sets (of *pitches*) equivalent to $\{19,1,50\}$ under T_n^p or T_n^pI or both.
7. $(0-1-6)_{T_n/T_nI}$	$[0-1-6]$	The class of all *lines* equivalent to $0-1-6$ under T_n or T_nI or both.
8. $(19-1-50)_{T_n^p/T_n^pI}$		The class of all *lines* (of *pitches*) equivalent to $19-1-50$ under T_n^p or T_n^pI or both.
9. $[0,1,6]_{M5}$		The class of all sets equivalent to $\{0,1,6\}$ under T_n or T_nI or T_nM5 or T_nM7.
10. $[0-1-6]_{M5}$		The class of all lines equivalent to $0-1-6$ under T_n or T_nI or T_nM5 or T_nM7.

Basic Atonal Theory

TABLE II: T_n/T_nI-Types of Sets

The leftmost entry gives a T_n/T_nI-type of set (section 4.13); the rightmost entry gives the type of the set complement of any of the equivalent sets in the type given in the leftmost entry. The next-to-left and rightmost entries list the degree of symmetry (section 4.31), followed by entries listing the interval vectors (section 5.13). The middle entry (e.g., "3—1/9—1") cross-references this table with Allen Forte's *The Structure of Atonal Music*, giving the list-labels of the set types from Forte's Appendix 1.

TRICHORDS   NONACHORDS

[0,1,2]	2	<2,1,0,0,0,0>	3—1/9—1	<8,7,6,6,6,3>	2	[0,1,2,3,4,5,6,7,8]
[0,1,3]	1	<1,1,1,0,0,0>	3—2/9—2	<7,7,7,6,6,3>	1	[0,1,2,3,4,5,6,7,9]
[0,1,4]	1	<1,0,1,1,0,0>	3—3/9—3	<7,6,7,7,6,3>	1	[0,1,2,3,4,5,6,8,9]
[0,1,5]	1	<1,0,0,1,1,0>	3—4/9—4	<7,6,6,7,7,3>	1	[0,1,2,3,4,5,7,8,9]
[0,1,6]	1	<1,0,0,0,1,1>	3—5/9—5	<7,6,6,6,7,4>	1	[0,1,2,3,4,6,7,8,9]
[0,2,4]	2	<0,2,0,1,0,0>	3—6/9—6	<6,8,6,7,6,3>	2	[0,1,2,3,4,5,6,8,10]
[0,2,5]	1	<0,1,1,0,1,0>	3—7/9—7	<6,7,7,6,7,3>	1	[0,1,2,3,4,5,7,8,10]
[0,2,6]	1	<0,1,0,1,0,1>	3—8/9—8	<6,7,6,7,6,4>	1	[0,1,2,3,4,6,7,8,10]
[0,2,7]	2	<0,1,0,0,2,0>	3—9/9—9	<6,7,6,6,8,3>	2	[0,1,2,3,5,6,7,8,10]
[0,3,6]	2	<0,0,2,0,0,1>	3—10/9—10	<6,6,8,6,6,4>	2	[0,1,2,3,4,6,7,9,10]
[0,3,7]	1	<0,0,1,1,1,0>	3—11/9—11	<6,6,7,7,7,3>	1	[0,1,2,3,5,6,7,9,10]
[0,4,8]	6	<0,0,0,3,0,0>	3—12/9—12	<6,6,6,9,6,3>	6	[0,1,2,4,5,6,8,9,10]

TETRACHORDS   OCTACHORDS

[0,1,2,3]	2	<3,2,1,0,0,0>	4—1/8—1	<7,6,5,4,4,2>	2	[0,1,2,3,4,5,6,7]
[0,1,2,4]	1	<2,2,1,1,0,0>	4—2/8—2	<6,6,5,5,4,2>	1	[0,1,2,3,4,5,6,8]
[0,1,2,5]	1	<2,1,1,1,1,0>	4—4/8—4	<6,5,5,5,5,2>	1	[0,1,2,3,4,5,7,8]
[0,1,2,6]	1	<2,1,0,1,1,1>	4—5/8—5	<6,5,4,5,5,3>	1	[0,1,2,3,4,6,7,8]
[0,1,2,7]	2	<2,1,0,0,2,1>	4—6/8—6	<6,5,4,4,6,3>	2	[0,1,2,3,5,6,7,8]
[0,1,3,4]	2	<2,1,2,1,0,0>	4—3/8—3	<6,5,6,5,4,2>	2	[0,1,2,3,4,5,6,9]
[0,1,3,5]	1	<1,2,1,1,1,0>	4—11/8—11	<5,6,5,5,5,2>	1	[0,1,2,3,4,5,7,9]
[0,1,3,6]	1	<1,1,2,0,1,1>	4—13/8—13	<5,5,6,4,5,3>	1	[0,1,2,3,4,6,7,9]
[0,1,3,7]	1	<1,1,1,1,1,1>	4—Z29/8—Z29	<5,5,5,5,5,3>	1	[0,1,2,3,5,6,7,9]
[0,1,4,5]	2	<2,0,1,2,1,0>	4—7/8—7	<6,4,5,6,5,2>	2	[0,1,2,3,4,5,8,9]
[0,1,4,6]	1	<1,1,1,1,1,1>	4—Z15/8—Z15	<5,5,5,5,5,3>	1	[0,1,2,3,4,6,8,9]
[0,1,4,7]	1	<1,0,2,1,1,1>	4—18/8—18	<5,4,6,5,5,3>	1	[0,1,2,3,5,6,8,9]
[0,1,4,8]	1	<1,0,1,3,1,0>	4—19/8—19	<5,4,5,7,5,2>	1	[0,1,2,4,5,6,8,9]
[0,1,5,6]	2	<2,0,0,1,2,1>	4—8/8—8	<6,4,4,5,6,3>	2	[0,1,2,3,4,7,8,9]
[0,1,5,7]	1	<1,1,0,1,2,1>	4—16/8—16	<5,5,4,5,6,3>	1	[0,1,2,3,5,7,8,9]
[0,1,5,8]	2	<1,0,1,2,2,0>	4—20/8—20	<5,4,5,6,6,2>	2	[0,1,2,4,5,7,8,9]
[0,1,6,7]	4	<2,0,0,0,2,2>	4—9/8—9	<6,4,4,4,6,4>	4	[0,1,2,3,6,7,8,9]

[0,2,3,5]	2	<1,2,2,0,1,0>	4—10/8—10	<5,6,6,4,5,2>	2	[0,2,3,4,5,6,7,9]
[0,2,3,6]	1	<1,1,2,1,0,1>	4—12/8—12	<5,5,6,5,4,3>	1	[0,1,3,4,5,6,7,9]
[0,2,3,7]	1	<1,1,1,1,2,0>	4—14/8—14	<5,5,5,5,6,2>	1	[0,1,2,4,5,6,7,9]
[0,2,4,6]	2	<0,3,0,2,0,1>	4—21/8—21	<4,7,4,6,4,3>	2	[0,1,2,3,4,6,8,10]
[0,2,4,7]	1	<0,2,1,1,2,0>	4—22/8—22	<4,6,5,5,6,2>	1	[0,1,2,3,5,6,8,10]
[0,2,4,8]	2	<0,2,0,3,0,1>	4—24/8—24	<4,6,4,7,4,3>	2	[0,1,2,4,5,6,8,10]
[0,2,5,7]	2	<0,2,1,0,3,0>	4—23/8—23	<4,6,5,4,7,2>	2	[0,1,2,3,5,7,8,10]
[0,2,5,8]	1	<0,1,2,1,1,1>	4—27/8—27	<4,5,6,5,5,3>	1	[0,1,2,4,5,7,8,10]
[0,2,6,8]	4	<0,2,0,2,0,2>	4—25/8—25	<4,6,4,6,4,4>	4	[0,1,2,4,6,7,8,10]
[0,3,4,7]	2	<1,0,2,2,1,0>	4—17/8—17	<5,4,6,6,5,2>	2	[0,1,3,4,5,6,8,9]
[0,3,5,8]	2	<0,1,2,1,2,0>	4—26/8—26	<4,5,6,5,6,2>	2	[0,1,3,4,5,7,8,10]
[0,3,6,9]	8	<0,0,4,0,0,2>	4—28/8—28	<4,4,8,4,4,4>	8	[0,1,3,4,6,7,9,10]

PENTACHORDS   SEPTACHORDS

[0,1,2,3,4]	2	<4,3,2,1,0,0>	5—1/7—1	<6,5,4,3,2,1>	2	[0,1,2,3,4,5,6]
[0,1,2,3,5]	1	<3,3,2,1,1,0>	5—2/7—2	<5,5,4,3,3,1>	1	[0,1,2,3,4,5,7]
[0,1,2,3,6]	1	<3,2,2,1,1,1>	5—4/7—4	<5,4,4,3,3,2>	1	[0,1,2,3,4,6,7]
[0,1,2,3,7]	1	<3,2,1,1,2,1>	5—5/7—5	<5,4,3,3,4,2>	1	[0,1,2,3,5,6,7]
[0,1,2,4,5]	1	<3,2,2,2,1,0>	5—3/7—3	<5,4,4,4,3,1>	1	[0,1,2,3,4,5,8]
[0,1,2,4,6]	1	<2,3,1,2,1,1>	5—9/7—9	<4,5,3,4,3,2>	1	[0,1,2,3,4,6,8]
[0,1,2,4,7]	1	<2,2,2,1,2,1>	5—Z36/7—Z36	<4,4,4,3,4,2>	1	[0,1,2,3,5,6,8]
[0,1,2,4,8]	1	<2,2,1,3,1,1>	5—13/7—13	<4,4,3,5,3,2>	1	[0,1,2,4,5,6,8]
[0,1,2,5,6]	1	<3,1,1,2,2,1>	5—6/7—6	<5,3,3,4,4,2>	1	[0,1,2,3,4,7,8]
[0,1,2,5,7]	1	<2,2,1,1,3,1>	5—14/7—14	<4,4,3,3,5,2>	1	[0,1,2,3,5,7,8]
[0,1,2,5,8]	1	<2,1,2,2,2,1>	5—Z38/7—Z38	<4,3,4,4,4,2>	1	[0,1,2,4,5,7,8]
[0,1,2,6,7]	1	<3,1,0,1,3,2>	5—7/7—7	<5,3,2,3,5,3>	1	[0,1,2,3,6,7,8]
[0,1,2,6,8]	2	<2,2,0,2,2,2>	5—15/7—15	<4,4,2,4,4,3>	2	[0,1,2,4,6,7,8]
[0,1,3,4,6]	1	<2,2,3,1,1,1>	5—10/7—10	<4,4,5,3,3,2>	1	[0,1,2,3,4,6,9]
[0,1,3,4,7]	1	<2,1,3,2,1,1>	5—16/7—16	<4,3,5,4,3,2>	1	[0,1,2,3,5,6,9]
[0,1,3,4,8]	2	<2,1,2,3,2,0>	5—Z17/7—Z17	<4,3,4,5,4,1>	2	[0,1,2,4,5,6,9]
[0,1,3,5,6]	2	<2,2,2,1,2,1>	5—Z12/7—Z12	<4,4,4,3,4,2>	2	[0,1,2,3,4,7,9]
[0,1,3,5,7]	1	<1,3,1,2,2,1>	5—24/7—24	<3,5,3,4,4,2>	1	[0,1,2,3,5,7,9]
[0,1,3,5,8]	1	<1,2,2,2,3,0>	5—27/7—27	<3,4,4,4,5,1>	1	[0,1,2,4,5,7,9]
[0,1,3,6,7]	1	<2,1,2,1,2,2>	5—19/7—19	<4,3,4,3,4,3>	1	[0,1,2,3,6,7,9]
[0,1,3,6,8]	1	<1,2,2,1,3,1>	5—29/7—29	<3,4,4,3,5,2>	1	[0,1,2,4,6,7,9]
[0,1,3,6,9]	1	<1,1,4,1,1,2>	5—31/7—31	<3,3,6,3,3,3>	1	[0,1,3,4,6,7,9]
[0,1,4,5,7]	1	<2,1,2,2,2,1>	5—Z18/7—Z18	<4,3,4,4,4,2>	1	[0,1,4,5,6,7,9]
[0,1,4,5,8]	1	<2,0,2,4,2,0>	5—21/7—21	<4,2,4,6,4,1>	1	[0,1,2,4,5,8,9]
[0,1,4,6,8]	1	<1,2,1,3,2,1>	5—30/7—30	<3,4,3,5,4,2>	1	[0,1,2,4,6,8,9]

142   Basic Atonal Theory

[0,1,4,6,9]	1	<1,1,3,2,2,1>	5—32/7—32	<3,3,5,4,4,2>	1	[0,1,3,4,6,8,9]
[0,1,4,7,8]	2	<2,0,2,3,2,1>	5—22/7—22	<4,2,4,5,4,2>	2	[0,1,2,5,6,7,9]
[0,1,5,6,8]	1	<2,1,1,2,3,1>	5—20/7—20	<4,3,3,4,5,2>	1	[0,1,2,4,7,8,9]
[0,2,3,4,6]	2	<2,3,2,2,0,1>	5—8/7—8	<4,5,4,4,2,2>	2	[0,2,3,4,5,6,8]
[0,2,3,4,7]	1	<2,2,2,2,2,0>	5—11/7—11	<4,4,4,4,4,1>	1	[0,1,3,4,5,6,8]
[0,2,3,5,7]	1	<1,3,2,1,3,0>	5—23/7—23	<3,5,4,3,5,1>	1	[0,2,3,4,5,7,9]
[0,2,3,5,8]	1	<1,2,3,1,2,1>	5—25/7—25	<3,4,5,3,4,2>	1	[0,2,3,4,6,7,9]
[0,2,3,6,8]	1	<1,2,2,2,1,2>	5—28/7—28	<3,4,4,4,3,3>	1	[0,1,3,5,6,7,9]
[0,2,4,5,8]	1	<1,2,2,3,1,1>	5—26/7—26	<3,4,4,5,3,2>	1	[0,1,3,4,5,7,9]
[0,2,4,6,8]	2	<0,4,0,4,0,2>	5—33/7—33	<2,6,2,6,2,3>	2	[0,1,2,4,6,8,10]
[0,2,4,6,9]	2	<0,3,2,2,2,1>	5—34/7—34	<2,5,4,4,4,2>	2	[0,1,3,4,6,8,10]
[0,2,4,7,9]	2	<0,3,2,1,4,0>	5—35/7—35	<2,5,4,3,6,1>	2	[0,1,3,5,6,8,10]
[0,3,4,5,8]	2	<2,1,2,3,2,0>	5—Z37/7—Z37	<4,3,4,5,4,1>	2	[0,1,3,4,5,7,8]

HEXACHORDS

For the twenty cases in which complementary hexachords are of the same type, no entry appears in the right-hand column. In the remaining cases, only the type of the complement is given, since mutually complementary hexachords have the same interval vector and degree of symmetry (section 5.16).

[0,1,2,3,4,5]	2	<5,4,3,2,1,0>	6—1	
[0,1,2,3,4,6]	1	<4,4,3,2,1,1>	6—2	
[0,1,2,3,4,7]	1	<4,3,3,2,2,1>	6—Z36/6—Z3	[0,1,2,3,5,6]
[0,1,2,3,4,8]	2	<4,3,2,3,2,1>	6—Z37/6—Z4	[0,1,2,4,5,6]
[0,1,2,3,5,7]	1	<3,4,2,2,3,1>	6—9	
[0,1,2,3,5,8]	1	<3,3,3,2,3,1>	6—Z40/6—Z11	[0,1,2,4,5,7]
[0,1,2,3,6,7]	1	<4,2,2,2,3,2>	6—5	
[0,1,2,3,6,8]	1	<3,3,2,2,3,2>	6—Z41/6—Z12	[0,1,2,4,6,7]
[0,1,2,3,6,9]	2	<3,2,4,2,2,2>	6—Z42/6—Z13	[0,1,3,4,6,7]
[0,1,2,3,7,8]	2	<4,2,1,2,4,2>	6—Z38/6—Z6	[0,1,2,5,6,7]
[0,1,2,4,5,8]	1	<3,2,3,4,2,1>	6—15	
[0,1,2,4,6,8]	1	<2,4,1,4,2,2>	6—22	
[0,1,2,4,6,9]	1	<2,3,3,3,3,1>	6—Z46/6—Z24	[0,1,3,4,6,8]
[0,1,2,4,7,8]	1	<3,2,2,3,3,2>	6—Z17/6—Z43	[0,1,2,5,6,8]
[0,1,2,4,7,9]	1	<2,3,3,2,4,1>	6—Z47/6—Z25	[0,1,3,5,6,8]
[0,1,2,5,6,9]	1	<3,1,3,4,3,1>	6—Z44/6—Z19	[0,1,3,4,7,8]
[0,1,2,5,7,8]	1	<3,2,2,2,4,2>	6—18	
[0,1,2,5,7,9]	1	<2,3,2,3,4,1>	6—Z48/6—Z26	[0,1,3,5,7,8]
[0,1,2,6,7,8]	4	<4,2,0,2,4,3>	6—7	
[0,1,3,4,5,7]	1	<3,3,3,3,2,1>	6—Z10/6—Z39	[0,2,3,4,5,8]
[0,1,3,4,5,8]	1	<3,2,3,4,3,0>	6—14	

[0,1,3,4,6,9]	1	<2,2,5,2,2,2>	6—27	
[0,1,3,4,7,9]	2	<2,2,4,3,2,2>	6—Z49/6—Z28	[0,1,3,5,6,9]
[0,1,3,5,7,9]	1	<1,4,2,4,2,2>	6—34	
[0,1,4,5,7,9]	1	<2,2,3,4,3,1>	6—31	
[0,1,3,6,7,9]	2	<2,2,4,2,2,3>	6—30	
[0,2,3,6,7,9]	2	<2,2,4,2,3,2>	6—Z29/6—Z50	[0,1,4,6,7,9]
[0,1,4,5,6,8]	1	<3,2,2,4,3,1>	6—16	
[0,1,4,5,8,9]	6	<3,0,3,6,3,0>	6—20	
[0,2,3,4,5,7]	2	<3,4,3,2,3,0>	6—8	
[0,2,3,4,6,8]	1	<2,4,2,4,1,2>	6—21	
[0,2,3,4,6,9]	1	<2,3,4,2,2,2>	6—Z45/6—Z23	[0,2,3,5,6,8]
[0,2,3,5,7,9]	1	<1,4,3,2,4,1>	6—33	
[0,2,4,5,7,9]	2	<1,4,3,2,5,0>	6—32	
[0,2,4,6,8,10]	12	<0,6,0,6,0,3>	6—35	

144 Basic Atonal Theory

ANSWERS TO SELECTED EXERCISES

Note: Answers have been provided for selected exercises only (normally for every other question) in order to supply answers both for teachers and for students teaching themselves—and at the same time to make the exercises usable as assignments for graded homework. The answers printed here provide enough unanswered exercises for the latter purpose and enough answered exercises for the former purpose.

CHAPTER 2

Exercises 2-1 (Nos. 13–24)

13. <0,5,8,10,9,1,7,3,4,2,11,6>
14. i<0,5> = 5 − 0 = 5
15. i<5,8> = 8 − 5 = 3
16. i<8,10> = 10 − 8 = 2
17. i<10,9> = 9 − 10 = 11
18. i<9,1> = 1 − 9 = 4
19. i<1,7> = 7 − 1 = 6
20. i<7,3> = 3 − 7 = 8
21. i<3,4> = 4 − 3 = 1
22. i<4,2> = 2 − 4 = 10
23. i<2,11> = 11 − 2 = 9
24. i<11,6> = 6 − 11 = 7

Answers to Selected Exercises 145

Exercises 2-II   (Nos. 36-47)

36. $i(0,5) = 5$

37. $i(5,8) = 3$

38. $i(8,10) = 2$

39. $i(10,9) = 1$

40. $i(9,1) = 4$

41. $i(1,7) = 6$

42. $i(7,3) = 4$

43. $i(3,4) = 1$

44. $i(4,2) = 2$

45. $i(2,11) = 3$

46. $i(11,6) = 5$

47. a) $$\begin{matrix} x: & \begin{pmatrix} 0 & 1 & 2 & 3 & 4 & 5 & 6 & 7 & 8 & 9 & 10 & 11 \\ 0 & 1 & 2 & 3 & 4 & 5 & 0 & 1 & 2 & 3 & 4 & 5 \end{pmatrix} \\ x \bmod 6: & \end{matrix}$$

b) It removes the distinction between 7 and 1 semitones, 8 and 2, 9 and 3, 10 and 4, 11 and 5. Such distinctions fit the music under study, while such identifications (e.g., of 7 with 1) do not.

Exercises 2-III   (Nos. 49, 51, 53, 55)

49. {1,2,4,5,7,8}. (Right hand is set complement {9,10,11,0,3,6}.)

51. {1,4,5,8}

53. {7,9,11,1}

55. {6,7,8,9,11,1}

CHAPTER 3

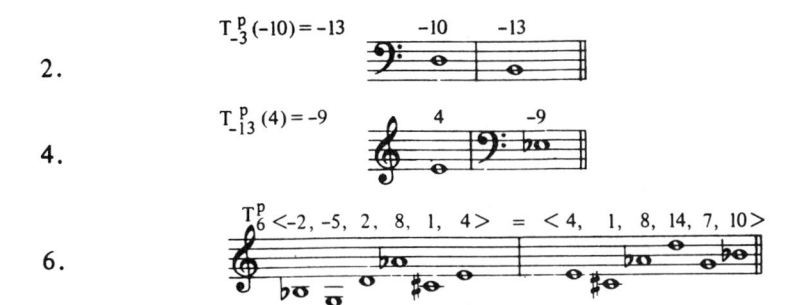

Exercises 3-I   (Nos. 2,4,6)

2. $T_{-3}^p(-10) = -13$

4. $T_{-13}^p(4) = -9$

6. $T_6^p \langle -2, -5, 2, 8, 1, 4 \rangle = \langle 4, 1, 8, 14, 7, 10 \rangle$

146 Basic Atonal Theory

Exercises 3-II   (Nos. 2,4,6,8,10,12,14,16)

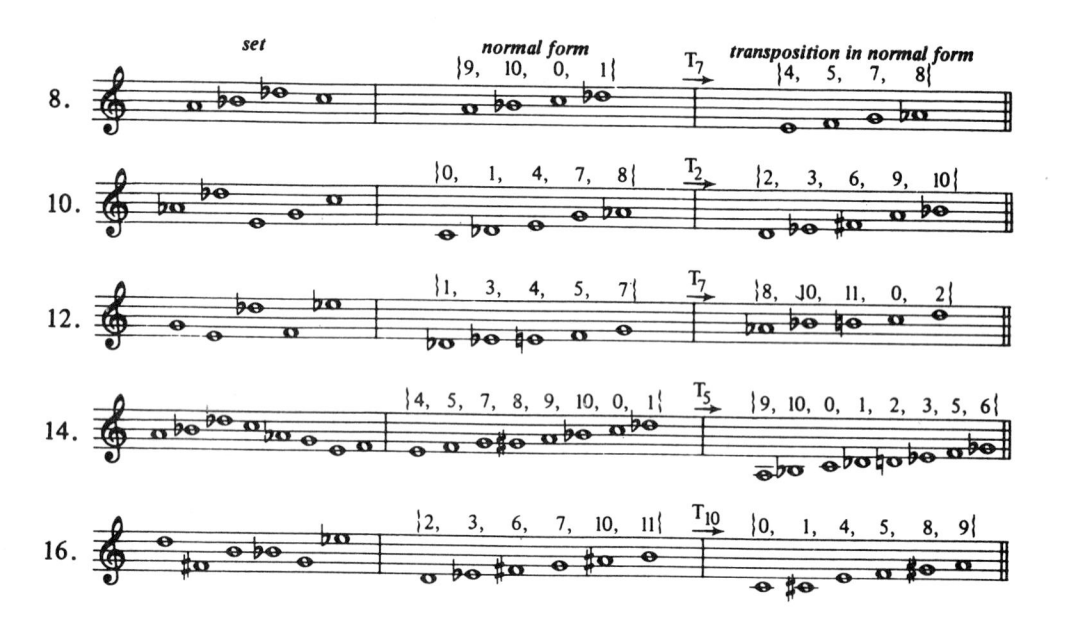

2. $T_2 \langle 0, 6, 8 \rangle = \langle 2, 8, 10 \rangle$

4. $T_{11} \langle 0, 8, 11, 4, 9 \rangle = \langle 11, 7, 10, 3, 8 \rangle$

6. $T_6 \langle 4, 1, 8, 2, 7, 10 \rangle = \langle 10, 7, 2, 8, 1, 4 \rangle$

8.   set — normal form $\{9, 10, 0, 1\}$ — T_7 — transposition in normal form $\{4, 5, 7, 8\}$

10. $\{0, 1, 4, 7, 8\}$ — T_2 — $\{2, 3, 6, 9, 10\}$

12. $\{1, 3, 4, 5, 7\}$ — T_7 — $\{8, 10, 11, 0, 2\}$

14. $\{4, 5, 7, 8, 9, 10, 0, 1\}$ — T_5 — $\{9, 10, 0, 1, 2, 3, 5, 6\}$

16. $\{2, 3, 6, 7, 10, 11\}$ — T_{10} — $\{0, 1, 4, 5, 8, 9\}$

Exercises 3-III   (Nos. 2,4)

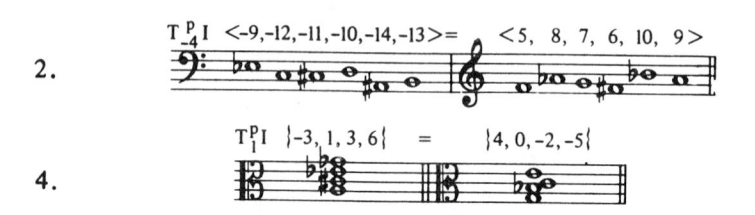

2. $T_{-4}^p I \langle -9, -12, -11, -10, -14, -13 \rangle = \langle 5, 8, 7, 6, 10, 9 \rangle$

4. $T_1^p I \{-3, 1, 3, 6\} = \{4, 0, -2, -5\}$

Answers to Selected Exercises   147

Exercises 3-IV   (Nos. 2,4,6,8)

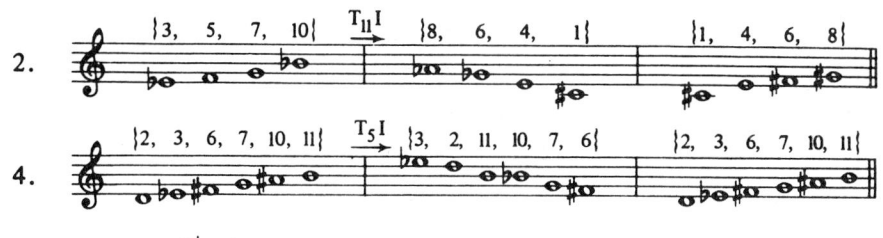

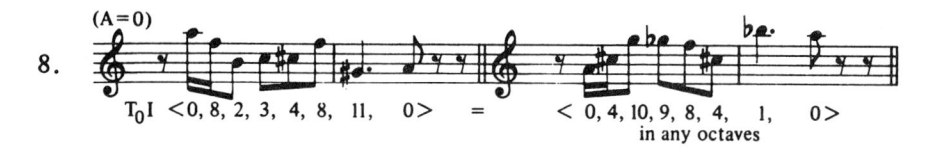

2. {3, 5, 7, 10} $\xrightarrow{T_{11}I}$ {8, 6, 4, 1}   {1, 4, 6, 8}

4. {2, 3, 6, 7, 10, 11} $\xrightarrow{T_5I}$ {3, 2, 11, 10, 7, 6}   {2, 3, 6, 7, 10, 11}

6. ($E^\flat = 0$) T_8I <8, 0, 2, 3> = <0, 8, 6, 5>

8. (A=0)
T_0I <0, 8, 2, 3, 4, 8, 11, 0> = < 0, 4, 10, 9, 8, 4, 1, 0>
in any octaves

Exercises 3-V   (Nos. 1; 3a-f; 6a, c, e)

1. $T_{7n}M5(T_nM5(x)) =$
$T_{7n}M5(5x + n) =$
$(25x + 5n) + 7n =$
$x + 12n = x + 0 \cdot n = x + 0 = x = T_0(x)$
$T_{5n}M7(T_nM7(x)) =$
$T_{5n}M7(7x + n) =$
$(49x + 7n) + 5n =$
$x + 12n = x + 0 = x = T_0(x)$

3. a) $\begin{pmatrix} 0 & 3 & 6 & 9 \\ 0 & 3 & 6 & 9 \end{pmatrix} \begin{matrix} x \\ M5(x) \end{matrix}$ d) $\begin{pmatrix} 0 & 3 & 6 & 9 \\ 0 & 9 & 6 & 3 \end{pmatrix} \begin{matrix} x \\ M7(x) \end{matrix}$

b) $\begin{pmatrix} 1 & 4 & 7 & 10 \\ 5 & 8 & 11 & 2 \end{pmatrix} \begin{matrix} x \\ M5(x) \end{matrix}$ e) $\begin{pmatrix} 1 & 4 & 7 & 10 \\ 7 & 4 & 1 & 10 \end{pmatrix} \begin{matrix} x \\ M7(x) \end{matrix}$

c) $\begin{pmatrix} 2 & 5 & 8 & 11 \\ 10 & 1 & 4 & 7 \end{pmatrix} \begin{matrix} x \\ M5(x) \end{matrix}$ f) $\begin{pmatrix} 2 & 5 & 8 & 11 \\ 2 & 11 & 8 & 5 \end{pmatrix} \begin{matrix} x \\ M7(x) \end{matrix}$

6. a) T_5M7 {1,4,7,10} = {0,9,6,3} = {0,3,6,9}

c) T_3M7 {6,8,9,10,11,1} = {9,11,6,1,8,10} = {6,8,9,10,11,1}

e) T_2M7 {4,5,6,10,11,0} = {6,1,8,0,7,2} = {0,1,2,6,7,8}

148   Basic Atonal Theory

CHAPTER 4

Exercises 4-I   (Nos. 1-10)

① {0,1,2,7}   (0,1,2,7)   [0,1,2,7]
② {3,5,8,11}   (0,2,5,8)   [0,2,5,8]
③ {4,6,9,10}   (0,2,5,6)   [0,1,4,6]
④ {7,8,11,1}   (0,1,4,6)   [0,1,4,6]
⑤ {6,9,0,2}   (0,3,6,8)   [0,2,5,8]
⑥ {3,4,5,10}   (0,1,2,7)   [0,1,2,7]
⑦ = ④
⑧ = ③
⑨ = ⑤
⑩ = ②

Exercises 4-II   (Nos. 1-8)

1. ⑤ = $T_5I($ ② $)$
2. ⑥ = $T_5I($ ① $) = T_3($ ① $)$; $T_5I($ ① $)$ is more consistent.
3. ⑦ = $T_5I($ ③ $)$
4. ⑧ = $T_0($ ③ $)$
5. ⑨ = $T_5I($ ② $)$
6. ⑩ = $T_0($ ② $)$
7. ⑪ = $T_0($ ① $)$
8. ⑫ = $T_5I($ ① $)$

Exercises 4-III   (Nos. 1,4,6,8)

1. T_0, T_2I; 7̄ 0̄ 1 2 7 (index = 2); 24/2 = 12

4. T_0, T_3I; 5̄ 6̄ 7 8 9 10 (index = 3); 24/2 = 12

6. T_0, T_6I; 3 6̄ 8̄ 9 10 0 3 (index = 6); 24/2 = 12

8. $T_0, T_2, T_4, T_6, T_8, T_{10}, T_0I, T_2I, T_4I, T_6I, T_8I, T_{10}I$

    1̄ 3̄ 5 7 9 11 (index = 0)   (other patterns possible)

Answers to Selected Exercises 149

$\overparen{3\ 5\ 7}$ 1 7 9 11 (index = 2)

$\overparen{9\ 11\ 1}$ 3 5 7 (index = 4)

$\overparen{9\ 11\ 1}$ 3 5 7 9 (index = 6)

$\overparen{11\ 1\ 3}$ 5 7 9 (index = 8)

$\overparen{11\ 1\ 3}$ 5 7 9 11 (index = 10)

24/12 = 2

Exercises 4-IV (Nos. 1a, c, e; 2b, d)

1. a) 3 4 5 ⌐6 7 8⌐ $\{3,4,5\}\cup\{6,7,8\} =$
   $\{3,4,5\}\cup T_{11}I\{3,4,5\}$
   $[0,1,2]$ type

   3 4 5 6 7 8 $\{3,4,6\}\cup\{5,7,8\} =$
   $\{3,4,6\}\cup T_{11}I\{3,4,6\}$
   $[0,1,3]$ type

   3 4 5 6 7 8 $\{3,5,7\}\cup\{4,6,8\} =$
   $\{3,5,7\}\cup T_{11}I\{3,5,7\}$
   $[0,2,4]$ type

   3 4 5 6 7 8 $\{4,5,8\}\cup\{3,6,7\} =$
   $\{4,5,8\}\cup T_{11}I\{4,5,8\}$
   $[0,1,4]$ type

1. c) 6 8 10 11 1 3 T_9I
   $[0,2,4]$

   6 8 10 11 1 3 T_9I
   $[0,2,5]$

   6 8 10 11 1 3 T_9I
   $[0,3,7]$

150   Basic Atonal Theory

      6 8 10 11 1 3   T₉I

                                [0,2,7]

1. e) 2 3 6 7 10 11   T₁I

                                [0,1,4]

      2 3 6 7 10 11   T₅I

                                [0,1,4]

      2 3 6 7 10 11   T₉I

                                [0,1,4]

      2 3 6 7 10 11   T₁I

                                [0,3,7]

      2 3 6 7 10 11   T₅I

                                [0,3,7]

      2 3 6 7 10 11   T₉I

                                [0,3,7]

      2 3 6 7 10 11   T₁I

                                [0,1,5]

      2 3 6 7 10 11   T₅I

                                [0,1,5]

      2 3 6 7 10 11   T₉I

                                [0,1,5]

      2 3 6 7 10 11   T₁I = T₅I = T₉I

                                [0,4,8]

2. b) 0 2 4 7 9   T₄I

                                [0,2,5,7]

      0 2 4 7 9   T₄I

                                [0,2,4,7]

0 2 4 7 9	T_4I [0,3,7]
0 2 4 7 9	T_4I [0,2,5]
0 2 4 7 9	T_4I [0,2,7]
2. d) 6 7 8 9 0 3	T_3I [0,2,5,8]
6 7 8 9 0 3	T_3I [0,1,4,7]
6 7 8 9 0 3 6 7 8 9	T_3I [0,1,2,5]
6 7 8 9 0 3 6 7 8 9	T_3I [0,1,2,6]
6 7 8 9 0 3 6 7 8 9	T_3I [0,1,3,6]
6 7 8 9 0 3 6 7 8 9	T_3I [0,2,3,6]
6 7 8 9 0 3 6 7 8 9	T_3I [0,1,4]
6 7 8 9 0 3 6 7 8 9	T_3I [0.2,5]
6 7 8 9 0 3 6 7 8 9	T_3I [0,2,6]
6 7 8 9 0 3 6 7 8 9	T_3I [0,1,6]

152   Basic Atonal Theory

CHAPTER 5

Exercises 5-I   (Nos. 2, 4)

2. {8,10,11,0,3}   (0,2,3,4,7)   [0,2,3,4,7]   <2,2,2,2,2,0>
4. {7,8,0,3}   (0,1,5,8)   [0,1,5,8]   <1,0,1,2,2,0>

Exercises 5-II   (Nos. 2, 4, 8)

2. No. Counterexample: {0,1,4,6}, or {0,1,3,7}: <1,1,1,1,1,1>. Each maps not into itself, but into the other.
4. Yes. Theorem in section 5.15.
8. Yes.

Exercises 5-V   (Nos. 1a, c, e, g, i, k; 3; 4a, c, e)

1. a) <1,2,3,4,5,6,5,4,3,2,1,0>
   c) <3,2,5,0,5,2,3,4,1,6,1,4>
   e) <3,6,3,0,3,6,3,0,3,6,3,0>
   g) from 1a: $r_{2 \cdot 2 + 1}R =$
   r_5R <1,2,3,4,5,6,5,4,3,2,1,0>
   = r_5 <0,1,2,3,4,5,6,5,4,3,2,1>
   = <5,4,3,2,1,0,1,2,3,4,5,6>
   i) from 1c: $r_{11}R$ <3,2,5,0,5,2,3,4,1,6,1,4>
   = r_{11}<4,1,6,1,4,3,2,5,0,5,2,3>
   = <1,6,1,4,3,2,5,0,5,2,3,4>
   k) from 1e: $r_{11}R$ <3,6,3,0,3,6,3,0,3,6,3,0>
   = <3,6,3,0,3,6,3,0,3,6,3,0>

3. B♭ = 0:   *interval vector*   *TICS vector*
   {0,1,2,7}   <2,1,0,0,2,1>   <1,2,4,2,1,0,0,2,2,2,0,0>
   {3,5,8,11}   <0,1,2,1,1,1>   <0,2,2,0,3,0,1,2,2,0,2,2>
   {4,6,9,10}   <1,1,1,1,1,1>   <1,2,2,2,2,0,1,2,2,0,2,0>

Remarks: The only operation under which all three sets have zero pc in common with their transformations is T_5I. T_2I preserves maximum pc content within each tetrachord: 4,2,2. Notice identical numbers of pc in common for {3,5,8,11} and {4,6,9,10} under T_5I, T_6I, T_7I, T_8I, T_9I, $T_{10}I$ (see TICS vectors), also T_1I and T_2I, and T_2, T_4, T_5, T_6. The common-tone structures of these two sets are much closer to each other than either is to that of {0,1,2,7}. Other patterns are evident.

4. a) {9,11,0,1,2,4} = T_9 {0,2,3,4,5,7} so

VTICS = $r_2 \cdot _9$ VTICS $_{\{0,2,3,4,5,7\}}$

= r_6 <3,0,3,2,3,4,3,6,3,4,3,2> (from 1h)

= <3,6,3,4,3,2,3,0,3,2,3,4>

interval vector = <3,4,3,2,3,0>

I) into itself: T_0, T_1I

II) into its complement: T_6, T_7I

4. c) {3,4,5,6,7,8} = T_3 {0,1,2,3,4,5}

so from 1a:

VTICS = r_6 <1,2,3,4,5,6,5,4,3,2,1,0>

= <5,4,3,2,1,0,1,2,3,4,5,6>

interval vector = <5,4,3,2,1,0>

I) into itself: T_0, $T_{11}I$

II) into its complement: T_6, T_5I

4. e) {1,2,5,6,9,10} = T_1 {0,1,4,5,8,9}

so from 1k:

VTICS = r_2 <3,6,3,0,3,6,3,0,3,6,3,0>

= <3,0,3,6,3,0,3,6,3,0,3,6>

interval vector = <3,0,3,6,3,0>

I) into itself: T_0, T_4, T_8, T_3I, T_7I, $T_{11}I$

II) into its complement: T_2, T_6, T_{10}, T_1I, T_5I, T_9I

INDEX

absolute value, 22, 133
adjacency-interval series, 88
aggregate, 68, 96n, 118–19
all-combinatorial hexachords, 94, 104–5, 110–11, 118–19
argument, 53
Arnold, S., 120
articulation, 16, 17
atonal music, 1, 2
atonal theory, v, 2, 19 see also set complexes, theory of

Babbitt, Milton, vii, 2, 25, 50, 51, 57n, 96n, 120, 123n, 137, 138n
Bach, Johann Sebastian, 2, 3
    Well-Tempered Clavier, 3, 27
Barkin, Elaine, 120
Batstone, Philip, 120
Baumslag, Benjamin, 57n, 58n
Bazelow, Alex, 120, 123n
Beethoven, Ludwig van, 2, 97
    Eroica Symphony, 89
Benjamin, William, 96n, 120
Berg, Alban, 2, 3, 18n, 51, 97, 98, 120
    Wozzeck, 3
Boretz, Benjamin, vii, viii, 39, 68n, 78, 120
    Meta-Variations, 39, 96n
Boulez, Pierre, 1, 2
Brahms, Johannes, 2, 97
Brickle, Frank, 120, 123n
Browne, Richmond, 120
Browning, Robert
    Pippa Passes, 3
Burkhart, Charles, 73n

canonical ordering, 88, 91
cardinality, 74–75
Carter, Elliott, 2
Chandler, Bruce, 57n, 58n
"Changing Chord, The," 61; see also Schoenberg, Arnold, "Farben"
circle of fifths transform; see multiplicative operations
circle of fourths transform; see multiplicative operations
Clifton, Thomas, 120

combinatorial matrix (CM), 118
combinatoriality, 53, 58n; see also all-combinatorial hexachords
    aggregate, 123n
    general, 123n
    hexachordal, 117–19
    special, 123n
common-tone, 92–93, 97–123
    definitions of, 111
common-tone theorems;
    for pitches, 109
    for T_n1 and T_n1-common-tone structures, 111
    for transpositions, 107–10
commutation, 52, 54
complement mod 12; see modulo 12
compound operations, 51–53, 54
    closed, 52, 54
Cone, Edward T., viii, 68n, 120
Coppock, Jane, 73n
counterdomain, 136

Dallapiccola, Luigi, 2
Davidovsky, Mario, 2
Debussy, Claude, 12
DeYoung, Lynden, 51
diatonic functionality, 19
direct interval, 25
domain, 136
duration patterns, 7, 16
dynamics, 16, 17, 18n

equivalence class, 74–77
    notations, 139–43
exclusivity, 75
exhaustivity, 75

Forte, Allen, viii, 73n, 96n, 102, 120, 140; see also *Structure of Atonal Music*
Foster, Stephen, 3

Gamer, Carlton, 51
general theory of music, 19
Group Theory, 57n, 58n

Hair, G., 120

155

156 Index

hexachord 105–7; *see also* combinatoriality
   aggregate combinatoriality, 119
   corollary, 107
   theorems of, 105–7
homomorphism, 58n, 103, 121n
Howe, Hubert, S., 58n, 120

IFF, 133
images, 136, 138
In Theory Only, 96n
indeterminate notation, 2
index, 50–51, 88–89, 91–92, 97, 111–13
instrumentation; *see* orchestration
integer model, 19–39; *see also* modulo 12
interval class, 29
interval content, 98–100; *see also* multiplicative operations
   definition of, 98
   invariance of, 102–3
interval mod 6, 29
interval vector, 100–2, 120n
   definition of, 100
intervalic expansion, 65
invariance, 51, 53, 55
inversion, 28, 45–51, 52, 55, 137
   definition of, 45
   inversion of, 49–51
      theorem of, 49
   multiplicative operations on, 54
   pitch, 45–47, 89
   pitch-class, 47–49, 89
      definition of, 47, 57n
inversional index, 50, 88, 91
inversional symmetry, 50-51, 88, 91–95, 118
   center of, 50–51
   theorem of, 91
isomorphism, 55, 58n, 103

Journal of Music Theory (JMT), viii, 96n, 120n, 138n

Kassler, Michael, 120
Klein four group, 57n

Lang, Paul Henry, viii
Lansky, Paul, 51, 98
"leaping (•out" motive, 60, 66
Lewin, David, 51, 57n, 96n, 120, 123n

Ligeti, György, 2
Linearity and verticality, 8

M5, M7; *see* multiplicative operations
Mahler, Gustav, 2
mapping, 40–41, 47, 49, 53, 55, 56n, 92–93, 133, 136–37
   one-to-one, 137
Martino, Donald, 2, 96n, 120, 123n
mathematics, 2
matrix, 54, 55
modulo 12 (mod 12), v, 23–24
   complementary mod 12, 28, 47
Morris, Robert, 58n, 120, 123n
multiplicative operations, 53–56, 58n, 98, 121n
   definition of, 98
   interval, 98–100
   interval content under, 103–5
      theorem of, 104
Musical Quarterly, 138n

nesting, 8–18
Nono, Luigi, 2
normal form, 31–39, 47
   definition of, 38
   invariance of, 48
   shortcut for finding, 38
normal order; *see* normal form
numerological fallacy, 19

oral tradition, v, vii
orchestration, 7, 16
order numbers, 138
order operations, 134–35

partition, 96n; *see also* subset
Perle, George, viii, 51, 98, 120
permutation, 137, 138
Perspectives of New Music (PNM), vii, viii, 57n, 58n, 73n, 96n, 120n, 123n; *see also Sounds and Words: Milton Babbitt at 60*
Perspectives on Contemporary Music Theory, viii
Perspectives on Schoenberg and Stravinsky, viii, 68n
pitch, integer model of, 19–39
pitch interval (ip)
   ordered, 20–21, 26, 28, 29
      definition of, 21

unordered, 22, 29
  definition of, 22
pitch-class (pc), 22–29, 31
  definition of, 23
  equivalence, 19, 22
    definition of, 22
  lines, 74
  sets, 74–75, 88–95
Pousseur, Henri, 120
preimages, 136, 138
Problems of Modern Music: The Princeton Seminar in Advanced Musical Studies, viii

Rahn, John, 120
range, 136
Regener, Eric, 120
residue class, 24
rests, 16
retrograde, 134–35
retrograde symmetry, 7, 8, 11, 14, 16, 17, 91, 92
Rogers, John 120
roman numeral analysis, 12
rotation, 33, 113, 134–135
Rothgeb, John, 120
row, twelve-tone, 137

Schenkerian-derived theory, 79
Schoenberg, Arnold, 1, 2, 3, 18n, 51, 97, 118, 120
  "Analysis of the Four Orchestral Songs, Opus 22," 68
  Drei Klavierstücke op. 11, 17
  Five Pieces for Orchestra op. 16, 17, 59
    "Farben" op. 16 no. 3, 53, 59–73, 103, 108, 109, 116
      arrangement of, 69–72
  Jakobsleiter, Die, 35
  Klavierstück op. 33a, 17, 80, 82, 83–87, 90, 95
  Orchestral Songs op. 22, 68
  Piano Concerto op. 42, 24–25, 26
  Pierrot Lunaire op. 21, 18
  Serenade op. 24, 18
  String Quartet (third) op. 30, 18
  String Quartet (fourth) op. 37, 119, 138
  Suite op. 29, 37, 100–2
Score and IMA Magazine, The, 96n
serial music, 2, 11
serial theory, v, 2, 118, 120
set, 27–29, 31, 134, 137–38
  equivalence class, 96n
  intersection, 135
  inversion, 47, 93–95
  number of members, 136
  transposition, 48, 88–89
  types, 74–96
  union and disunion of inversionally symmetrical, 93–95, 135
set complexes, theory of, viii; *see also* atonal theory
Simple Composition, viii
Serial Composition and Atonality, viii
Sounds and Words: Milton Babbitt at 60, vii
Spies, Claudio, 68n, 120
Starr, Daniel, 58n, 120, 123n
Stockhausen, Karlheinz, 2
Stravinsky, Igor, 2, 79, 110
  Octet for Wind Instruments, 79
Structure of Atonal Music, The, viii, 73n, 96n, 140
subset, 80, 94–95, 136
  content, 115–117
  partitioning, 94
  proper, 136
surjective, 136
Swift, Richard, 120
symbols (algebra, logic), 133–38
symmetry, 90–95, 96n, 97–98, 105; *see also* inversional symmetry and transpositional symmetry
  degree of, theorem of, 91, 96n
  theorems of, 91

TICS, 111–12
  vectors, 113–15
  corollary, 114
  proofs of, 122n
  theorems of, 114
T_n-types, 75–80, 140–43
  definitions of, 76
tonal music, 1–2, 68
tonal theory, 19
transposed inversion; *see* inversion
transposition
  common-tone theorem, 67
  complementary, theorem of, 121n
  equivalency, 33
  identity, 44
  inverse, 44–45
    theorem of, 45
  pitch, 40–41, 52, 57n, 89, 137
    definition of, 40

158 Index

pitch class, 42–45, 89
   definition of, 42
   related, 88–90
transpositional symmetry, 91–93, 118
twelve pitch-class, system of, v

undirected interval, 29

Wagner, Richard, 2, 78
Webern, Anton, 2, 3, 18n, 51, 60, 73n, 97, 120
   "Farben" arrangement, 69–72
   Fünf Sätze op. 5, no. 4, 34

Symphonie op. 21, 3, 4–18, 30, 31, 51, 59
Variationen op. 27, 18
Westergaard, Peter, 51, 120, 123n
Winham, Godfrey, 58n, 120
Wintle, Christopher, 120
Wuorinen, Charles, viii, 2, 120

Xenakis, Yannis, 2

Z-related sets, 102, 104, 105, 121n
Zuckerman, Mark, 120
Zyklus, 2